SUNNI PATTIWAL

The Rules of UX Design

Copyright © 2024 by Sunni Pattiwal

All rights reserved. No part of this publication may be reproduced, stored, or transmitted in any form or by any means, electronic, mechanical, photocopying, recording, scanning, or otherwise without written permission from the publisher. It is illegal to copy this book, post it to a website, or distribute it by any other means without permission.

First edition

*This book was professionally typeset on Reedsy.
Find out more at reedsy.com*

Contents

Preface   viii
Special Thanks   x

I Foundations of UX Design

1. Chapter 1: What is UX Design?   3
2. Chapter 2: The History of UX Design   10
3. Chapter 3: The Difference Between UX and UI   16
4. Chapter 4: Understanding User-Centered Design (UCD)   23
5. Chapter 5: The Psychology of Users   30
6. Chapter 6: Core UX Principles   38
7. Chapter 7: Human-Computer Interaction Basics   47
8. Chapter 8: The Role of Empathy in UX   55
9. Chapter 9: Balancing Business and User Needs   64
10. Chapter 10: Key Skills for a UX Designer   70

II User Research and Analysis

11. Chapter 11: Understanding the User: Research Methods   79

12	Chapter 12: Conducting User Interviews	86
13	Chapter 13: Creating Personas	91
14	Chapter 14: User Journey Mapping	95
15	Chapter 15: Gathering Data: Surveys, Polls, and...	101
16	Chapter 16: Heuristic Evaluation	110
17	Chapter 17: Competitive Analysis	116
18	Chapter 18: Analyzing User Data and Feedback	118
19	Chapter 19: Behavioral and Attitudinal Research	124
20	Chapter 20: Translating Research into Actionable Insights	131
III	Information Architecture	
21	Chapter 21: The Basics of Information Architecture (IA)	139
22	Chapter 22: Creating Site Maps	144
23	Chapter 23: Card Sorting Techniques	148
24	Chapter 24: Navigation Design	154
25	Chapter 25: Taxonomy and Classification Systems	161
26	Chapter 26: Designing for Searchability	167
27	Chapter 27: The Role of Metadata in UX Design	173
28	Chapter 28: Effective Labeling and Terminology	180
29	Chapter 29: The Importance of Content Hierarchy	187
30	Chapter 30: Optimizing Information Architecture for...	196

IV Interaction Design

31	Chapter 31: Introduction to Interaction Design	205
32	Chapter 32: Designing User Flows	211
33	Chapter 33: Wireframing: From Concept to Creation	220
34	Chapter 34: Prototyping for Interaction	228
35	Chapter 35: Design Patterns in Interaction Design	233
36	Chapter 36: Microinteractions: Small Details, Big Impact	239
37	Chapter 37: Gestures, Taps, and Clicks	244
38	Chapter 38: Designing for Different Devices (Mobile, Web,...	251
39	Chapter 39: Feedback and Responsiveness in Interaction	257
40	Chapter 40: Error Handling in UX	264

V Visual Design in UX

41	Chapter 41: Visual Hierarchy in UX Design	271
42	Chapter 42: Designing for Accessibility	276
43	Chapter 43: Color Theory in UX	282
44	Chapter 44: Typography in User Interfaces	286
45	Chapter 45: Creating Consistent Visual Design Systems	291
46	Chapter 46: Using Imagery and Icons Effectively	299
47	Chapter 47: Designing for Brand and Identity	305
48	Chapter 48: Simplicity and Minimalism in UX Design	310

49	Chapter 49: The Role of White Space	315
50	Chapter 50: Designing Engaging Call-to-Actions	318

VI Usability Testing and Iteration

51	Chapter 51: Usability Testing and Iteration	325
52	Chapter 52: Different Types of Usability Tests	331
53	Chapter 53: How to Conduct Usability Testing	337
54	Chapter 54: Analyzing Usability Test Results	341
55	Chapter 55: A/B Testing for UX	347
56	Chapter 56: The Role of Analytics in UX Iteration	354
57	Chapter 57: Iterative Design: Continuous Improvement	357
58	Chapter 58: Balancing Data-Driven and Intuitive Design...	365
59	Chapter 59: The Importance of Feedback Loops	370

VII UX Design in Practice

60	Chapter 60: Agile UX and Working in Sprints	377
61	Chapter 61: Collaboration Between UX and Development	381
62	Chapter 62: Working with Stakeholders	385
63	Chapter 63: Design Handoff: From Design to Development	390
64	Chapter 64: UX Writing: Crafting the Perfect Microcopy	398

65	Chapter 65: Ethics in UX Design	405
66	Chapter 66: The Future of UX Design	409
67	Chapter 67: AI and Machine Learning in UX	414
68	Chapter 68: How AI Fits into the UX Process	418
69	Chapter 69: How AI Thinks	424
70	Chapter 70: How AI Creates an Image	431
71	Chapter 71: How AI Creates a Website Design	436
72	Chapter 72: Designing for Inclusivity and Diversity	442
73	Chapter 73: UX Beyond the Screen: Voice and Gesture...	448

VIII Book References

74	A Good Book Reading List	459

Preface

In today's digital world, user experience (UX) has become a cornerstone of successful design. As technology evolves at an unprecedented pace, understanding how to create intuitive, engaging, and meaningful interactions between users and digital products is more important than ever. **"The Rules of UX Design"** aims to be your comprehensive guide to navigating this complex yet fascinating field.

This book is a culmination of years of experience, research, and passion for design. Whether you are a seasoned UX professional, a budding designer, or someone curious about the principles that shape our digital interactions, this book offers valuable insights and practical advice for every reader.

In the chapters that follow, we will explore the foundational concepts of UX design, delve into the intricacies of user research, and discuss the essential elements of information architecture and interaction design. We will also examine the importance of visual design, usability testing, and iterative processes, equipping you with the tools and knowledge needed to create user-centered solutions.

What sets this book apart is its focus on actionable principles—what I call the "rules" of UX design. These rules are derived from established practices, industry standards, and emerging trends. They serve not only as guidelines but also as a framework for fostering creativity and innovation within your design process.

I believe that design should be inclusive and accessible to everyone. Therefore, this book emphasizes the importance of understanding diverse user needs and experiences. By prioritizing empathy and inclusivity, we can create designs that resonate with all users, regardless of their backgrounds or abilities.

As you embark on this journey through the rules of UX design, I encourage you to think critically, experiment boldly, and remain open to new ideas. Design is not just about aesthetics; it is about solving real problems and enhancing the lives of users.

Thank you for joining me on this exploration of user experience design. I hope you find inspiration, guidance, and a deeper understanding of this dynamic field as we uncover the rules that can transform your design practice.

Kind regards,

Sunni Pattiwal

the author of this book

Special Thanks

This book would not have been possible without the support, guidance, and inspiration of many incredible people.

First and foremost, I would like to thank my family for their unwavering support, patience, and encouragement throughout this journey. Your belief in me kept me moving forward.

To my friends, peers, and collaborators — thank you for the conversations, feedback, and honest perspectives that helped shape my thinking and refine this work.

A special thank you to:
Rob Swallow, Vanessa Jaramillo, Ian Dunstan, Jamil Shehadeh, Nikki Oakes, Sarah Fenn, Karmen Blazevic, Mihovil Karac, Matea, Bhavesh Barve, Dan Maxted, Ivan Barac, Natalia Consumi, Abbie Truman, Nikola Šubić, Sadie Playle, Vilim, Amanda, and Adam Lancaster.

Your support, insights, and encouragement have played an important role in bringing this book to life.

To the designers, developers, and product teams I've had the privilege to work with over the years — your collaboration and shared passion for creating better user experiences have deeply influenced this book.

I would also like to thank the wider UX community. The shared knowledge, discussions, and continuous learning within this field continue to inspire and push the boundaries of what great design can achieve.

Finally, thank you to you, the reader. Your curiosity and commitment to improving user experiences are what drive this industry forward.

— **Sunni Pattiwal**
Author of the book

I

Foundations of UX Design

Understand the basics of UX design, its history, and core principles.
This section lays the groundwork for UX by explaining fundamental concepts, the difference between UX and UI, and the importance of empathy and user-centered design. It provides a strong foundation for both beginners and those looking to refresh their knowledge.

1

Chapter 1: What is UX Design?

Introduction to UX Design

User Experience (UX) Design is all about creating products, services, or systems that are not only functional but also enjoyable for users. It focuses on how a person feels when interacting with a product, be it a website, an app, or even a physical device. UX design covers everything from how easy it is to use a product to how it makes the user feel. The goal of UX design is to improve the quality of the interaction between the user and the product by making it simple, intuitive, and pleasant.

But UX design is not just about making things look pretty or usable. It is about understanding the needs and behaviours of users and aligning those insights with the goals of a business. A good UX designer considers both the user and the business, creating a balance between what users want and what businesses need.

UX design is a crucial aspect of product development, and it plays a significant role in ensuring that products are effective and easy to use. However, as we will explore throughout this book, collaborating between different teams, such as UX designers, project managers (PMs), and developers, can sometimes be challenging. But before we dive into the collaboration issues, let's break down what UX design really involves and why it is so essential.

What UX Design Involves

UX design is a multi-disciplinary field, requiring a range of skills from research to visual design. It involves understanding users through research, testing prototypes, and refining designs to meet user needs. Here's a breakdown of the main areas that UX design covers:

User Research
Before a designer starts sketching ideas, they need to know who their users are and what they want. This can be done through interviews, surveys, or observing users as they interact with products. User research is the foundation of good UX design because it allows the designer to create a product that fits the users' needs.

Information Architecture (IA)
Once the research is done, designers need to organise the information in a way that makes sense to users. Information architecture is about structuring content so users can easily find what they're looking for.

Wireframing and Prototyping
After the information is organised, designers create wireframes and prototypes. Wireframes are basic layouts, while prototypes are working models used to test ideas and gather feedback.

Usability Testing
No design is perfect on the first try. Usability testing involves real users interacting with a product and giving feedback so designers can improve the experience.

Visual Design
This focuses on how the product looks. Good UX design is not only functional but visually clear, consistent, and aligned with the brand.

Interaction Design
This covers how users interact with the product, including navigation, button behaviour, transitions, and responsiveness.

The Importance of UX Design

A well-designed user experience can determine whether a product succeeds or fails. Poor UX leads to frustration and abandonment, while good UX builds trust and engagement.

UX design is also cost-effective. Fixing problems early in the design phase is far cheaper than fixing them after launch.

The Role of UX Designers in a Team

UX designers do not work alone. They collaborate with project managers, developers, marketers, and other stakeholders.

This can create tension. UX designers focus on user needs, PMs focus on timelines and budgets, and developers focus on technical execution. These different priorities can lead to misalignment if not managed carefully.

Why It's Hard to Collaborate with UX Designers, PMs, and Developers

Collaboration challenges often come from differences in priorities, communication styles, and working methods.

- **Different priorities:** UX focuses on usability, PMs on delivery, developers on feasibility
- **Communication gaps:** Designers use visuals, developers use code, PMs use business language
- **Different workflows:** UX is iterative, development prefers fixed specifications

Different Team Sizes and Their Impact

UX teams vary depending on company size.
Small Teams
Fast-paced, flexible, but often resource-limited. People wear multiple hats, and decisions are made quickly.

Medium Teams
More structured roles and better balance, but risk of silos forming between departments.

Large Teams
Highly specialised roles and strong expertise, but more complex communication and coordination challenges.

Cross-Functional Teams
Teams made up of UX, PMs, and developers working closely together. Often Agile-based, improving collaboration but still requiring clear communication and shared expectations.

AI in the UX Design Process

In recent years, Artificial Intelligence (AI) has become an important supporting tool in UX design. While UX remains a human-centred discipline, AI is increasingly used to speed up research, design exploration, and content creation.

It is important to understand that AI does not think like a human. Instead, it analyses large amounts of data, recognises patterns, and predicts likely outcomes based on what it has learned. It does not understand emotion, intent, or user context in the way a UX designer does.

AI can support UX in several ways:

- **User research support:** analysing large volumes of feedback and identifying patterns
- **Ideation:** generating layout ideas, wireframes, and design variations quickly

- **Content creation:** producing placeholder text, microcopy, and tone variations
- **Prototyping:** turning simple prompts into visual concepts or interface ideas

However, AI outputs are based on existing patterns. This means it is strong at speed and variation, but weaker in originality, emotional understanding, and ethical judgement.

In simple terms, AI processes what is most likely, while UX design requires understanding what is most meaningful for users.

The role of AI in UX teams is not to replace designers, but to support them. It can help speed up repetitive tasks and generate ideas, but human judgement is still essential to interpret results, test with real users, and ensure the design truly meets user needs.

How This Book Will Help

In this book, we will explore practical strategies for improving collaboration between UX designers, PMs, and developers. We will dive deeper into common pain points and offer tips on how to streamline communication, align priorities, and work more effectively together, regardless of team size.

Whether you're working in a small startup or a large corporation, this book will help iron out the awkward parts of working together and ensure that everyone is pulling in the same direction. By the end, you'll have a better understanding of how to navigate these challenges and deliver products that are not only successful but also enjoyable for users.

2

Chapter 2: The History of UX Design

User Experience (UX) design has become a critical field in today's digital world, but it didn't start with websites, apps, or even computers. The history of UX design is rooted in a much older human desire: to create tools and systems that make life easier and more enjoyable. In this chapter, we will explore the development of UX design from its early beginnings to its current importance in the technology-driven era.

1. Early Beginnings of UX: Tools and Systems
UX design, in its most basic form, has been part of human history for centuries. Long before we had digital interfaces, people were designing tools, structures, and systems with the user in mind. Think about the earliest tools made by humans – stones shaped into axes or spears. These were designed to be efficient, easy to handle, and comfortable to use. They had to meet the needs of the users who relied on them for survival.

In ancient times, engineers and architects had a similar

approach when designing buildings, cities, and public spaces. The Romans, for example, built aqueducts to provide fresh water to their cities. They had to carefully consider how the water would travel, how people would access it, and how the design would meet the needs of the population. Even in ancient Egypt, the way the pyramids were built took into account the effort and skill needed to construct them, considering how people would work with the materials available.

These early examples highlight the idea that people have always been thinking about how objects, systems, and environments can be shaped to meet human needs. Although these may not have been called "UX design" at the time, the principles of making things functional, efficient, and user-friendly were present.

2. The Industrial Revolution: The Birth of Ergonomics and Usability

Fast forward to the Industrial Revolution in the 18th and 19th centuries, where the concept of user-centred design began to formalise. Factories and mass production changed the way products were made, and with that came a new focus on efficiency and usability. Machines and tools used in factories needed to be designed in ways that made them easy and safe to use. Workers had to be able to operate machines effectively, and this led to the development of ergonomics – the study of how people interact with machines and equipment.

One of the pioneers in this field was Frederick Winslow Taylor, an American engineer who is known for his work in scientific management. In the late 19th century, Taylor studied how workers performed tasks in factories, breaking down processes into steps to make them more efficient. His work laid the foundation for designing tools and systems that would optimise human performance.

Another key figure was Henry Dreyfuss, an American industrial designer who published *Designing for People* in 1955. Dreyfuss focused on how products, from telephones to thermostats, should be designed with the user in mind. His work helped establish the importance of considering human factors in design, ensuring that products were not only functional but also comfortable and easy to use.

During this period, the idea that design should consider the user experience became more established, though the term "UX" was not yet in use. The focus on ergonomics, usability, and human-centred design would continue to evolve, laying the groundwork for modern UX design.

3. The Digital Age: Birth of Human-Computer Interaction

The real turning point in the history of UX design came with the advent of computers in the 20th century. Early computers were complex machines that were difficult to use, requiring specialist knowledge. However, as computers became more accessible, it became clear that they needed to be designed with the user in mind.

In the 1970s and 1980s, the field of Human-Computer Interaction (HCI) emerged. HCI focused on how people interact with computers and digital systems, with the goal of making these interactions easier and more intuitive. Researchers and designers began to study how people used computers, looking at things like screen layouts, input methods, and how information was displayed.

One of the most important developments during this time was the creation of graphical user interfaces (GUIs). Before GUIs, people had to type commands to interact with computers, which was not user-friendly for the average person. The introduction of icons, windows, and pointing devices like the mouse made computers much more accessible. One of the key pioneers in this area was Douglas Engelbart, who invented the computer mouse and demonstrated the first modern GUI in 1968.

Companies like Apple and Microsoft played a significant role in popularising user-friendly interfaces in the 1980s and 1990s. Apple's Macintosh, released in 1984, was one of the first commercially successful computers to feature a GUI, making it much easier for non-experts to use a computer. Microsoft followed with Windows, bringing GUI-based computing to a wider audience.

This period marked the beginning of UX design as we know it today. Designers started to focus on how users interacted with digital products, aiming to create experiences that were easy, intuitive, and even enjoyable. The field of HCI laid the foundation for the development of UX as a discipline, with a focus on usability, human factors, and interface design.

4. The Rise of the Internet and the Birth of UX Design

With the rise of the internet in the 1990s, the need for UX design became even more important. Websites and web applications became a new frontier for user interaction, and companies quickly realised that they needed to create online experiences that were not only functional but also user-friendly.

During this time, the term "User Experience" (UX) was first coined by Don Norman, a cognitive scientist and designer. In the mid-1990s, Norman was working at Apple and introduced the term to describe the holistic experience that users have when interacting with a product. He argued that UX goes beyond just usability – it includes every aspect of the interaction, from the look and feel of the product to the emotional response it evokes in the user.

This broader view of UX design gained traction as the internet grew, and companies began to invest more in designing their websites and digital products with the user in mind. The early 2000s saw the rise of web design as a profession, with designers focusing on creating websites that were visually appealing, easy to navigate, and functional.

Around the same time, mobile devices started to become more common, adding another layer of complexity to UX design. Designers now had to consider how users would interact with smaller screens and touch interfaces, leading to the development of mobile-first design principles.

5. UX Design in the Modern Era
Today, UX design is a well-established field that is central to

the development of digital products. Companies across all industries recognise the importance of creating positive user experiences, whether they are designing websites, apps, or physical products.

The tools and methodologies used in UX design have become more sophisticated, with designers relying on user research, prototyping, and testing to create products that meet the needs of their users. Design thinking, a problem-solving approach that focuses on understanding the user's needs, has become a popular framework for UX design.

In recent years, the rise of artificial intelligence (AI), virtual reality (VR), and augmented reality (AR) has opened up new possibilities for UX design. Designers are now exploring how these technologies can be used to create immersive and personalised experiences. At the same time, there is a growing emphasis on ethical design, with designers considering the broader impact of their work on society.

The history of UX design is a story of evolution, from the earliest tools and systems to the complex digital products we use today. As technology continues to advance, UX design will undoubtedly continue to play a critical role in shaping the way we interact with the world around us.

3

Chapter 3: The Difference Between UX and UI

In the world of digital design, two terms are often used interchangeably, but they have distinct meanings and roles: **UX (User Experience)** and **UI (User Interface)**. While they are closely related, they serve different purposes and require different approaches. Understanding the difference between UX and UI is crucial for anyone involved in creating products, whether it's a website, app, or any digital service. This chapter will explain the differences, clarify the roles of each, and show how they work together to create successful, user-centred designs.

What is UX?

UX, or **User Experience**, refers to how a person feels when interacting with a product or service. It's about the overall experience, whether it's pleasant, frustrating, easy, or complicated. A good UX ensures that users can accomplish their goals smoothly and without unnecessary friction. The main focus of UX is on solving user problems, making their interaction with the product seamless and enjoyable. It's all about functionality and user satisfaction.

When we talk about UX design, we are not just referring to visual aspects; it's much broader. UX encompasses research, strategy, wireframing, testing, and iteration. A UX designer's job is to think about how users will interact with the product from start to finish. They gather insights into what users want and need and use that information to create solutions that meet those needs.

This process involves several key steps:

1. **Research and Analysis**: Before any design work begins, UX designers conduct thorough research to understand users' needs, behaviours, and pain points. They might interview users, conduct surveys, or analyse user behaviour on existing platforms. The goal is to gather data that will guide design decisions.

2. **User Personas and User Journeys**: After gathering insights, UX designers create user personas – fictional characters that represent the different types of users. These personas help the design team stay focused on real user needs. Alongside personas, designers map out user journeys, which describe the steps a user might take to achieve their goals. For example, how does a user find information on a website, or how do they complete a purchase?

3. **Information Architecture**: This is about organising the content and features of a product in a way that makes sense to users. It involves structuring the navigation and layout so users can easily find what they're looking for.

4. **Wireframing and Prototyping**: Before creating the final product, UX designers sketch wireframes, which are basic outlines of a product's layout. Wireframes focus on functionality rather than aesthetics. Once these are refined, prototypes are built to test the design. Prototyping allows for testing how users will interact with the product before fully building it.

5. **Usability Testing**: Testing is a critical part of UX design. Designers observe real users interacting with the prototype to identify any issues or areas of confusion. This allows for revisions and improvements before the product is finalised.

UX is, in essence, about making sure the user's journey through a product is as smooth and satisfying as possible. It's not just about the look but how it works. No matter how beautiful a design is, if users struggle to use it, the UX has failed.

What is UI?

UI, or **User Interface**, is often confused with UX because it is also focused on how users interact with a product. However, UI deals specifically with the **visual** and **interactive** elements. If UX is the structure and function of a product, UI is the look and feel. It's about the layout of buttons, icons, typography, colours, and other visual aspects that users engage with directly.UI designers are responsible for ensuring that the visual aspects of the product align with the brand's identity and are intuitive to users. They work closely with UX designers to ensure that the visual design supports the overall experience. For example, if the UX design determines where a button should be placed for optimal usability, the UI designer decides what that button will look like and how it will behave when clicked.

Some of the key tasks involved in UI design include:

1. **Visual Design**: This involves choosing colours, fonts, and imagery that align with the brand and appeal to the user. The visual hierarchy must be clear, guiding users to the most important elements on the screen.

2. **Interactive Design**: UI designers focus on how interactive elements, like buttons and menus, behave. For example, when a button is clicked, does it change colour or shape to indicate it's been pressed? These subtle interactions improve usability by giving users feedback on their actions.

3. **Responsiveness**: UI design also ensures that a product looks and works well across different devices and screen sizes. For example, a website should be just as functional and visually appealing on a mobile phone as it is on a desktop computer.

4. **Consistency**: Consistency is vital in UI design. Every page or screen of a product should follow the same design principles, so users can predict how to interact with it. This helps create a sense of familiarity and reduces the learning curve for users.

In summary, UI design is about creating a visually appealing and functional interface that enhances the user's interaction with the product. It's about ensuring that everything the user sees and interacts with is clear, consistent, and aligned with the brand's goals.

How Do UX and UI Work Together?

Although UX and UI are different, they are deeply interconnected and must work together to create a successful product. Neither can exist in isolation – a beautifully designed interface (UI) is useless if the experience is frustrating (UX), and a well-structured UX is ineffective if the UI is confusing or unattractive.
Here's how they complement each other:

- **UX focuses on functionality and solving user problems**, while **UI focuses on the visual elements and how the product feels**. Together, they ensure that the product not only works well but also looks good and is enjoyable to use.

- **UX design often comes first** in the process. The structure, user flows, and functionality are mapped out before the visual design elements are added. Once the UX foundation is in place, UI designers step in to bring the interface to life with visuals and interactions.

- **Both require collaboration**. UX and UI designers often work together, sharing feedback and ideas to ensure that the design is cohesive. For example, a UI designer may suggest a new way of displaying information that improves the user's experience, or a UX designer might recommend changes to the interface layout to make it more user-friendly.

In the end, UX and UI design both aim to enhance the user's interaction with the product. When done well, users don't even notice these elements – they simply enjoy a smooth, intuitive experience.

Common Misconceptions About UX and UI

There are several common misconceptions about UX and UI that are worth addressing:

1. **"UI is more important than UX"**: Some people think that as long as a product looks good, users will enjoy it. However, if the experience is frustrating or confusing, users are likely to leave, no matter how attractive the interface is.

2. **"UX is only about wireframes and prototypes"**: While wireframing and prototyping are part of UX design, they are just one aspect. UX is about the entire process

of researching, planning, testing, and iterating on a product to make it work well for users.

3. **"UI is just about making things look pretty"**: While aesthetics are part of UI design, it's much more than that. UI designers also think about how users will interact with each element, ensuring the interface is intuitive and easy to use.

4. **"UX and UI are the same thing"**: As we've discussed, UX and UI are different but related. UX is about the overall experience and functionality, while UI is about the visual and interactive elements.

Conclusion

In summary, UX and UI are two sides of the same coin. UX design focuses on solving user problems and ensuring a seamless experience, while UI design focuses on creating an appealing and intuitive interface. Both are crucial to the success of any product. By working together, UX and UI designers ensure that users can achieve their goals easily and enjoyably, which ultimately leads to a more successful and engaging product. Understanding the difference between the two is essential for anyone involved in digital design.

4

Chapter 4: Understanding User-Centered Design (UCD)

User-Centered Design (UCD) is a design philosophy that places the needs, preferences, and limitations of the end-user at the forefront of the design process. It's not just about how something looks or works, but how it meets the goals and expectations of the people using it. UCD ensures that products are easy to use, accessible, and satisfying to interact with. This chapter will break down what UCD is, why it's essential, and how to apply its principles in real-world UX design projects.

Part 1: What is User-Centered Design?

UCD is a design approach where the user is at the core of every decision made during the development of a product. This methodology differs from traditional design approaches where designers or stakeholders might focus more on aesthetics, technology, or business goals rather than prioritising user needs. The key principle of UCD is simple: design with empathy. This means stepping into the shoes of the end-user to fully understand their context, needs, and frustrations. By making users the centre of attention, you ensure that the product will be functional and enjoyable to use.

The process of UCD generally involves several iterative stages, such as:

1. **Research and Discovery** – Understanding who the users are, what they need, and what problems they face.
2. **Ideation and Prototyping** – Designing possible solutions and creating prototypes to visualise and test ideas.
3. **Testing and Feedback** – Engaging with real users to test prototypes and get feedback, which leads to revisions.
4. **Implementation and Evaluation** – Developing the final product and continuously evaluating its performance and usability in real-world settings.

Every stage of this process involves users in some capacity, ensuring that the product is designed to solve real problems and meet real needs.

Part 2: The Importance of UCD in UX Design

When we talk about the importance of User-Centered Design, it goes beyond just making something "usable." It's about creating products that improve the quality of life for users, providing an enjoyable experience that fits naturally into their lives.

1. **Reduces the risk of failure**: By involving users from the start, UCD helps designers avoid assumptions that could lead to failure. Designers often make decisions based on what they think users want, but these assumptions can be wrong. By gathering user insights early on, you reduce the risk of launching a product that doesn't meet user needs.

2. **Increases user satisfaction**: Products designed with UCD principles tend to be more intuitive and user-friendly, which leads to greater satisfaction. Users feel more in control and confident in their interactions, which in turn, leads to higher engagement and loyalty.

3. **Improves accessibility**: UCD pushes designers to think about a wide range of users, including those with disabilities. By incorporating accessibility into the design process, you ensure your product is usable by the widest possible audience, which is not only ethically responsible but also increases your potential market.

4. **Boosts efficiency**: Products that are easy to use help users complete tasks more efficiently, reducing frustration and saving time. This is particularly important in areas like web design, where people are often looking to complete specific tasks quickly, such as finding information or making a purchase.

5. **Enhances brand reputation**: Companies known for user-centered products often build strong reputations, as users tend to trust and recommend products that pro-

vide positive experiences. When users enjoy interacting with a product, they're more likely to spread the word, leading to organic growth and brand loyalty.

In essence, UCD is not just about the user—it benefits the business as well. By creating products that are easy, efficient, and satisfying to use, companies can drive customer satisfaction, loyalty, and even profitability.

Part 3: Applying UCD Principles in UX Design

Applying User-Centered Design requires more than just understanding its importance; it requires a deliberate, structured process that places users at the heart of every decision. Here's how to apply UCD in practice:

1.User Research

The foundation of UCD is understanding your users. Start by identifying who your target users are and conduct user research to gather insights. This might include:

- **Surveys and Questionnaires**: Useful for gathering quantitative data from a large group of users.
- **Interviews**: One-on-one conversations with users to explore their behaviours, needs, and frustrations.
- **User Observation**: Watching users interact with products to identify pain points and opportunities for improvement.

This research will help you create **user personas**, which are fictional characters that represent the key segments of your audience. Personas help guide design decisions by keeping user goals and challenges front of mind.

2.Task Analysis

Once you know who your users are, the next step is understanding what they need to accomplish. Task analysis involves breaking down the tasks that users need to complete and understanding the steps involved in each task. This can help you identify bottlenecks or areas where users struggle, giving you the insight you need to simplify the process.

Usability Testing

Usability testing is a critical part of the UCD process. This involves creating prototypes of your product and having real users interact with them. The goal is to identify areas of friction and uncover potential problems before the final product is developed.

Key aspects of usability testing include:

- **Task Completion**: Can users successfully complete the tasks set before them?
- **Efficiency**: How long does it take users to complete tasks?
- **Error Rate**: How often do users make mistakes?
- **Satisfaction**: How do users feel about their experience?

This feedback loop is crucial for refining your design and ensuring that the product works well in real-life scenarios.

3. Iterative Design

UCD is an iterative process. After usability testing, you'll need to refine and revise your design based on the feedback you've gathered. This might involve adjusting features, rethinking navigation, or even reworking the overall design approach. Each iteration should bring you closer to a solution that meets the needs of your users. The cycle of designing, testing, and refining doesn't stop after launch. Continuous feedback from users can help you improve the product over time, ensuring it remains relevant and useful as user needs evolve.

4. Collaboration

UCD is a collaborative effort that often involves cross-functional teams, including designers, developers, product managers, and stakeholders. It's important that everyone involved in the project shares a user-focused mindset. Regular communication and feedback loops ensure that the user's perspective is always considered throughout the development process.

5. Accessibility and Inclusivity

One of the most critical components of UCD is ensuring that your product is accessible to everyone, including people with disabilities. This means considering things like screen reader compatibility, colour contrast for users with vision impairments, and keyboard navigation for those who can't use a mouse. Inclusivity also means thinking about diverse user groups in terms of age, culture, and technical proficiency. Designing for inclusivity helps ensure that your product is usable and enjoyable for all users, not just a specific subset.

In summary, User-Centered Design is a holistic approach that places the user's needs, behaviours, and context at the centre of the design process. It's a way to ensure that your products are not just functional, but also intuitive, enjoyable, and accessible to a broad range of users. By prioritising the user in every decision, you can create experiences that not only meet their needs but also exceed their expectations.

5

Chapter 5: The Psychology of Users

5.1 Understanding Human Behaviour

When designing user experiences (UX), it's crucial to understand human behaviour. People are not robots; they have emotions, habits, and preferences. Good UX design relies on psychology to anticipate how users will act.

At its core, human behaviour is driven by goals. Users approach products, websites, or apps with specific objectives in mind, whether that's finding information, completing a task, or being entertained. As a UX designer, your job is to make sure that the user's journey towards their goal is as smooth as possible.

Mental Models
A key concept in psychology is the mental model. Mental models are the assumptions or expectations users bring with them based on their past experiences. For example,

if someone has used a website before, they expect certain buttons to be in familiar places, like a search bar at the top or a menu on the left. If your design breaks these expectations, users can feel confused or frustrated.

To create effective designs, it's important to align with users' mental models. However, this doesn't mean you should never innovate. It simply means that when you do something different, it should be intuitive enough that users can adapt quickly. A good rule of thumb is to respect convention when it helps users navigate, but don't be afraid to improve on those conventions if they lead to a better experience.

Cognitive Load
Cognitive load refers to the amount of mental effort required to use a product. If a design is too complex or requires too much thinking, users may become overwhelmed. They might make mistakes or abandon the task altogether.

To reduce cognitive load, keep things simple. Use clear language, familiar icons, and well-organised layouts. Break tasks into small, manageable steps. For instance, a long form on a website can be split into sections, which makes it feel less daunting. Avoid forcing users to remember too much information, such as entering the same details multiple times. In UX design, every decision you make should aim to reduce unnecessary friction. By keeping cognitive load in check, you help users achieve their goals with less effort, creating a more satisfying experience.

Attention and Perception

People's attention is limited, and it's important to design with that in mind. Most users will scan a page rather than reading it in detail. This means you should place the most important information where it's most likely to be seen – usually near the top of a page, in larger text, or in a highlighted area.

Users also tend to perceive things in certain patterns. For example, people often group items that are close together or that share the same colour. By using these psychological principles, you can guide users through your design in a logical way. You want their attention to flow naturally from one element to the next, helping them find what they're looking for without unnecessary delays.

5.2 Emotional Design and User Engagement

Design is not just about solving problems; it's also about creating experiences that resonate emotionally. People are more likely to engage with a product that makes them feel positive emotions. If a user enjoys using a product, they're more likely to return to it, recommend it, or even overlook minor flaws.

The Role of Emotions in UX

Emotion plays a significant role in decision-making. When users feel happy, excited, or reassured, they're more inclined to continue using a product. On the other hand, frustration, confusion, or boredom can lead to abandonment. Successful UX designers use emotional design to make the user experience both effective and enjoyable.

One way to achieve this is through the aesthetics of the design. Clean layouts, attractive colour schemes, and smooth animations all contribute to a more pleasant user experience. However, emotional design goes beyond looks. It also involves creating interactions that feel intuitive and rewarding. For instance, when a user completes a task, offering feedback in the form of a sound, message, or visual cue can reinforce a sense of accomplishment.

Trust and UsabilityTrust is another emotional factor that impacts UX. Users need to feel confident that a product is reliable, secure, and capable of meeting their needs. Clear, transparent design choices – such as clearly labelled buttons, obvious privacy policies, and secure payment methods – help build trust. Usability and trust go hand in hand. If a website or app is difficult to use, users are likely to lose trust in it, especially if it involves sensitive actions like making a purchase or entering personal information. By ensuring that your design is easy to navigate and free of errors, you can strengthen users' confidence in your product.

Engaging Users with PersonalisationAnother powerful tool for emotional design is personalisation. People appreciate feeling recognised and valued. When a product can adapt to their preferences, it creates a more tailored experience that keeps them coming back. For example, many websites and apps offer personalised recommendations based on previous interactions. This not only makes the user feel catered to but also reduces effort, as they don't need to search for what they want. However, personalisation must be handled with care. Too much personalisation, or irrelevant suggestions, can feel intrusive and push users away.

5.3 Motivation and User Behaviour

Understanding what motivates users is key to encouraging certain behaviours. If you want users to complete tasks, explore features, or return regularly to a product, you need to tap into their motivations.

Extrinsic vs Intrinsic Motivation
There are two main types of motivation: extrinsic and intrinsic. Extrinsic motivation comes from external rewards, such as badges, points, or discounts. For example, many apps use gamification techniques, like rewarding users for completing certain tasks or logging in daily. While extrinsic rewards can be effective, intrinsic motivation is often more powerful. Intrinsic motivation comes from within – it's the satisfaction users get from simply enjoying the experience or reaching a personal goal. For example, social media apps tap into the intrinsic desire for connection and self-expression.

A well-designed product will often combine both types of motivation. For instance, a fitness app might offer badges for milestones (extrinsic motivation), but users are more likely to keep using it because they feel healthier and fitter (intrinsic motivation). Striking the right balance between these two can create a compelling user experience that drives long-term engagement.

The Hook Model

The Hook Model, created by Nir Eyal, is a framework that helps explain how products can build habits in users. It involves four stages: trigger, action, reward, and investment.

1. **Trigger:** A trigger is what prompts a user to take action. It can be external, like a notification, or internal, like a desire to relieve boredom.

2. **Action:** This is the behaviour the user performs in response to the trigger. For example, clicking on a notification or opening an app.

3. **Reward:** After the action, users expect some kind of reward. The more immediate and satisfying the reward, the stronger the habit becomes. For example, in social media, the reward might be seeing new content or receiving likes and comments.

4. **Investment:** The final stage involves the user investing time, effort, or data into the product, which increases the likelihood of them returning. This could be personalising their profile, saving preferences, or contributing content. The more users invest, the more attached they become to the product.

Understanding and using the Hook Model allows UX designers to create experiences that are not only engaging but also habit-forming. However, it's important to use these techniques ethically. Designs should aim to add value to the user's life, rather than manipulating them into unnecessary behaviours.

Behavioural Economics in UX

Behavioural economics is the study of how people make decisions. In UX design, understanding these decision-making processes helps create experiences that guide users towards desired actions.

For instance, people often suffer from **choice paralysis** when presented with too many options. Simplifying choices or offering defaults can make decisions easier for users. Similarly, using **social proof** – showing that others have made a certain choice – can influence users to follow suit. This is why many websites highlight popular products or feature customer reviews.

Another concept from behavioural economics is **loss aversion**, which suggests that people are more motivated to avoid losses than to gain equivalent rewards. For example, limited-time offers or "last chance" messages can spur users to take action because they fear missing out on something valuable.

Conclusion

In UX design, understanding the psychology of users is just as important as mastering design tools or techniques. By recognising how people think, feel, and act, you can create experiences that are not only functional but also deeply satisfying. The key is to reduce cognitive load, engage emotions, and tap into motivations, helping users achieve their goals in the most seamless and enjoyable way possible. By aligning design with the natural behaviours and desires of users, you create a product that feels intuitive, trustworthy, and even delightful.

6

Chapter 6: Core UX Principles

In this chapter, we'll explore the fundamental principles that guide user experience (UX) design. Understanding these principles is key to creating digital products that users will enjoy and find valuable. The core principles are focused on enhancing the overall experience by making products useful, easy to use, and delightful. They apply to all forms of UX design, whether you're working on websites, apps, or physical products.

1. User-Centred Design

User-centred design is the heart of UX. This principle ensures that every decision in the design process is made with the user's needs in mind. It's not about what the designer thinks looks good or what the business wants; it's about how users will interact with and experience the product.

To achieve a user-centred design, it's important to:

- **Understand the users:** Research is critical. It's important to know who your users are, what they want, what problems they face, and what they expect from the product.

- **Involve users in the design process:** User testing and feedback are essential. By involving users in every stage of design, you ensure the product meets their expectations and solves their problems.

- **Design for real people:** Users come from different backgrounds, and they have different levels of digital literacy. A user-centred approach takes this into account and creates designs that work for a wide range of people.

2. Consistency

Consistency is one of the simplest but most effective ways to improve the user experience. When a product is consistent, it becomes predictable, and users feel more comfortable using it. Consistency applies to both visual elements and functionality.

Key aspects of consistency include:
Visual consistency: Ensure that the visual elements of your design (like buttons, fonts, and colours) remain the same across the entire product. This helps users navigate and understand the interface more easily.
Functional consistency: Functions and interactions should work in a predictable way. For example, if a swipe gesture performs a certain action in one part of an app, it should perform the same action everywhere in the app.

Internal and external consistency: Internal consistency refers to the design being uniform within itself, while external consistency refers to following broader design conventions across the industry. External consistency can reduce the learning curve, as users are already familiar with certain standards, like the meaning of common icons.

3. Simplicity

Good UX design is often about keeping things simple. Simplicity means making a product easy to understand and use. It's about removing unnecessary complexity and presenting only what is essential to the user.

Here are a few ways to maintain simplicity in UX design:

- **Minimise cognitive load:** Don't overwhelm users with too much information or too many choices. Focus on what is important and make actions clear and straightforward.

- **Use clear language:** Avoid jargon or complicated terms. Use language that is easy to understand, so users can quickly grasp what they need to do.

- **Reduce the number of steps**: Every additional step a user has to take is an opportunity for confusion or frustration. Simplify the journey by reducing the number of actions required to achieve a goal.

4. Feedback

Feedback is crucial in UX design because it helps users understand the result of their actions. Without feedback, users may feel uncertain or frustrated. Feedback can take many forms, such as visual cues, sound, or text notifications.

Types of feedback in UX design include:

- **Visual feedback:** This could be a button changing colour when clicked, or a progress bar indicating that a task is being completed. It reassures users that their actions have been registered.

- **Audio feedback:** Sounds can be used to confirm actions, like a click sound when a button is pressed or a notification chime when a message is received.

- **Textual feedback:** Displaying messages like "Your file has been uploaded" or "Error: Please try again" gives users a clear understanding of what's happening and what they should do next.

Providing feedback not only improves the user's experience but also makes the interaction feel more human.

5. Accessibility

Accessibility is about designing for everyone, including people with disabilities. A good UX design ensures that all users, regardless of their abilities, can use the product comfortably. Designing with accessibility in mind not only helps people with disabilities but often improves the experience for all users.

Some key elements of accessibility are:

- **Colour contrast:** Make sure there is enough contrast between text and background colours to make reading easier for people with visual impairments.

- **Keyboard navigation:** Ensure that your product can be navigated using a keyboard for users who may not be able to use a mouse or touchscreen.

- **Screen readers:** Provide text alternatives for images and other non-text content so screen readers can describe them to visually impaired users.

Making your product accessible isn't just the right thing to do; it's often a legal requirement in many countries.

6. Hierarchy and Structure

Hierarchy in design refers to the arrangement of elements in a way that indicates their importance. A well-structured design guides the user's attention to the most important information first and makes the interface easier to scan.

There are several ways to create hierarchy in design:

- **Size and scale:** Larger elements tend to attract more attention, so use size to highlight important features.

- **Colour and contrast:** High-contrast elements often stand out more, so use colour strategically to guide users through the interface.

- **Spacing and alignment:** Proper spacing between elements and a clear layout make the design feel organised and reduce the mental effort required to understand it.

A clear hierarchy not only makes the design more visually appealing but also makes it easier to use.

7. Usability

Usability is at the core of good UX design. It refers to how easily and effectively users can interact with a product. If a product is not usable, even the most visually stunning design will fail.

Key aspects of usability include:

- **Ease of learning:** Users should be able to quickly learn how to use the product, even if they've never seen it before.

- **Efficiency:** Once users have learned how to use the product, they should be able to accomplish tasks quickly and with minimal effort.

- **Error prevention and recovery:** The design should prevent errors as much as possible, but when mistakes happen, it should offer clear instructions on how to recover.

Usability testing is an important part of the design process, as it reveals potential problems and areas for improvement.

8. Emotion and Delight

While usability is essential, great UX design goes beyond just functionality. It's about creating a product that delights users and evokes positive emotions. Emotionally engaging designs can make users feel satisfied, motivated, and even excited to use a product.

Ways to incorporate emotion into design include:

- **Micro-interactions:** Small, delightful animations or responses when users perform an action can make the experience more enjoyable. For example, a subtle animation when a user adds an item to their cart can make the process feel more satisfying.

- **Personalisation:** Allowing users to customise their experience can create a sense of ownership and make them feel more connected to the product.

- **Surprise and delight:** Sometimes, adding a small unexpected element, like a playful error message or a creative loading animation, can make users smile and improve their overall experience.

While focusing on emotion, it's important to strike a balance between delight and usability. A design that is fun but not functional won't succeed in the long run.

9. Responsiveness and Flexibility

In today's world, people use a wide variety of devices to access digital products, from smartphones and tablets to desktop computers. Responsive design ensures that your product

looks and works well on all screen sizes and devices.
Key elements of responsiveness and flexibility include:

- **Adaptive layouts:** Create designs that automatically adjust to different screen sizes, ensuring a seamless experience across devices.

- **Touch-friendly elements:** On mobile devices, interactive elements need to be large enough and spaced appropriately so that they're easy to tap.

- **Cross-platform compatibility:** Ensure your product functions properly on different operating systems and browsers, providing a consistent experience regardless of the platform.

With more users accessing products on mobile devices, responsive design is no longer optional — it's a necessity. In conclusion, these core principles of UX design provide a solid foundation for creating products that are not only functional but also enjoyable to use. By focusing on the user, maintaining consistency, ensuring simplicity, and keeping accessibility in mind, designers can build experiences that resonate with users and stand the test of time.

7

Chapter 7: Human-Computer Interaction Basics

Understanding Human-Computer Interaction

Human-Computer Interaction, often shortened to HCI, is the study of how people interact with computers and other digital devices. The goal of HCI is to create user-friendly systems that allow people to perform their tasks efficiently and effectively. In this chapter, we will explore the key principles of HCI and how they relate to user experience (UX) design.

At its core, HCI is about understanding the relationship between humans and computers. This involves studying how users think, what they expect from technology, and how they use different interfaces. The better we understand these factors, the better we can design systems that meet the needs of users. HCI combines elements from computer science, cognitive psychology, design, and social sciences to create a comprehensive approach to understanding how users interact with technology.

The Importance of HCI

HCI is vital for several reasons. Firstly, technology is an integral part of our lives. We use computers, smartphones, and tablets for work, communication, and entertainment. If these devices are difficult to use or frustrating, it can lead to a poor experience. Good HCI design ensures that users can achieve their goals with ease and satisfaction.

Secondly, poor design can have serious consequences. For example, if a medical device is complicated to use, it can result in incorrect diagnoses or treatments. In contrast, a well-designed interface can improve productivity and reduce errors. Therefore, understanding HCI principles can lead to safer, more efficient, and more enjoyable user experiences.

Key Concepts in HCI

To understand HCI, we must consider several key concepts that shape the way we design interfaces. These include usability, accessibility, interaction styles, and user feedback.

Usability

Usability refers to how easy and pleasant a system is to use. A usable system should be intuitive, efficient, and satisfying. To ensure usability, designers must consider the needs and abilities of users. This includes understanding their prior experience, familiarity with technology, and expectations.

One way to assess usability is through user testing. By observing real users as they interact with a system, designers can identify pain points and areas for improvement. For example, if users struggle to find a specific feature, the designer may need to reconsider its placement or design.

Accessibility

Accessibility is about making sure that all users can use a system, including those with disabilities. This can involve providing alternative text for images, ensuring that interfaces can be navigated using a keyboard, and using colour contrasts that are easy to see. Designing for accessibility means considering the diverse range of users who may interact with a system and ensuring that no one is excluded.

A key principle of accessibility is that it benefits everyone. For example, captions on videos not only help people who are hard of hearing but also those who may be in a noisy environment. Thus, accessibility should be a fundamental aspect of HCI design.

Interaction Styles

Interaction styles refer to the ways users can interact with a system. This includes traditional methods like using a mouse and keyboard, as well as touch, voice, and gestures. Different interaction styles are suitable for different contexts. For instance, touchscreens are common on mobile devices, while keyboard and mouse are typically used on computers.

Designers should choose interaction styles that best suit the users and tasks at hand. For example, if users are often on the go, touch interactions may be more appropriate. On the other hand, for complex tasks requiring precision, a mouse and keyboard may be preferable.

User Feedback

User feedback is essential for improving HCI design. It provides valuable insights into how users perceive and interact with a system. Feedback can come in many forms, including surveys, interviews, and usability tests. By gathering feedback, designers can understand users' frustrations, needs, and preferences.

Incorporating user feedback into the design process is crucial. It helps ensure that the final product meets the expectations of its users and provides a positive experience. Continuous feedback also allows for ongoing improvements, making the system more effective over time.

Cognitive Psychology in HCI

Cognitive psychology plays a significant role in HCI. It examines how people think, learn, and remember, which is vital for designing intuitive interfaces. Understanding cognitive processes helps designers create systems that align with how users naturally think and behave.

One key concept from cognitive psychology is the notion of mental models. Mental models are the internal representations that users create in their minds to understand how a system works. Designers should strive to create systems that align with users' mental models, making it easier for them to predict outcomes and navigate the interface.

Another important aspect is the limited capacity of human memory. People can only hold a small amount of information in their working memory at one time. Therefore, designers should minimize cognitive load by simplifying tasks and presenting information in clear, manageable chunks.

Affordances and Signifiers

Affordances and signifiers are critical concepts in HCI that help users understand how to interact with an interface. Affordances refer to the properties of an object that suggest its function. For example, a button that appears raised suggests that it can be pressed. Designers should consider affordances when creating interfaces to make them more intuitive.

Signifiers are visual cues that indicate how to use an object. For instance, a play button on a video player is a signifier that suggests the user can start the video by clicking it. Effective use of affordances and signifiers can greatly enhance usability, as they guide users in their interactions.

Designing for Different Users

When designing for HCI, it is essential to consider the diversity of users. People come from various backgrounds, have different levels of experience with technology, and possess unique preferences and abilities. This diversity means that a one-size-fits-all approach does not work in design.

User personas are a valuable tool for understanding different users. A user persona is a fictional representation of a target user group based on research and data. By creating user personas, designers can better empathise with users and tailor their designs to meet specific needs.

The Role of Prototyping in HCI

Prototyping is an essential part of the HCI design process. A prototype is an early version of a product that allows designers to test ideas and gather feedback before finalising the design. Prototypes can range from simple sketches to fully interactive digital models.

Creating prototypes enables designers to explore different concepts and quickly identify what works and what doesn't. It also allows users to interact with a tangible representation of the design, providing valuable feedback that can guide further development.

The Iterative Design Process

HCI is fundamentally an iterative process. This means that designers continuously refine their work based on user feedback and testing.

The iterative design process typically involves the following steps:

1. **Research:** Understand users' needs, behaviours, and goals through surveys, interviews, and observations.

2. **Design:** Create initial design concepts and prototypes.

3. **Test:** Conduct usability tests with real users to gather feedback on the designs.

4. **Refine:** Use the feedback to improve the design and address any identified issues.

5. **Repeat:** Continue this cycle until the design meets user needs and expectations.

The iterative nature of HCI ensures that the final product is user-centered and well-suited to the target audience. It allows designers to make informed decisions based on actual user experiences rather than assumptions.

Conclusion

In conclusion, Human-Computer Interaction is a vital field that focuses on how people interact with technology. Understanding the principles of HCI, including usability, accessibility, interaction styles, and user feedback, is essential for creating effective user experiences. By considering cognitive psychology, affordances, and the diversity of users, designers can create intuitive and engaging interfaces.

The role of prototyping and the iterative design process is crucial in HCI, allowing designers to refine their work based on real user feedback. By following these principles, designers can create systems that enhance productivity, reduce errors, and ultimately provide users with a positive experience.

As technology continues to evolve, the importance of HCI will only grow. By prioritising the needs and experiences of users, we can create technology that enriches our lives and empowers us to achieve our goals.

8

Chapter 8: The Role of Empathy in UX

Understanding Empathy in User Experience Design

Empathy is a crucial aspect of user experience (UX) design. It refers to the ability to understand and share the feelings of others. In UX design, empathy helps designers create products and services that genuinely meet the needs of users. When designers practise empathy, they put themselves in the users' shoes. This means considering how users feel, think, and behave when they interact with a product.

At its core, empathy allows designers to see the world from the users' perspectives. This viewpoint is essential for designing intuitive interfaces and seamless experiences. When designers understand users' emotions and motivations, they can create solutions that address real problems. Instead of just focusing on aesthetics or technology, empathetic design prioritises the user's journey. This holistic approach results in products that are not only functional but also enjoyable to use.

In the past, many designers focused solely on technical specifications and design trends. However, this approach often led to products that were difficult to use or didn't resonate with the target audience. As the field of UX has evolved, the importance of empathy has become more widely recognised. Designers now strive to connect with users on a deeper level, leading to more successful products.

Why Empathy Matters in UX Design

Empathy is vital in UX design for several reasons. Firstly, it allows designers to identify user needs accurately. By understanding what users want and need, designers can create features that enhance usability. For example, if users struggle to find a specific function in a mobile app, an empathetic designer will take note and adjust the layout to make navigation easier. This responsiveness leads to a better overall experience for users.

Secondly, empathy fosters better communication between designers and users. When designers listen to users and take their feedback seriously, they create a two-way conversation. This dialogue not only helps to refine the product but also builds trust between the designer and the user. Users are more likely to feel valued when their opinions matter, leading to a positive relationship with the brand.

Thirdly, empathetic design can result in increased user satisfaction and loyalty. When users feel understood and catered to, they are more likely to return to the product and recommend it to others. This positive word-of-mouth can be invaluable for a brand. For instance, if a user enjoys using a website because it meets their needs and expectations, they will likely share their experience with friends and family.

Finally, empathy helps to create inclusive designs. By considering a diverse range of users, designers can create products that are accessible to everyone. This means thinking about users with different abilities, backgrounds, and experiences. An inclusive approach not only broadens the user base but also ensures that no one is left behind. For example, websites that incorporate features for users with visual impairments demonstrate how empathy can lead to more accessible design.

Techniques to Cultivate Empathy in UX Design

Designers can use several techniques to cultivate empathy in their work. One effective method is user research. This involves gathering information about users through surveys, interviews, and observations. By asking questions and listening to users' experiences, designers can gain insights into their needs and challenges. For example, a designer might conduct interviews with users to learn about their frustrations when using a particular app. These insights can then inform design decisions and lead to improvements.

Another useful technique is creating user personas. A persona is a fictional character that represents a specific segment of users. By developing detailed profiles of these personas, designers can better understand the motivations, behaviours, and goals of their target audience. For instance, a designer might create a persona for a busy professional who needs a time-management app. By considering this persona's needs, the designer can tailor the app's features to be more useful for users like them.

Additionally, empathy mapping is a helpful tool in the design process. This technique involves visually organising information about users, including what they think, feel, say, and do. By mapping out these elements, designers can gain a comprehensive view of the user experience. For example, an empathy map might reveal that users feel frustrated when they cannot easily find information on a website. This understanding can prompt designers to make changes that improve navigation and overall usability.

Testing prototypes with real users is another effective way to foster empathy. When designers observe users interacting with their designs, they can see firsthand how users respond to different elements. This feedback can be invaluable for making adjustments and improvements. For instance, if users struggle with a particular button or function, designers can revise it based on this feedback, leading to a more intuitive experience.

The Importance of Active Listening

Active listening is a key component of empathy in UX design. It involves fully concentrating on what users are saying and understanding their perspectives without interrupting or making assumptions. When designers practise active listening, they can uncover valuable insights about user needs and pain points. This skill is especially important during user interviews or feedback sessions.

By demonstrating that they are genuinely interested in users' opinions, designers can create a safe space for honest dialogue. This openness encourages users to share their thoughts and feelings more freely, leading to richer feedback. For example, a designer who listens actively might discover that users have specific concerns about data privacy when using an app. This information can be crucial for addressing user fears and improving the product.

Furthermore, active listening helps to build rapport with users. When users feel heard and valued, they are more likely to engage with the design process. This connection can lead to deeper insights and a better understanding of user needs. Ultimately, active listening enhances the empathetic design process and contributes to creating more effective products.

Creating User-Centred Design Solutions

Empathy in UX design leads to user-centred solutions. This means placing the user at the heart of the design process and prioritising their needs above all else. When designers adopt a user-centred approach, they create products that are not only functional but also enjoyable to use. This shift in focus can lead to innovative design solutions that truly resonate with users.

To create user-centred designs, designers must continuously gather user feedback and iterate on their solutions. This process of testing and refining is essential for ensuring that the final product meets users' expectations. For instance, if users report difficulty in understanding a particular feature, designers can revisit that feature and make necessary adjustments. This commitment to improvement reflects an empathetic approach that values user input.

Moreover, user-centred design encourages collaboration among team members. When designers, developers, and stakeholders work together to consider user needs, the outcome is often more effective. This collaborative spirit fosters creativity and innovation, as different perspectives can lead to unique solutions. For example, a developer might suggest a technical solution that aligns with user needs, resulting in a more cohesive product.

The Impact of Empathy on Brand Loyalty

Empathy in UX design can significantly impact brand loyalty. When users feel understood and appreciated, they are more likely to remain loyal to a brand. This loyalty stems from the positive experiences users have when interacting with empathetic designs. When a product meets their needs and enhances their lives, users develop a sense of attachment to the brand.

Furthermore, empathetic design can lead to increased customer satisfaction. When users enjoy using a product, they are more likely to share their experiences with others.

Positive word-of-mouth recommendations can be powerful in attracting new customers. For instance, if a user finds a travel booking website easy to navigate and enjoyable, they may recommend it to friends and family, expanding the brand's reach.

In contrast, when users feel neglected or misunderstood, they are more likely to abandon a product. Negative experiences can lead to frustration and disappointment, driving users away from a brand. Therefore, it is essential for designers to prioritise empathy in their work to foster positive relationships with users.

The Challenges of Practising Empathy

While empathy is vital in UX design, it can also present challenges. One of the main difficulties is the potential for bias. Designers may unconsciously project their own experiences onto users, leading to assumptions that do not reflect the actual needs of the target audience. To counteract this bias, designers must actively seek diverse perspectives and avoid making assumptions based on their own experiences.

Another challenge is the fast-paced nature of design projects. In some cases, time constraints may lead designers to skip important empathetic practices, such as user research and testing. This haste can result in designs that do not fully address user needs, ultimately harming the product's success. Therefore, it is crucial for designers to prioritise empathy, even when working under tight deadlines.

Lastly, designers may face resistance from stakeholders who prioritise aesthetics or technical specifications over user needs. This can create tension in the design process and hinder the ability to create empathetic solutions. To overcome this challenge, designers must advocate for the importance of empathy and educate stakeholders on its benefits. By demonstrating how empathetic designs lead to better user experiences, designers can foster a shared commitment to user-centred design.

Conclusion: The Lasting Value of Empathy in UX Design

In conclusion, empathy plays a vital role in UX design. It allows designers to understand users' needs, create user-centred solutions, and foster positive relationships between users and brands. By cultivating empathy through user research, active listening, and collaboration, designers can create products that genuinely resonate with users.

Empathy not only enhances the user experience but also contributes to brand loyalty and customer satisfaction. As designers continue to prioritise empathy in their work, they will create innovative solutions that meet the diverse needs of users. In an increasingly competitive market, empathetic design will be a key differentiator for successful products and brands.

As the field of UX design evolves, the importance of empathy will only grow. Designers must remain committed to understanding and addressing user needs, ensuring that their work has a lasting positive impact on users'

9

Chapter 9: Balancing Business and User Needs

In today's digital landscape, finding the right balance between business goals and user needs is crucial for successful UX design. This chapter explores how designers can create experiences that satisfy both the requirements of the business and the expectations of users. At its core, UX design aims to provide value to users while also driving business success. Achieving this balance begins with understanding the fundamental needs of both parties. Businesses typically seek to increase revenue, reduce costs, and enhance brand reputation. Users, on the other hand, desire a seamless, enjoyable experience that helps them achieve their goals efficiently.

Therefore, the first step in balancing these needs is conducting thorough research. This research should include user interviews, surveys, and usability testing to gain insights into user preferences and pain points. Simultaneously, businesses should outline their objectives clearly, defining what success looks like for them. By understanding the intersection of user needs and business goals, designers can create a product that serves both effectively.

Once the research is completed, it is essential to identify key performance indicators (KPIs) that measure success from both perspectives. KPIs for business might include conversion rates, average order value, or customer retention rates, while user-centric KPIs could focus on task completion time, user satisfaction scores, or the Net Promoter Score (NPS). By aligning these metrics, designers can create a balanced scorecard that highlights how user experience initiatives contribute to business objectives. For example, improving the usability of a website could lead to higher conversion rates, as a smoother user journey encourages more customers to complete their purchases. It is vital to communicate this alignment clearly to stakeholders, ensuring that everyone understands how user-focused design translates into business success.

Another critical aspect of balancing business and user needs is prioritisation. Designers must learn to prioritise features and changes based on both user feedback and business impact. Techniques such as the MoSCoW method—where features are categorised into Must have, Should have, Could have, and Won't have—can help streamline this process. By prioritising user needs that also support business goals, designers can create a roadmap that drives meaningful improvements. However, it is also essential to remain flexible. Business needs can shift due to market trends, competitive pressures, or internal strategy changes, while user preferences may evolve over time. Therefore, an iterative design process is necessary, allowing teams to adapt based on ongoing feedback and data analysis. Regularly revisiting research findings and KPIs ensures that the design remains relevant and effective.

Collaboration plays a significant role in balancing these needs. Designers should work closely with stakeholders from various departments, including marketing, sales, and customer support, to ensure a holistic understanding of business objectives. Regular workshops and brainstorming sessions can facilitate this collaboration, fostering a shared vision that prioritises both users and business outcomes. Involving users in the design process through co-design sessions or feedback loops can also enhance this collaboration, ensuring that their voice is heard and considered in decision-making. By creating a culture of collaboration, teams can foster innovation and generate creative solutions that meet both user needs and business goals.

Furthermore, understanding user personas can help bridge the gap between business and user needs. User personas are fictional representations of different user types based on research data. These personas help designers empathise with users and consider their specific needs and behaviours. By developing personas that reflect the target audience, designers can create tailored experiences that align with users' expectations while also supporting business objectives. For instance, if a persona represents a busy professional who needs quick access to information, the design should focus on efficiency, ensuring that critical information is easily accessible. This way, user needs guide the design decisions while still aligning with the business's overarching goals.

In addition to research and collaboration, creating a clear value proposition is essential for balancing business and user needs. A value proposition outlines the unique benefits a product or service offers to users and why it is better than the competition. By clearly communicating this value, businesses can attract users while ensuring that their offerings meet user needs effectively. Designers can play a vital role in crafting this value proposition through user-centric design. By showcasing how the product addresses specific user pain points or desires, designers can help the business differentiate itself in the market.

Moreover, it is essential to consider the long-term implications of design decisions. Short-term gains might boost revenue or user engagement, but they could lead to negative user experiences over time. For example, implementing too many ads to increase immediate revenue might frustrate users, leading to decreased engagement and loyalty. Therefore, designers should advocate for solutions that support sustainable business practices and foster long-term user satisfaction. This approach helps ensure that business needs do not overshadow user needs, ultimately leading to a stronger brand reputation and user loyalty.

To effectively balance business and user needs, it is crucial to foster a culture of empathy within the design team and the broader organisation. Empathy allows designers to understand the user experience deeply, which can lead to more thoughtful design decisions. Encouraging team members to engage with users, whether through observation, interviews, or usability testing, can help build this empathy. When the entire team understands and values user needs, they are more likely to prioritise them in their work. This shift in mindset can lead to innovative solutions that satisfy both users and business objectives.

Furthermore, it is vital to advocate for user needs at every stage of the design process. Designers should develop strong communication skills to articulate the importance of user experience to stakeholders. This communication involves presenting research findings, user feedback, and case studies that illustrate the link between user experience and business success. By making a compelling case for user-centric design, designers can ensure that user needs are prioritised alongside business objectives.

As businesses evolve, so do user expectations. Keeping abreast of industry trends, emerging technologies, and changing user behaviours is essential for maintaining this balance. Designers should engage in continuous learning, attending workshops, conferences, and networking events to stay informed about the latest developments in UX design and business strategies. By staying current, designers can anticipate changes in user needs and adjust their designs accordingly, ensuring that the final product remains relevant and valuable.

Finally, measuring the impact of design decisions is

crucial for understanding the balance between business and user needs. Using analytics tools, designers can track user behaviour, conversion rates, and other key metrics. This data-driven approach allows teams to assess the effectiveness of their designs and make informed decisions about future iterations. Regularly reviewing performance metrics not only helps identify areas for improvement but also provides insights into how well the design meets both user needs and business objectives. By establishing a feedback loop, designers can ensure that their work continually aligns with the evolving landscape of user expectations and business goals.

In conclusion, balancing business and user needs in UX design is an ongoing process that requires careful consideration, collaboration, and empathy. By conducting thorough research, defining clear KPIs, prioritising effectively, fostering collaboration, creating user personas, crafting a strong value proposition, advocating for user needs, and measuring impact, designers can create experiences that delight users while achieving business success. This balance is essential for building a strong brand reputation, driving customer loyalty, and ultimately, ensuring the long-term viability of a product in a competitive market. As the digital landscape continues to evolve, maintaining this balance will be more important than ever, enabling businesses to thrive while providing exceptional user experiences.

10

Chapter 10: Key Skills for a UX Designer

Part 1: Understanding Users

The first and most important skill for any UX designer is understanding users. This involves knowing who the users are, what they need, and how they behave. To achieve this, a designer must engage in user research, which is a process that collects information about users through various methods.

User research can take many forms, including interviews, surveys, and observations. For example, in interviews, designers can ask users about their experiences and expectations when using a product. Surveys can reach a larger audience and gather quantitative data about user preferences. Observations allow designers to see how users interact with a product in real time, revealing pain points and areas for improvement.

Empathy is a key component of understanding users. Designers need to put themselves in the users' shoes and think about their feelings, thoughts, and motivations. This helps designers create more intuitive and user-friendly experiences. Empathy can be cultivated through activities like creating user personas, which are fictional characters that represent different user types based on research. These personas help designers keep the users in mind throughout the design process.

Another important aspect of understanding users is creating user journeys. A user journey maps out the steps a user takes when interacting with a product. It highlights the user's goals, emotions, and challenges at each stage. By visualising this journey, designers can identify areas where users may struggle and find opportunities for improvement.

In addition to empathy, designers need strong analytical skills. They must be able to gather data from various sources and make sense of it. This involves looking for patterns and trends in user behaviour and using this information to inform design decisions. Analytical skills also help designers evaluate the effectiveness of their designs through methods like A/B testing, where different versions of a product are tested to see which one performs better.

Lastly, communication skills are crucial in understanding users. Designers must effectively share their findings and insights with other team members, such as developers, marketers, and stakeholders. This ensures everyone is on the same page and understands the users' needs and preferences.

In summary, understanding users is the foundation of UX design. It involves conducting thorough research, practising empathy, analysing data, and communicating effectively. By honing these skills, designers can create products that truly meet the needs of their users.

Part 2: Design Thinking

The second key skill for a UX designer is design thinking. Design thinking is a problem-solving approach that emphasises understanding users, challenging assumptions, and redefining problems in an attempt to identify alternative strategies and solutions. This process is iterative, meaning designers repeatedly refine their ideas based on user feedback and testing.

The design thinking process typically consists of five stages: empathise, define, ideate, prototype, and test. In the **empathise** stage, designers gather insights about users through research methods, as discussed in the previous section. This information forms the basis for understanding user needs and pain points.

In the **define** stage, designers synthesise the insights gained from the empathy stage. They create a clear problem statement that articulates what the users need and what challenges they face. This statement helps focus the design efforts on solving a specific problem rather than making vague improvements.

The **ideate** stage is where creativity comes into play. Designers brainstorm a wide range of ideas and solutions to the defined problem. It is essential to encourage free thinking and explore even the most outlandish ideas, as this can lead to innovative solutions. Techniques such as mind mapping or sketching can be helpful during this stage to visualise ideas and concepts.

After ideation, the next step is to create a **prototype**. A prototype is a tangible representation of the ideas generated in the ideation stage. It can be a simple sketch, a wireframe, or an interactive mock-up. Prototyping allows designers to bring their ideas to life and gives users something to interact with. It is important to remember that prototypes don't have to be perfect; they should simply serve as a tool for testing and gathering feedback.

Finally, the **test** stage involves presenting the prototype to users and observing how they interact with it. This is an opportunity to gather valuable feedback and make adjustments based on user experiences. Testing should be seen as a learning process, where designers continuously refine their solutions to create a better user experience.

Design thinking also encourages collaboration. It is often a team effort, bringing together people with different perspectives and expertise. Collaborating with others can lead to richer ideas and more comprehensive solutions. Designers should be open to feedback and willing to iterate on their designs based on input from teammates and users.

In conclusion, design thinking is a vital skill for UX designers. It provides a structured yet flexible framework for problem-solving that centres around the user. By mastering design thinking, designers can develop innovative solutions that effectively meet user needs and enhance their overall experience.

Part 3: Technical Skills and Tools

The third essential skill for a UX designer is proficiency in technical skills and tools. While a strong understanding of user behaviour and design thinking is crucial, being able to implement those ideas is equally important. This requires familiarity with various design tools and technologies that help bring concepts to life.

One of the fundamental tools in UX design is wireframing software. Wireframes are basic layouts that show the structure of a webpage or application without the distractions of colour, typography, or images. They help designers focus on functionality and user flow. Popular wireframing tools include Sketch, Adobe XD, and Figma. These tools allow designers to create interactive prototypes, making it easier to communicate ideas to stakeholders and test with users.

In addition to wireframing, knowledge of graphic design is beneficial. UX designers often need to create visual elements such as icons, buttons, and images. Familiarity with graphic design software like Adobe Photoshop or Illustrator can be helpful in creating these assets. Designers should also understand the principles of visual design, including colour theory, typography, and layout, to ensure their designs are aesthetically pleasing and effective.

Responsive design is another vital technical skill for UX designers. With the increasing use of mobile devices, it is essential to create designs that adapt to various screen sizes and orientations. Designers should know how to create flexible layouts and understand the principles of mobile-first design. This means prioritising the mobile experience before expanding to larger screens, ensuring usability across all devices.

Familiarity with front-end development languages such as HTML, CSS, and JavaScript can also be beneficial for UX designers. While designers don't need to be expert developers, understanding how websites and applications are built can inform design decisions and improve communication with development teams. Knowing the limitations and capabilities of coding can help designers create feasible designs that can be effectively implemented. Additionally, UX designers should be comfortable using analytics tools to measure user behaviour. Understanding tools like Google Analytics can help designers gain insights into how users interact with their products. This data is invaluable for making informed design decisions and continuously improving user experiences.

Lastly, staying updated with industry trends and emerging technologies is crucial for UX designers. The field of UX design is constantly evolving, and new tools and techniques emerge regularly. Participating in workshops, attending conferences, and following industry leaders on social media can help designers stay informed about the latest developments and best practices.

In summary, technical skills and familiarity with design tools are essential for UX designers. Mastering wireframing, graphic design, responsive design, front-end development, and analytics will enable designers to create effective and engaging user experiences. By combining these technical abilities with a strong understanding of users and design thinking, UX designers can excel in their roles and make a significant impact in their field.

II

User Research and Analysis

Discover the importance of understanding your users and how to gather meaningful insights. This section explores various research methods to understand user behavior, needs, and motivations. Learn how to create personas, conduct interviews, analyze user feedback, and transform data into actionable design strategies.

11

Chapter 11: Understanding the User: Research Methods

Understanding users is at the heart of effective UX design. Knowing who your users are, what they need, and how they behave can significantly enhance the design process. This chapter explores various research methods that help designers gather valuable insights about users. By employing these methods, designers can create products that meet users' needs, resulting in a better overall experience.

1. Surveys and Questionnaires

Surveys and questionnaires are popular research tools used to gather quantitative data from users. They allow designers to reach a large audience and obtain a wide range of opinions. Surveys typically consist of closed questions, which provide respondents with specific options to choose from. This format makes it easier to analyse the data statistically. For example, a survey might ask users to rate their satisfaction with a product on a scale of one to five.

On the other hand, questionnaires can also include open-ended questions, allowing users to express their thoughts in their own words. This qualitative data can provide deeper insights into user preferences and pain points. For instance, a questionnaire might ask, "What features do you think would improve our website?" By analysing the responses, designers can identify common themes and make informed design decisions.

When conducting surveys and questionnaires, it is essential to consider the target audience. The questions should be clear and concise to avoid confusion. Additionally, the timing of the survey can impact the response rate. Sending surveys immediately after a user has interacted with a product can lead to more accurate feedback.

Finally, it's crucial to analyse the data collected effectively. Statistical tools can help identify trends and patterns, but qualitative data should also be considered. Combining both quantitative and qualitative insights can lead to a comprehensive understanding of user needs.

2. Interviews

Interviews are a powerful qualitative research method that allows designers to engage directly with users. They provide an opportunity to gather in-depth information about user experiences, motivations, and behaviours. During an interview, a designer can ask open-ended questions, encouraging users to share their thoughts and feelings about a product or service.

The setting for interviews can vary. They can take place in person, over the phone, or through video calls. Regardless of the format, creating a comfortable environment is crucial. Users should feel at ease to express their honest opinions without fear of judgment.

To conduct effective interviews, it is essential to prepare a list of questions beforehand. However, it is equally important to be flexible during the conversation. Sometimes, users might reveal valuable insights that were not initially anticipated. Active listening plays a significant role in this process; designers should pay close attention to users' responses and ask follow-up questions to delve deeper into specific topics.

After conducting interviews, it is vital to analyse the findings systematically. Taking detailed notes or recording the conversations (with permission) can help designers remember key insights. Thematic analysis can be used to identify recurring patterns and trends across different interviews. This information can then be used to inform design decisions and improve user experiences.

3. Usability Testing

Usability testing is a method that focuses on evaluating a product's user-friendliness. This technique involves observing users as they interact with a product, identifying any challenges or frustrations they encounter. The primary goal is to ensure that the product is easy to use and meets user needs effectively.

To conduct usability testing, designers typically create specific tasks for users to complete while interacting with the product. For example, if testing a website, users might be asked to find a particular piece of information or complete a transaction. Observers watch how users navigate the product, taking note of any difficulties they face.

There are different types of usability testing, including moderated and unmoderated tests. Moderated tests involve a facilitator guiding the session and asking questions, while unmoderated tests allow users to complete tasks independently. Each approach has its advantages and disadvantages, and the choice depends on the research goals and available resources.

After the testing session, designers should analyse the data collected. This includes both qualitative feedback from users and quantitative metrics, such as task completion rates and time taken to complete tasks. Identifying common usability issues is crucial for making improvements to the product.

Incorporating usability testing into the design process helps ensure that products are intuitive and user-friendly. By addressing usability concerns early on, designers can avoid costly changes later in the development cycle.

4. Contextual Inquiry

Contextual inquiry is a research method that combines observation and interviews. It allows designers to see how users interact with a product in their natural environment. By observing users in context, designers gain insights into the real-world challenges and tasks users face.

During a contextual inquiry, designers visit users at their workplace or home, observing their behaviours and interactions with the product. This immersive approach provides valuable context that might be missed in traditional interviews. For instance, seeing how users navigate a website while multitasking can reveal insights into their needs and preferences.

While observing, designers should take detailed notes and ask questions to clarify users' actions and decisions. It's essential to strike a balance between observation and interaction; designers should not disrupt the user's natural workflow but also seek to understand their thought process.

After the inquiry, analysing the collected data is vital. This method often yields rich qualitative insights, and thematic analysis can help identify key patterns. Designers can use these insights to inform design decisions and create products that better align with user needs.

5. Ethnographic Studies

Ethnographic studies involve in-depth research into users' lives and environments. This method aims to understand users' behaviours, motivations, and challenges in their everyday contexts. Ethnographers spend extended periods with users, observing their interactions and collecting qualitative data through interviews and informal conversations.

This approach allows designers to gain a holistic understanding of users, uncovering hidden needs that might not surface in other research methods. For example, an ethnographic study might reveal how users incorporate technology into their daily routines, highlighting areas for improvement in existing products.

Ethnographic studies require a significant investment of time and resources. Researchers must build trust with users to encourage open and honest feedback. The insights gathered can be incredibly valuable, as they provide a comprehensive view of users' experiences.

After completing the study, researchers should carefully analyse the findings, looking for patterns and themes that emerge. The data can inform design decisions and help create user-centred products that resonate with real-world needs.

Conclusion

In conclusion, understanding the user is a fundamental aspect of UX design. By employing various research methods such as surveys, interviews, usability testing, contextual inquiries, and ethnographic studies, designers can gather valuable insights into user needs and behaviours. Each method offers unique advantages, and combining them can lead to a more comprehensive understanding of the target audience. This understanding ultimately informs design decisions, leading to products that provide better user experiences. By investing time in user research, designers can create solutions that not only meet user needs but also delight them, resulting in successful products that stand out in the marketplace.

12

Chapter 12: Conducting User Interviews

Importance of User Interviews

User interviews are an essential method for gathering insights about how people interact with your product or service. Conducting these interviews effectively can help you understand the needs, preferences, and pain points of your users.

Preparation for Interviews

The first step in conducting user interviews is to prepare thoroughly. Begin by defining the goals of the interview. What specific information are you hoping to gather? Are you looking to understand how users navigate your website, what features they find most useful, or what challenges they encounter? Having clear objectives will guide your questions and ensure that the interview stays focused.

Selecting Participants

Next, it's important to select the right participants. Choose users who represent your target audience. If your product is aimed at young professionals, ensure that the interviewees are young professionals. This way, the feedback you gather will be relevant and insightful. To recruit participants, you can reach out to your existing user base, use social media, or even collaborate with research firms.

Crafting Interview Questions

Once you have your participants, it's time to prepare your interview questions. Open-ended questions are particularly useful as they encourage participants to share their thoughts and experiences in detail. Instead of asking, "Did you find our website easy to use?" you might ask, "Can you describe your experience navigating our website?" This approach gives users the freedom to express themselves fully. It's also important to avoid leading questions, as these can bias the responses. For instance, instead of asking, "How did you like our new feature?" you could ask, "What are your thoughts on our new feature?" This way, you allow users to express any opinions, whether positive or negative.

Using Prompts and Scenarios

Another helpful technique is to use prompts or scenarios to encourage discussion. You might say, "Imagine you are trying to book a flight on our website. Can you walk me through what you would do?" This can help users think aloud, providing valuable insights into their thought processes.

Setting the Right Environment

Before the interviews, make sure to set the right environment. Conduct the interviews in a quiet, comfortable space, whether it's in person or online. Ensure that the technology works smoothly if you are using video conferencing tools. This will help participants feel at ease and encourage open communication.

Building Rapport

It's also crucial to build rapport with the interviewees. Start the conversation with some casual chit-chat to help them relax. You might ask about their day or comment on something light-hearted before diving into the questions. Building a connection can lead to more honest and detailed responses.

Practicing Active Listening

During the interview, practice active listening. Pay close attention to what the participants say, and be open to follow-up questions. If they mention something interesting or unexpected, don't hesitate to dig deeper. For example, if a user mentions they had trouble finding a specific feature, ask them to explain what made it difficult.

Documenting the Interviews

Another important aspect of conducting user interviews is to take thorough notes or record the session, with permission from the participants. This documentation will be invaluable for later analysis. If you are recording the interview, make sure to inform participants beforehand and reassure them that their privacy will be respected.

Analyzing Findings

After the interview, take time to review your notes or recordings while the information is still fresh in your mind. Look for common themes or patterns that emerged during the discussions. This can help you identify key insights that can inform your design decisions. It's also a good idea to summarise the findings and share them with your team. This collaborative approach encourages everyone to learn from the user feedback and integrate it into their work.

Ongoing Process

Finally, remember that conducting user interviews is an ongoing process. You may need to conduct several rounds of interviews as your product evolves or as you explore new features. Regular user feedback will help you stay in tune with your audience and make informed design choices.

Conclusion

By following these guidelines, you can conduct effective user interviews that yield valuable insights and ultimately enhance the user experience of your product. In summary, conducting user interviews is a powerful tool in the UX design process. By carefully preparing your questions, selecting the right participants, and creating a comfortable environment, you can gather insights that will help shape your design decisions. Always listen actively and be open to exploring new ideas that emerge during the conversation. With practice, you will become skilled at conducting interviews that not only inform your design work but also build a deeper understanding of your users.

13

Chapter 13: Creating Personas

Understanding Personas

In the world of user experience (UX) design, creating personas is an essential step that helps designers understand the people who will use their products. A persona is a fictional character that represents a specific user type. It is built based on real data gathered from research and insights about users. When designers create personas, they bring together various aspects of the users' lives, such as their goals, behaviours, needs, and challenges. This process is crucial because it shifts the focus away from general assumptions about users and helps the design team to empathise with them.

To create effective personas, it is vital to conduct thorough research. This can include interviews, surveys, and observations of real users. By collecting qualitative and quantitative data, designers can develop a comprehensive understanding of their target audience. For example, if a design team is creating an app for elderly users, they might gather data about their technological proficiency, daily routines, and common challenges. This information helps designers create personas that reflect the true diversity of users.

Each persona should include specific details like a name, age, job, hobbies, and challenges they face. By providing these details, the team can picture the user as a real person, making it easier to design solutions that meet their needs. Moreover, personas should not only represent a single user but should encapsulate different segments of the target audience. This approach ensures that the final design is inclusive and caters to various user types.

Using Personas in the Design Process

Once personas are created, they become a powerful tool throughout the design process. They guide decision-making by helping the team stay focused on the users' needs and expectations. Whenever a design choice needs to be made, the team can refer back to the personas to ask themselves, "How would this affect our persona?" This practice helps avoid design choices that might be based on personal preferences rather than user needs.

Personas also play a crucial role in creating user scenarios. A user scenario is a story that describes how a persona interacts with the product in a specific context. For example, if a persona represents a busy professional who uses a task management app, a scenario might illustrate how this user schedules their day and prioritises tasks. These scenarios help the design team understand how users will engage with their product in real life.

In addition to aiding in design decisions, personas can also be helpful in usability testing. During testing sessions, designers can refer to the personas to ensure that the tasks and features are relevant to the users they represent. This ensures that feedback collected during testing is actionable and aligned with the personas' expectations.

Furthermore, sharing personas with stakeholders is a great way to foster understanding and alignment within the team. When everyone is on the same page regarding who the users are, it creates a shared vision and helps avoid misunderstandings. This collective understanding also leads to better collaboration among team members, as they can all reference the same personas throughout the project.

Keeping Personas Updated

Creating personas is not a one-time task. User behaviours and needs can change over time, so it is crucial to keep personas updated. Regularly revisiting and refining personas based on new research ensures that they remain relevant and accurate. This might involve conducting new interviews, analysing user feedback, or observing changes in market trends.

It's also essential to recognise when to create new personas. If significant changes in user demographics or technology occur, it may be necessary to develop additional personas to capture these shifts. For instance, if a new technology emerges that a certain segment of users begins to adopt, creating a new persona can help the design team address the specific needs of that group.

Moreover, involving the team in the persona creation and updating process can lead to a more comprehensive understanding of the users. Encouraging team members to share their insights and experiences with users can lead to richer, more nuanced personas. This collaborative approach fosters a culture of empathy towards users and strengthens the design process.

In conclusion, creating personas is a fundamental part of UX design that helps teams empathise with users and make informed design decisions. By understanding users through research, utilising personas throughout the design process, and keeping them updated, designers can create products that genuinely meet the needs of their audience. Ultimately, this practice leads to better user experiences and increases the chances of a product's success in the market.

14

Chapter 14: User Journey Mapping

User journey mapping is a crucial process in understanding how users interact with a product or service. It allows designers to visualise the steps a user takes, from their first encounter with a brand to the final goal they want to achieve. In this chapter, we will explore what user journey mapping is, why it is important, and how to create effective user journey maps.

Understanding User Journey Mapping

User journey mapping involves creating a visual representation of the user's experience. It outlines every touchpoint a user has with a product, from the initial awareness stage to the moment they become a loyal customer. Each touchpoint is an opportunity for the user to interact with the brand. These can include visiting a website, engaging with customer service, or using the product itself.

When creating a user journey map, it is essential to consider the user's perspective. This means looking at the process through their eyes and understanding their thoughts, feelings, and motivations at each stage. By doing this, designers can identify pain points or areas where users may struggle. A user journey map typically includes several key components: the user persona, stages of the journey, touchpoints, user emotions, and pain points.

User Persona: A user persona is a fictional character that represents a segment of your target audience. It is based on real data and research about your users. By defining a user persona, you can better understand their needs, goals, and behaviours. This understanding is crucial when mapping their journey.

Stages of the Journey: The user journey can be broken down into several stages, including awareness, consideration, decision, and post-purchase. Each of these stages represents a different phase in the user's experience. During the awareness stage, users become aware of a problem they need to solve. In the consideration stage, they start researching potential solutions. The decision stage is when they choose a product, and the post-purchase stage involves using the product and seeking support if needed.

Touchpoints: Touchpoints are the various points of interaction between the user and the brand. They can be physical or digital, such as social media ads, website visits, product demonstrations, or customer service calls. Identifying these touchpoints is vital for understanding how users engage with your product.

User Emotions: Mapping out user emotions at each stage helps identify how they feel during their journey. Are they excited, frustrated, or confused? Understanding these emotions can help designers create a better experience for users. For instance, if users feel frustrated during the consideration stage, you may need to simplify your product information.

Pain Points: Pain points are the challenges or obstacles that users face during their journey. Identifying these pain points allows designers to focus on improving the user experience. By addressing these issues, you can enhance user satisfaction and increase the likelihood of repeat business.

Why User Journey Mapping is Important

User journey mapping is essential for several reasons. Firstly, it helps designers empathise with users. By understanding their needs and frustrations, designers can create products and services that genuinely meet user expectations. This empathy is vital in building a user-centric design approach.

Secondly, user journey mapping provides valuable insights into user behaviour. By visualising the entire journey, designers can identify patterns and trends in how users interact with a product. This data can inform design decisions and help improve the overall user experience. For example, if many users drop off at a particular stage, it may indicate a problem with that part of the journey that needs addressing.

Moreover, user journey maps can serve as a communication tool among team members. They provide a clear visual representation of the user experience that can be easily shared with stakeholders. This visual clarity helps align everyone's understanding of the user journey, leading to more cohesive design strategies.

Finally, user journey mapping is a dynamic process. It is not a one-time task but rather an ongoing effort that should evolve as user needs and behaviours change. Regularly updating the journey map based on user feedback and data ensures that your product remains relevant and user-friendly.

How to Create an Effective User Journey Map

Creating an effective user journey map involves several steps. Here is a simple guide to help you through the process:

Step 1: Define Your User Persona
Start by defining your user persona. Gather data about your target audience through surveys, interviews, and research. Understand their demographics, needs, goals, and behaviours. Creating a detailed user persona will guide you throughout the mapping process.

Step 2: Identify the Stages of the Journey
Next, outline the stages of the user journey. Determine the key phases your users go through when interacting with your product. Common stages include awareness, consideration, decision, and post-purchase. Be sure to tailor these stages to your specific product and audience.

Step 3: List Touchpoints
Once you have the stages defined, identify the touchpoints associated with each stage. Consider all the ways users interact with your product, including online and offline channels. This could include social media, your website, customer support, and product usage. Listing all touchpoints will help you understand where users engage with your brand.

Step 4: Map User Emotions and Pain Points
At this point, you can begin mapping user emotions and pain points for each stage of the journey. Ask yourself questions like: How does the user feel at this stage? What challenges are they facing? Consider using a scale to represent emotions, such as happy, neutral, and frustrated. This emotional mapping will highlight areas for improvement.

Step 5: Visualise the User Journey
With all the information gathered, it's time to create the visual representation of the user journey. You can use various tools for this, from simple pen and paper to specialised software like Miro or Lucidchart. The map should be clear and easy to understand, showcasing the stages, touchpoints, emotions, and pain points in a cohesive way.

Step 6: Review and Validate
Once the user journey map is complete, it is essential to review it with your team and stakeholders. Gather feedback and validate the findings. This collaboration will help ensure that your journey map accurately reflects the user experience.

Step 7: Iterate and Update

User journey mapping is not a one-time activity. As you gather more data and feedback, be prepared to iterate and update your journey map. This ongoing process will help you stay aligned with user needs and improve the overall experience continuously.

Conclusion

User journey mapping is a powerful tool for understanding and improving the user experience. By visualising the user's journey, designers can empathise with users, identify pain points, and create solutions that enhance satisfaction. Following the steps outlined in this chapter, you can create effective user journey maps that guide your design decisions and ultimately lead to a better product. Remember, the user journey is not static; it evolves as user needs change, so stay committed to iterating and improving based on user feedback. In doing so, you will create a product that not only meets but exceeds user expectations.

15

Chapter 15: Gathering Data: Surveys, Polls, and Questionnaires

In the world of User Experience (UX) design, understanding what users think and feel about a product or service is vital. One of the best ways to gather this information is through surveys, polls, and questionnaires. These tools help designers and businesses collect valuable data from their users, allowing them to make informed decisions and improve their offerings. In this chapter, we will explore the differences between these methods, how to design effective surveys, and the best practices for analysing the data you collect.

Understanding Surveys, Polls, and Questionnaires

At first glance, surveys, polls, and questionnaires may seem quite similar, but they serve different purposes and are used in different ways.

Surveys are comprehensive tools designed to collect

detailed information about users' experiences, opinions, and behaviours. They often include a mix of open-ended and closed-ended questions. Open-ended questions allow respondents to express their thoughts freely, providing richer data. Closed-ended questions, such as multiple choice or rating scales, make it easier to analyse responses statistically. Surveys can be lengthy, usually taking 10 to 30 minutes to complete, depending on the number of questions and the depth of information required.

Polls, on the other hand, are typically much shorter and focus on a specific topic or question. They usually consist of a single question with limited response options, making them quick to answer. Polls are often used in real-time situations, like social media, where you want immediate feedback or insights. Because of their brevity, polls may not provide as much detail as surveys, but they can still yield valuable insights into users' preferences or trends.

Questionnaires are a set of questions designed to gather specific information. While they can resemble surveys, they are often less comprehensive and can be used in various contexts, such as research studies or market analysis. Questionnaires can include both closed and open-ended questions, but they are typically more focused on specific areas of interest rather than the broader insights gathered in a survey.

When choosing which method to use, consider your objectives. If you want in-depth insights into user experiences, a survey may be the best option. For quick feedback on a specific topic, a poll could suffice. If you need targeted information on a particular aspect, a questionnaire might be the way to go.

Designing Effective Surveys

Designing a successful survey is crucial for gathering meaningful data. Here are some essential tips for creating effective surveys that engage respondents and yield reliable results.

Define Your Objectives

Before you begin designing your survey, clearly define your objectives. What specific information do you want to gather? Are you looking to understand user satisfaction, gather feedback on a new feature, or assess usability issues? Having clear goals will help you formulate relevant questions and guide the structure of your survey. Write down your objectives, and keep them in mind throughout the design process.

Keep it Short and Focused

While it may be tempting to ask numerous questions to cover all possible areas of interest, it is essential to keep your survey short and focused. Long surveys can lead to respondent fatigue, causing users to abandon the survey before completing it. Aim for a length that takes no more than 10 to 15 minutes to complete. Prioritise the most important questions that align with your objectives, and avoid unnecessary or redundant questions.

Use Clear and Simple Language

When formulating questions, use clear and simple language. Avoid jargon or technical terms that respondents may not understand. The goal is to gather accurate responses, so make sure your questions are straightforward and easy to comprehend. For example, instead of asking, "How would you rate the usability of our application on a Likert scale?" consider a simpler phrasing, such as, "How easy is it to use our app?"

Mix Question Types

To maintain respondent engagement and gather a variety of data, use a mix of question types. Include closed-ended questions, such as multiple-choice and rating scales, alongside open-ended questions that allow respondents to elaborate on their thoughts. This combination will provide quantitative data for analysis while also capturing qualitative insights that can enrich your understanding of user experiences.

Pilot Test Your Survey

Before launching your survey to a wider audience, conduct a pilot test with a small group of users. This test will help identify any issues with question clarity, survey length, or technical glitches. Ask participants for feedback on their experience, and use this information to make necessary adjustments. Pilot testing can help ensure that your survey is effective and user-friendly.

Use Logical Flow and Structure

Organise your survey in a logical manner, grouping related questions together. Start with general questions and gradually move to more specific topics. This approach helps respondents ease into the survey and keeps them engaged. Use clear section headings or progress indicators to show users how far along they are in the survey, as this can encourage completion.

Ensure Anonymity and Confidentiality

To encourage honest responses, reassure respondents that their answers will remain anonymous and confidential. This is particularly important for sensitive topics or when gathering feedback about a product or service. If possible, provide an option for respondents to skip questions they are uncomfortable answering. Building trust with participants can lead to more accurate and valuable data.

Provide Incentives

Offering incentives can increase participation rates in your survey. Consider providing small rewards, such as discounts, gift cards, or entries into a prize draw for completing the survey. Make sure to clearly communicate the incentive in your survey invitation, as this can motivate more users to take part.

Conducting Polls for Quick Feedback

Polls are an excellent way to gather quick insights from your users. They can be used in various settings, including social media, websites, or during events. Here are some tips for conducting effective polls.

Choose the Right Platform

When conducting a poll, choose the platform that best reaches your target audience. Social media platforms like Twitter, Instagram, and Facebook offer built-in polling features that can engage users effectively. Alternatively, you can use survey tools that allow for easy integration into your website or email campaigns. Consider where your audience is most active and select the platform accordingly.

Craft Clear and Concise Questions

Since polls are typically focused on a single question, make sure it is clear and concise. Avoid ambiguity and ensure respondents understand exactly what you are asking. For example, instead of asking, "What do you think of our new feature?" consider phrasing it as "Do you find our new feature helpful?" with simple yes/no options. This makes it easier for respondents to provide quick feedback.

Limit Response Options

To keep your poll straightforward, limit the response options to three or four choices. Too many options can overwhelm respondents and lead to indecision. Focus on the most relevant choices that align with your objective. For example, if you're polling about colour preferences for a new product, you could provide options like "Red," "Blue," "Green," and "Yellow."

Promote Your Poll

Once your poll is live, promote it across your channels to maximise participation. Share it on social media, include it in newsletters, or highlight it on your website. Encourage users to participate by explaining the purpose of the poll and how their feedback will be used. Creating a sense of urgency can also help drive engagement, so consider setting a deadline for responses.

Analyse and Act on the Results

After the poll has closed, analyse the results and share them with your audience. Highlight key insights and trends that emerged from the data. If the poll is related to a specific product or feature, communicate any changes or updates that will be made based on the feedback received. This not only shows users that their opinions matter but also builds trust and encourages future participation.

Creating Questionnaires for Targeted Information

Questionnaires can be a valuable tool for collecting specific information from users. They allow you to gather data on particular areas of interest, helping you make informed design decisions. Here are some tips for creating effective questionnaires.

Determine Your Focus

Before creating a questionnaire, identify the specific focus or topic you want to explore. This could be user demographics, feedback on a particular feature, or user satisfaction levels. Having a clear focus will guide the questions you include and ensure that the data collected is relevant to your goals.

Use Clear and Direct Questions

As with surveys, clarity is key when designing questionnaires. Use direct and straightforward language to avoid confusion. Ensure that respondents understand what you are asking and how they should respond. For instance, instead of asking, "What are your thoughts on our new interface?" you could ask, "What do you like most about our new interface?" This specificity encourages more precise responses.

Include a Mix of Question Types

Just as with surveys, including a mix of question types can enhance the quality of your questionnaire. Use closed-ended questions for easy quantitative analysis and open-ended questions for richer qualitative insights. This blend allows you to gather a range of data that can inform your design decisions effectively.

Keep It User-Friendly

Design your questionnaire to be user-friendly and easy to navigate. Use a clean layout with clear instructions and progress indicators. Avoid overly complicated question formats that may confuse respondents. Aim for a design that is visually appealing and accessible, ensuring users can complete the questionnaire without frustration.

Test and Revise

Before distributing your questionnaire widely, test it with a small group of users. Gather feedback on the clarity and flow of the questions, and make any necessary adjustments. Revise the questionnaire based on user input to ensure it effectively gathers the information you need.

Follow Up and Thank Participants

After respondents complete your questionnaire, follow up with a thank you message. This gesture shows appreciation for their time and feedback. If appropriate, consider sharing key findings from the questionnaire to demonstrate how their input is contributing to your work.

16

Chapter 16: Heuristic Evaluation

Heuristic evaluation is an essential method in user experience (UX) design that helps identify usability problems in a user interface. This technique allows designers and usability experts to evaluate a product by examining it against a set of established principles known as heuristics. These heuristics serve as general rules of thumb that can guide the evaluation process, making it easier to identify potential issues that may hinder user experience.

One of the most widely recognised sets of heuristics was developed by Jakob Nielsen, a leading expert in usability. His list includes ten key principles that address various aspects of user interaction. These principles include visibility of system status, match between system and the real world, user control and freedom, consistency and standards, error prevention, recognition rather than recall, flexibility and efficiency of use, aesthetic and minimalist design, help users recognise, diagnose, and recover from errors, and help and documentation. Each of these principles provides a lens through which evaluators can assess how well a design meets user needs and expectations.

The process of heuristic evaluation typically involves a small group of evaluators who independently examine the user interface. Each evaluator uses the heuristics as a guide to identify issues related to usability, accessibility, and overall user experience. After this individual evaluation, the group comes together to discuss their findings, combining insights to create a comprehensive list of usability problems. This collaborative aspect of heuristic evaluation can lead to a richer understanding of user experience and a more effective design solution.

One of the key benefits of heuristic evaluation is its efficiency. It can be conducted relatively quickly compared to other usability testing methods, such as user testing, which often requires extensive planning and coordination. Heuristic evaluations can be done at various stages of the design process, from early prototypes to final designs, allowing designers to identify and address usability issues before the product is launched. This early intervention can save time and resources in the long run, as fixing problems in the design stage is often less costly than making changes after a product has been released.

Despite its many advantages, heuristic evaluation is not without its challenges. One significant limitation is that it relies heavily on the expertise of the evaluators. If the evaluators are not well-versed in usability principles or do not have a solid understanding of the target audience, their findings may not accurately reflect user needs. Additionally, because heuristic evaluations are subjective, different evaluators may identify different issues, leading to potential inconsistencies in the evaluation results.

To mitigate these challenges, it is crucial to select evaluators who have a strong background in UX design and usability principles. Ideally, the team should include a mix of experts, including designers, developers, and even potential users, to ensure a well-rounded evaluation. Furthermore, providing evaluators with context about the target audience and their needs can enhance the evaluation process, allowing for more relevant and actionable insights.

In conclusion, heuristic evaluation is a valuable technique in the field of UX design that helps identify usability problems in a user interface. By examining a product against established principles, designers can gain valuable insights into how to improve user experience. Although there are challenges associated with this method, careful selection of evaluators and providing adequate context can lead to effective outcomes. Ultimately, incorporating heuristic evaluation into the design process can result in more user-friendly products that better meet the needs of their intended audience.

Summary of Heuristic Evaluation Principles

To help clarify the principles of heuristic evaluation, we can briefly summarise them here:

1. **Visibility of System Status**: Users should always be informed about what is happening in the system, such as loading processes or actions that are being performed.

2. **Match Between System and the Real World**: The interface should speak the user's language, using familiar terms and concepts rather than technical jargon.

3. **User Control and Freedom**: Users often make mistakes. They should be able to undo or redo actions easily to correct any errors.

4. **Consistency and Standards**: Users should not have to wonder whether different words, situations, or actions mean the same thing. Consistency in design helps create a smoother experience.

5. **Error Prevention**: The design should be proactive in preventing errors before they occur, rather than merely providing error messages.

6. **Recognition Rather than Recall**: The interface should minimise the user's memory load by making options and information easily accessible.

7. **Flexibility and Efficiency of Use**: The design should cater to both novice and experienced users, allowing them to tailor frequent actions for greater efficiency.

8. **Aesthetic and Minimalist Design**: Interfaces should

not contain irrelevant or rarely needed information. A clean and uncluttered design enhances user experience.

9. **Help Users Recognise, Diagnose, and Recover from Errors**: Error messages should be expressed in plain language, indicating the problem and suggesting a solution.

10. **Help and Documentation**: Although ideally the system should be usable without documentation, it may still be necessary to provide help information that is easy to search and focused on the user's task.

By keeping these principles in mind, designers can create more intuitive and user-friendly interfaces, ultimately enhancing the overall user experience.

Conclusion

In summary, heuristic evaluation is a fundamental method in UX design that enables professionals to identify usability problems efficiently and effectively. By relying on established principles, evaluators can gain insights into how a design meets user needs and expectations. Despite its reliance on the expertise of evaluators, this method can lead to significant improvements in user experience when implemented correctly. Incorporating heuristic evaluation into the design process not only saves time and resources but also ultimately results in products that better serve their intended audience. As the field of UX continues to evolve, heuristic evaluation remains a critical tool for designers striving to create exceptional user experiences.

17

Chapter 17: Competitive Analysis

1. Understanding the Importance of Competitive Analysis

In this section, we'll explore why competitive analysis is a crucial step in the UX design process and how it can influence design decisions.

2. Identifying Your Competitors

This part discusses how to identify your main competitors in the market and what criteria to use for selection.

3. Analyzing Competitors' Designs

Here, we'll look into how to examine competitors' websites and applications, focusing on design elements, usability, and overall user experience.

4. Evaluating Strengths and Weaknesses

This section highlights the importance of recognising the strengths and weaknesses of competitors, which can guide your design choices.

5. Gathering User Feedback

We'll cover methods for collecting user feedback about competitors, such as reviews and surveys, and how this information can inform your design.

6. Understanding Target Audiences

In this section, we'll discuss how to analyse the target audience of competitors to better understand user preferences and behaviours.

7. Summarising Findings

Here, we'll outline how to compile your analysis into a comprehensive report, including key insights and visual representations.

8. The Ongoing Nature of Competitive Analysis

This section will emphasise that competitive analysis should be a continuous process, adapting to changes in the market and user needs.

18

Chapter 18: Analyzing User Data and Feedback

Understanding user data and feedback is essential in creating effective user experiences. In the digital world, the decisions we make should be guided by the needs and preferences of our users. Analyzing user data involves collecting various forms of information about how users interact with a product or service. This data can come from surveys, usability tests, and analytics tools, and it provides valuable insights into user behaviour. Feedback, on the other hand, refers to the opinions and suggestions from users regarding their experience with a product. By combining both data and feedback, designers can gain a deeper understanding of user needs, allowing them to improve their designs more effectively.

Importance of Analyzing User Data

The analysis of user data is vital for several reasons. Firstly, it helps identify patterns in user behaviour. For example, tracking how long users spend on a particular page can reveal if the content is engaging or if there are elements causing confusion. Understanding where users click the most can indicate what they find most useful, while also highlighting areas that might need improvement.

Secondly, user data can uncover usability issues. If a significant number of users abandon their carts at checkout, this might signal a problem in the process that needs addressing. Identifying such issues through data allows designers to make informed changes that enhance the overall user experience.

Finally, analyzing user data allows for continuous improvement. UX design is not a one-time process; it requires ongoing refinement. By regularly reviewing user data, designers can adapt to changes in user behaviour and preferences. This adaptability is key to maintaining a competitive edge in a rapidly changing digital landscape.

Collecting User Data

The collection of user data can take various forms. One effective method is the use of analytics tools, such as Google Analytics, which provide insights into user traffic, behaviour, and demographics. These tools can track page views, bounce rates, and the paths users take through a website. By examining this data, designers can gain insights into how well the website is performing and identify areas that may need improvement.

Surveys and questionnaires are another valuable way to gather feedback directly from users. These can be distributed after users interact with a product or service, allowing them to express their thoughts and feelings. Questions can cover aspects such as usability, design, and overall satisfaction. This direct feedback is crucial, as it captures users' perceptions, which may not always align with what data suggests.

Usability testing is also an essential method for gathering user data. This involves observing real users as they interact with a product, noting where they struggle or succeed. It provides qualitative data that can highlight specific issues that might not be apparent through quantitative data alone.

In addition, feedback forms and customer support channels can serve as valuable sources of user insights. Users often express their concerns or suggestions through these channels, offering designers a chance to address issues they may not have been aware of.

Analyzing User Feedback

Once user data has been collected, the next step is analysis. This involves organising the data to identify trends and draw conclusions. Start by categorising feedback into themes, such as usability, design, functionality, and content. This organisation helps to focus on specific areas that need attention.

Quantitative data, such as the number of users who reported an issue or the average time spent on a page, can be analysed using statistical methods. This analysis can reveal significant trends or anomalies, helping designers understand where they should direct their efforts. For example, if a high percentage of users indicate difficulty with a specific feature, it's crucial to investigate and resolve the underlying problem.

Qualitative data, like open-ended survey responses, requires a different approach. This type of data is often richer and provides deeper insights into user experiences. To analyse qualitative feedback, look for recurring themes and sentiments. Using tools like thematic analysis can help in identifying common patterns in user responses. It's important to approach this analysis with an open mind, allowing the data to guide your conclusions rather than seeking to confirm existing beliefs.

Applying Insights from User Data and Feedback

Once insights have been gathered from user data and feedback, it's time to apply these learnings to improve the design. Start by prioritising the issues identified in the analysis phase. Not every piece of feedback can be acted upon at once, so focus on changes that will have the most significant impact on user experience. For example, if a particular feature is causing frustration for many users, addressing this issue should take precedence.

Collaboration with the design team is essential during this phase. Sharing insights and discussing potential changes fosters a user-centered design approach. Consider creating prototypes or mock-ups based on user feedback to test proposed changes before full implementation. This iterative process allows for ongoing refinement and ensures that the final design effectively addresses user needs.

Additionally, keep users informed about updates and improvements. This communication can take the form of emails, blog posts, or notifications within the product. By showing users that their feedback is valued and acted upon, you build trust and encourage continued engagement.

Lastly, remember that the analysis of user data and feedback is an ongoing process. Once changes have been implemented, continue to monitor user behaviour and gather feedback. This cycle of analysis, application, and evaluation ensures that the design remains relevant and effective in meeting user needs.

Conclusion

In conclusion, analysing user data and feedback is a crucial aspect of UX design. It allows designers to understand user needs, identify issues, and continually improve their products. By employing various methods of data collection, analysing the information effectively, and applying insights, designers can create user experiences that are not only effective but also enjoyable. Ultimately, the goal of UX design is to serve users better, and understanding their behaviours and opinions is key to achieving that aim.

19

Chapter 19: Behavioral and Attitudinal Research

Understanding Behavioral and Attitudinal Research

Behavioral and attitudinal research is crucial in user experience (UX) design. This type of research helps designers understand how people interact with products and what they think about them. Behavioral research focuses on what users do—this means looking at their actions, like clicking on buttons, scrolling through pages, or making purchases. On the other hand, attitudinal research explores what users feel and believe about a product. This includes their opinions, preferences, and satisfaction levels. Together, these two types of research provide valuable insights into user needs and expectations.

To start, behavioral research often involves tracking user actions through various methods. One common technique is usability testing, where real users perform tasks while observers watch and take notes. This testing helps identify any problems users face when interacting with a product. For instance, if users struggle to find a checkout button, designers know they need to make it more visible or easier to use. Another method is A/B testing, where two versions of a webpage are compared to see which one performs better. This could involve changing the color of a button or the wording of a headline to find out what leads to more clicks or sales. By analysing user behaviour in these ways, designers can make informed decisions to improve the overall user experience.

On the other hand, attitudinal research provides insight into users' thoughts and feelings. Surveys and interviews are commonly used to gather this information. Surveys can be distributed online, asking users about their satisfaction with a product or what features they would like to see improved. For example, a survey might ask, "How likely are you to recommend our app to a friend?" This helps designers gauge overall user sentiment. Interviews allow for more in-depth conversations, giving users the chance to express their feelings in detail. By listening to what users say, designers can uncover valuable insights that numbers alone might not reveal.

Combining both types of research is essential for a complete understanding of user experience. While behavioral data shows what users do, attitudinal data explains why they do it. For instance, if a lot of users abandon their shopping carts, behavioral research reveals the action but attitudinal research might show they feel the checkout process is too complicated. This combination helps designers pinpoint the root cause of issues, allowing for more effective solutions.

The Importance of Context

Context plays a significant role in both behavioral and attitudinal research. The environment in which users interact with a product can greatly influence their behaviour and attitudes. For instance, a user browsing a website at home may behave differently than when using the same site on a mobile device while commuting. Understanding the context of use is vital for creating relevant and effective designs.

When conducting research, it's essential to consider various factors that could impact user behaviour. These can include the user's location, the device they're using, and even the time of day. For example, users might be more focused and less distracted when at home compared to when they are at work. This is where contextual inquiry comes into play, which involves observing users in their natural environments to understand their experiences better. By gathering data in real-life settings, designers can gain insights into how context affects user interactions and satisfaction.

Additionally, cultural factors can also shape user attitudes and behaviours. Different regions may have varying preferences and expectations when it comes to design. For instance, users in some cultures may prefer minimalistic designs, while others may appreciate more vibrant and elaborate aesthetics. Therefore, when conducting research, it's essential to consider the cultural backgrounds of users to ensure that designs resonate with them. By tailoring products to meet specific cultural needs, designers can create more engaging and effective user experiences.

Practical Applications of Research Findings

Once behavioral and attitudinal research has been conducted, the next step is to apply the findings to improve the design. This involves translating user insights into actionable design decisions. For example, if research indicates that users find a particular feature confusing, designers can simplify it or provide clearer instructions. This might involve redesigning a user interface to make it more intuitive or adding tooltips to guide users through complex processes.

Moreover, research findings can help prioritize features and functionalities. If users express a strong desire for a specific feature during interviews, this should be taken seriously in the design process. Prioritizing user-requested features not only enhances the product but also builds trust and loyalty among users. When users see that their feedback has been considered, they feel more valued and engaged with the product.

Additionally, research can inform marketing strategies. Understanding user attitudes can help craft more effective messaging and promotional campaigns. For instance, if research shows that users value sustainability, marketing efforts can highlight eco-friendly aspects of the product. This alignment between user values and marketing can enhance the overall brand image and attract a loyal customer base.

Finally, ongoing research is essential for continuous improvement. User needs and preferences can change over time, and staying attuned to these shifts is vital for maintaining a successful product. Regularly conducting follow-up surveys or usability tests ensures that the design remains relevant and user-friendly. It also shows users that their opinions matter and that the company is committed to providing the best experience possible.

Challenges in Behavioral and Attitudinal Research

While behavioral and attitudinal research offers valuable insights, it also comes with challenges. One common issue is the difficulty in accurately capturing user behaviour. Users may not always act as they would in real life during testing scenarios. For instance, they might feel pressured to perform well in a usability test, leading to behaviour that doesn't reflect their typical usage. To mitigate this, it's essential to create a comfortable testing environment and encourage users to act naturally.

Another challenge lies in the interpretation of data. Quantitative data, such as the number of clicks or survey scores, can provide useful insights, but they don't always tell the whole story. Qualitative data, gathered from interviews and open-ended survey questions, can be rich in detail but may also be subjective and harder to analyse. Striking the right balance between these two types of data is crucial. It's important for designers to develop a clear framework for interpreting data, ensuring that findings lead to meaningful insights rather than assumptions.

Moreover, recruiting the right participants for research can be challenging. It's essential to involve a diverse group of users that represent the target audience. If the sample is not representative, the findings may not be applicable to the broader user base. This can lead to designs that don't resonate with the majority of users. Therefore, planning recruitment strategies carefully and considering various demographic factors is essential for gathering accurate data.

Lastly, there is often a time and resource constraint associated with conducting research. UX designers may be under pressure to deliver projects quickly, leading to less thorough research. However, investing time in proper research upfront can save time and resources in the long run by preventing costly redesigns later on. It's crucial for teams to prioritise research and advocate for its importance within the development process.

Conclusion

In conclusion, behavioral and attitudinal research are fundamental components of successful UX design. By understanding user behaviour and attitudes, designers can create products that genuinely meet user needs and expectations. Combining both research types provides a comprehensive view of the user experience, guiding design decisions effectively. While challenges exist, overcoming them through careful planning and execution is vital for achieving a successful user experience. Ultimately, prioritising research not only leads to better designs but also fosters a deeper connection between users and products, creating lasting loyalty and satisfaction.

20

Chapter 20: Translating Research into Actionable Insights

Understanding the Importance of Research

Research is a cornerstone of user experience (UX) design. It provides the foundation upon which effective design decisions are made. Understanding users' needs, behaviours, and motivations is crucial for creating products that resonate with them. In this context, translating research into actionable insights becomes essential. The goal is to convert the raw data collected from user interviews, surveys, usability tests, and other methods into concrete steps that can guide design and development teams. This translation process is not merely about reporting findings but involves a deeper understanding of what these findings mean for the design process and how they can lead to practical improvements in the user experience.

Defining Research Goals

The first step in translating research into actionable insights is to clearly define your research goals. Why are you conducting the research? Are you trying to identify pain points in an existing product, understand user behaviours, or explore potential features for a new product? Having well-defined objectives helps focus your data collection efforts and ensures that the insights you derive are relevant to your project. For example, if your goal is to improve the usability of a mobile app, your research should centre on understanding how users interact with the app, what frustrates them, and what they find intuitive. This clarity helps in guiding your research methods and ensures that the insights generated will directly inform your design decisions.

Collecting and Analysing Data

Once you have established your research goals, the next step is to collect data. This can involve a variety of methods, including user interviews, surveys, usability tests, and field studies. Each method has its strengths and can provide different perspectives on user behaviour. For instance, interviews offer in-depth insights into user thoughts and feelings, while surveys can provide quantitative data that highlights broader trends.

After collecting data, the next step is analysis. This process involves sifting through the information to identify patterns, trends, and key insights. For instance, you may notice that several users struggle with the same feature or express similar frustrations. This analysis can be made easier by using tools such as affinity mapping, which allows you to group similar insights together visually. This not only helps in identifying common themes but also fosters collaboration within the team, as everyone can contribute to the analysis and see how different insights interconnect.

Synthesising Insights

After analysing the data, the next crucial step is to synthesise your findings. This involves distilling the vast amounts of information into key insights that can guide your design process. During synthesis, it's important to focus on the insights that are most relevant to your research goals and have the potential to significantly impact user experience.

For instance, if your research indicates that users find a particular feature confusing, this insight should be emphasised as a priority for improvement. Synthesising insights can also involve creating user personas or journey maps, which provide a visual representation of user behaviours and needs. These tools help to keep the user at the forefront of your design process, ensuring that the final product aligns with user expectations and preferences.

Prioritising Insights

Once you have synthesised your insights, the next step is prioritisation. Not all insights carry the same weight; some will have a more substantial impact on user experience than others. Assessing which insights align with your project goals and can lead to meaningful changes is crucial.

One effective approach is to use the impact-effort matrix, which helps evaluate insights based on their potential impact on the user experience versus the effort required to implement them. This visual tool allows teams to focus on quick wins that can significantly enhance the user experience without demanding extensive resources. Engaging your team in this process is essential, as it brings diverse perspectives that can shed light on insights you might have overlooked. Collaborative discussions can foster a sense of ownership among team members, ensuring that everyone is aligned on the priorities moving forward.

Translating Insights into Recommendations

After prioritising your insights, the next stage is to translate them into actionable recommendations. This is where the research truly begins to inform design decisions. Each recommendation should be clear and directly linked to the insights you've gathered. For instance, if users have expressed difficulty navigating a website, your recommendation could involve redesigning the navigation menu to make it more intuitive.

In this stage, it's also helpful to create user stories or scenarios that illustrate how users will interact with the proposed changes. This contextualises your recommendations, making it easier for the design team to understand the rationale behind them. Clear documentation of these recommendations is vital, as it serves as a reference point for the design and development teams throughout the project.

Communicating Insights Effectively

Effective communication of insights is crucial to ensure that all stakeholders understand and appreciate the findings. This involves more than simply presenting data; it requires storytelling techniques to make the insights relatable and compelling.

Consider using visual aids, such as infographics or presentations, to convey your findings in an engaging way. These tools can help illustrate user pain points and successes, making it easier for your audience to grasp the significance of the insights. By framing your findings in a narrative format, you can create a shared understanding of the user experience challenges and opportunities, fostering a collaborative approach to problem-solving among team members.

Iteration and Continuous Improvement

Translating research into actionable insights is not a one-time task; it is an iterative process that requires ongoing refinement. UX design is constantly evolving, and user needs can change over time. Therefore, it is essential to revisit your insights regularly, especially after implementing design changes.

Gathering feedback from users post-launch can provide valuable information on whether the changes have addressed the identified pain points. This feedback loop allows you to adjust your design solutions based on real user experiences. Moreover, being open to adapting your approach as new insights emerge is key to maintaining a user-centred design process. Regularly testing and iterating on your design not only improves the user experience but also keeps the team engaged and invested in the process.

Conclusion

In conclusion, translating research into actionable insights is a critical aspect of the UX design process. By defining clear research goals, collecting and analysing data, synthesising insights, prioritising recommendations, and communicating findings effectively, design teams can create products that truly meet user needs. Remember, this process is iterative and requires continuous refinement based on user feedback. By embracing this approach, you can ensure that your design solutions remain relevant, effective, and aligned with user expectations, ultimately leading to a more satisfying user experience.

III

Information Architecture

Learn how to organize and structure information to create intuitive experiences.
Information architecture (IA) is critical to helping users navigate digital products efficiently. This section covers IA principles, including site mapping, navigation design, and content hierarchy, helping you design products that make sense to your users.

21

Chapter 21: The Basics of Information Architecture (IA)

Understanding Information Architecture

Information Architecture (IA) is an essential part of creating user-friendly digital experiences. It involves organizing and structuring content so that users can easily find and navigate it. Just like a physical building needs a clear layout for people to move around, a website or app needs a well-thought-out structure for users to locate the information they seek. The main goal of IA is to make sure that the content is accessible, understandable, and usable.

User Research: The Foundation of IA

One of the first steps in developing IA is understanding the needs of the users. This requires conducting user research to gather insights about what users are looking for and how they behave online. Surveys, interviews, and usability testing are common methods used to collect this information. By knowing the users' goals and preferences, designers can create a structure that meets their needs effectively.

Creating a Content Inventory

Once the user needs are identified, the next step is to create a content inventory. This involves listing all the content that exists on the site, including pages, images, videos, and documents. This inventory helps designers see what content is available, what needs to be created, and how it can be organized logically. It is essential to evaluate the content's relevance and quality, ensuring that only valuable and necessary information is included in the architecture.

Developing a Site Map

After gathering user insights and creating a content inventory, designers can begin developing a site map. A site map is a visual representation of the structure of the website. It shows how different pages and sections relate to one another, helping to create a hierarchy that makes sense. For example, the home page typically links to main categories, which then link to subcategories and individual pages. This hierarchical structure guides users through the site, enabling them to find information quickly.

Effective Navigation Design

When designing the IA, it is also important to consider navigation. Good navigation helps users move through the site effortlessly. Designers must choose the right navigation style, such as top navigation bars, side menus, or breadcrumb trails. Each type of navigation has its pros and cons, and the choice will depend on the site's complexity and the users' preferences. Consistency in navigation is crucial; users should be able to predict where they can find information based on previous experiences.

The Importance of Labelling

Another key aspect of IA is labelling. Labels help users understand what to expect when they click on a link. Clear and descriptive labels guide users and reduce confusion. For instance, using labels like "Contact Us" or "About Us" makes it obvious what content lies behind those links. Avoiding jargon and technical terms is essential, as these can alienate users who may not be familiar with the terminology. The aim is to use simple language that everyone can understand.

Aligning with Users' Mental Models

In addition to labels, the organization of content must also reflect the users' mental models. This means structuring the information in a way that aligns with how users think and what they expect. For instance, if users are searching for recipes, they might expect to find categories like "Breakfast," "Lunch," and "Dinner." By aligning the structure with users' expectations, designers can create a more intuitive experience.

Testing and Validation

Testing is a critical phase in developing Information Architecture. Once the initial design is complete, it is essential to test it with real users. Usability testing helps identify any problems or areas of confusion within the IA. By observing users as they navigate the site, designers can gain valuable insights into how well the structure works. If users struggle to find information or become frustrated, designers can make necessary adjustments before the site goes live.

Documentation for Consistency

Documentation of the IA is also crucial. Creating guidelines that outline the structure, labels, and navigation can help maintain consistency throughout the site. This documentation serves as a reference for current and future team members, ensuring that everyone is on the same page when it comes to the site's architecture.

Conclusion: The Importance of Information Architecture

In conclusion, Information Architecture is a vital aspect of user experience design. It involves understanding user needs, organizing content logically, and creating a navigational structure that is easy to use. By focusing on user research, content inventory, site maps, navigation, and testing, designers can create effective Information Architectures that enhance user satisfaction and engagement. As the digital landscape continues to evolve, mastering the basics of IA will remain a crucial skill for anyone involved in UX design.

22

Chapter 22: Creating Site Maps

Understanding the Importance of Site Maps

Creating site maps is a crucial step in the design process that helps ensure a website's structure is clear, logical, and user-friendly. A site map serves as a visual representation of a website's architecture, outlining the various pages and their relationships to one another. By providing a bird's-eye view of the site, a site map enables designers, developers, and stakeholders to understand how content is organized and how users will navigate through it. This is particularly important in user experience (UX) design, where the primary goal is to create a seamless and intuitive experience for users.

Defining Goals and Objectives

The process of creating a site map begins with gathering information about the content and purpose of the website. This involves understanding the target audience and identifying the main goals of the site. Are users looking for information, products, or services? What are the key actions they need to take? By answering these questions, designers can establish a clear vision of what the site should achieve and how it should be structured.

Organizing Content Hierarchically

Once the objectives are defined, the next step is to outline the main categories and subcategories of content. This hierarchical structure should reflect the way users think and search for information. For example, a retail website might have primary categories such as "Men's Clothing," "Women's Clothing," and "Accessories," with subcategories under each. This organization not only makes it easier for users to find what they are looking for but also helps search engines index the content more effectively, improving the site's visibility in search results.

Creating the Site Map

After outlining the categories, designers can begin to create the site map itself. This can be done using various tools, from simple pen and paper to more advanced software designed for wireframing and mapping. A common method is to use boxes to represent pages and lines to connect them, showing the relationships between different sections. As the site map takes shape, it's essential to consider how users will navigate from one page to another. Each page should be easily accessible, with clear pathways leading from the homepage to subpages and back again.

Detailing Page Content and Functionality

An effective site map should also include details about the type of content each page will contain. This can help ensure that the design process is focused on creating valuable and relevant content for users. Additionally, including notes about functionality—such as forms, e-commerce features, or interactive elements—can provide clarity for developers during the build phase.

Iterating and Refining the Site Map

It is important to remember that a site map is not a static document; it is a living part of the design process. As feedback is gathered from users and stakeholders, it may be necessary to revisit and revise the site map to better meet their needs. This iterative process ensures that the final design is user-centric and effectively addresses the challenges identified during the initial planning stages.

Using the Site Map as a Guiding Tool

Once the site map is completed, it serves as a foundational tool for many other aspects of the design process. It can inform wireframes, which are more detailed representations of page layouts, and guide the development of user journeys, helping to illustrate how different users might interact with the site. By establishing a clear site structure upfront, designers can save time and resources later on, reducing the need for extensive revisions and adjustments during the development phase.

Enhancing Team Collaboration

Moreover, a well-structured site map enhances collaboration among team members. Designers, developers, content creators, and stakeholders can refer to the site map as a shared reference point, ensuring that everyone is on the same page regarding the site's structure and content. This alignment is vital in larger projects where multiple team members contribute to various aspects of the website.

Conclusion

In conclusion, creating a site map is a fundamental step in the UX design process. It provides a visual representation of a website's structure, ensuring that content is organized logically and that users can easily navigate through it. By gathering information about the target audience and site objectives, outlining categories and subcategories, and continuously refining the map based on feedback, designers can create an effective blueprint that guides the entire design and development process. A clear and detailed site map not only improves the user experience but also fosters collaboration among team members, leading to a more cohesive and successful website. In a world where users have many choices online, a well-designed site can be the difference between a satisfied visitor and a lost opportunity.

23

Chapter 23: Card Sorting Techniques

Understanding Card Sorting

Card sorting is a method used in user experience (UX) design to help organize and structure information. It involves taking a set of items, often called "cards," which can represent content, features, or topics, and asking participants to arrange these cards into groups that make sense to them. This technique helps designers understand how users think about and categorize information. When designing a website or an application, it is crucial to know how users expect to find information. Card sorting can reveal patterns in how users naturally group items, which can guide the creation of a more intuitive layout. By aligning the structure of your content with users' mental models, you can create a more user-friendly experience.

Card sorting is particularly useful when you have a large amount of content or when you are unsure about how to organize it. For example, if you are designing a new e-commerce website, card sorting can help you determine the best way to categorize products. Rather than guessing how users might want to browse, you can see how they naturally group items and use this data to inform your design choices. This process not only improves the usability of your site but also enhances user satisfaction, as people are more likely to find what they are looking for quickly and easily.

Types of Card Sorting

There are two main types of card sorting: open card sorting and closed card sorting. In an open card sorting exercise, participants are given a set of cards without predefined categories. They can create their own categories and labels based on how they perceive the relationships between the items. This method is particularly helpful for exploring new ideas or when you have no prior categories established. It allows users to express their thought processes freely, providing valuable insights into their expectations and preferences.

On the other hand, closed card sorting provides participants with predefined categories. Users are asked to sort the cards into these existing groups. This method is useful when you want to test the effectiveness of your current structure or see if your categories make sense to the users. It can highlight any gaps or issues in your existing organization, allowing you to make adjustments before finalizing the design.

Conducting a Card Sorting Session

When conducting a card sorting session, it is important to keep a few key steps in mind to ensure the process runs smoothly. First, prepare your cards. Each card should represent a single item, such as a page title or a feature name. It is essential to keep the wording clear and concise, as this will help participants understand the content without confusion. You may want to create around 20 to 30 cards, which is usually a manageable number for participants to sort effectively.

Next, select your participants. It is best to involve real users or potential users of your product. Their input is invaluable as they can provide insights based on their experiences and expectations. Aim for a diverse group of participants to capture different perspectives. Ideally, you should have at least five to ten participants to gather a range of data, but even small groups can yield helpful results.

Once you have your cards and participants, set up a comfortable environment for the sorting session. This can be done in person or online using card sorting software. Explain the purpose of the exercise to the participants and give them clear instructions on what you expect them to do. Encourage them to think aloud as they sort the cards. This will provide you with valuable information about their thought processes and reasoning behind their choices.

As the participants sort the cards, take notes or record the session if possible. This will help you analyze the data later.

After the sorting is complete, discuss the results with the participants. Ask them to explain their choices and how they came to their conclusions. This discussion can uncover deeper insights that may not be apparent from the card sorting alone.

Analyzing the Results

Once you have completed your card sorting sessions, it is time to analyze the results. If you conducted an open card sort, look for common patterns in the categories created by the participants. Take note of how many users grouped specific cards together and whether they used similar labels. This can help you identify themes and structures that resonate with your users.

For closed card sorts, you can create a matrix to compare how each participant categorized the cards. This matrix will allow you to see which categories were consistently used and which caused confusion. Highlight any discrepancies between participants' sorting and your existing structure. This information can inform necessary adjustments to your design.

It can also be helpful to create visual representations of the results, such as dendrograms or affinity diagrams, which can make it easier to see the relationships between the cards. These visuals can help you communicate your findings to stakeholders and team members, ensuring everyone is on the same page about the proposed structure.

Best Practices for Card Sorting

To get the most out of your card sorting sessions, follow some best practices. First, keep your cards simple. Use clear, straightforward language and avoid jargon or technical terms that participants may not understand. This will help ensure that users can focus on sorting rather than deciphering the content.

Second, consider running multiple rounds of card sorting. Each round can provide new insights, especially as you refine your categories and understand more about your users' needs. You can start with an open sort to gather initial ideas and then follow up with a closed sort to test specific categories.

Finally, ensure you keep your participants engaged. Make the session interactive and encourage feedback throughout the process. Participants are more likely to provide honest and helpful insights if they feel comfortable and valued during the session.

Conclusion

In summary, card sorting is a valuable technique in UX design that helps structure and organize information in a way that aligns with users' mental models. By conducting card sorting sessions—whether open or closed—you can gather essential insights into how users categorize information. Analyzing the results can lead to a more intuitive design that enhances user experience. Following best practices can ensure your sessions are effective and engaging. Ultimately, card sorting helps create a design that resonates with users, leading to increased satisfaction and improved usability.

24

Chapter 24: Navigation Design

Part 1: Understanding the Basics of Navigation Design

Navigation design is a key part of user experience (UX) design. It focuses on helping users find what they are looking for quickly and easily. Good navigation ensures that visitors to your website or app can move around smoothly without feeling lost or confused. Without effective navigation, even the best content or services can be difficult to access, leading users to leave your site or app in frustration.

At its core, navigation design is about structuring and organising the information on your site or app so that users can access it efficiently. It involves designing menus, links, buttons, and other elements that allow users to browse, explore, and take action. Think of navigation like a roadmap that guides users through their journey. If the road is clear, well signposted, and easy to follow, users will have a better experience.

A well-designed navigation system needs to be intuitive. Users should not have to think too hard about where to go or what to do next. The layout and labelling of your navigation should be clear, with a logical flow from one section to another. Imagine walking into a supermarket. The aisles are labelled, and products are grouped in logical categories – vegetables with vegetables, cleaning supplies with other cleaning supplies. In the same way, your website or app needs to make sense to its users.

There are several key components of navigation design:

- **Menus:** These are the primary way users move around a site. They can appear at the top of the page, in a sidebar, or as a dropdown.
- **Breadcrumbs:** These show the user where they are within the structure of the site, making it easier to backtrack.
- **Search Bar:** A search function helps users quickly find specific information without browsing through every page.
- **Calls to Action (CTAs):** Buttons or links that encourage users to take specific actions, such as "Buy Now" or "Learn More."

The goal is to create a seamless experience, where users can move through the site with minimal effort and find the information or products they need.

Part 2: Principles of Good Navigation Design

Good navigation design isn't just about making sure that links and buttons work. It's about making the experience easy and enjoyable for the user. Here are some key principles to keep in mind when designing navigation for your website or app:

1. **Consistency:** One of the most important rules in navigation design is to keep things consistent. This means using the same layout, labels, and design patterns throughout your site or app. If a user learns how to navigate one part of your site, they should be able to apply that knowledge everywhere else. Changing the location of the navigation bar or using different terminology in different sections can confuse users and disrupt their experience.

2. **Clarity:** Everything in your navigation system should be clear and easy to understand. Avoid jargon or overly complex language in your labels. Use familiar terms and icons that users will recognise. For example, a house icon usually represents the homepage, and a magnifying glass represents search.

3. **Simplicity:** Less is often more when it comes to navigation. Too many options can overwhelm users and make it harder for them to find what they need. Focus on providing the most important options in your main navigation and keep secondary links in dropdowns or footers.

4. **Hierarchy:** A clear hierarchy helps users understand the relationships between different pages and sections of your site. Primary navigation should highlight the most important areas, while secondary navigation can provide links to more specific content. For instance, an e-commerce site might have main categories like "Clothing," "Footwear," and "Accessories," with subcategories under each one.

5. **Feedback:** It's important to let users know where they are within your site. Highlight the current page or section they're in using visual cues like colours or underlining. This makes it easier for users to keep track of their journey and navigate back to earlier sections if needed.

6. **Mobile-Friendly Navigation:** More users are browsing on mobile devices than ever before, so your navigation needs to work well on smaller screens. Mobile-friendly navigation often involves using hamburger menus (three horizontal lines), collapsing content, and ensuring that buttons and links are large enough to tap easily.

7. **Accessibility:** Navigation should be accessible to all users, including those with disabilities. This means designing for screen readers, using high-contrast colours for visibility, and making sure links are keyboard navigable.

By following these principles, you can create a navigation system that helps users find what they need without frustration, leading to a better overall user experience.

Part 3: Common Navigation Patterns and When to Use Them

There are several common navigation patterns that designers use depending on the type of site or app they are working on. Choosing the right pattern can help guide users through the content more effectively. Here are a few of the most popular patterns:

1. **Top Navigation (Horizontal Menu):** This is one of the most common types of navigation, where the main menu is placed horizontally at the top of the page. It's ideal for websites with a relatively small number of top-level categories. For example, a corporate website might use this pattern to show options like "About Us," "Services," "Careers," and "Contact."

2. **Side Navigation (Vertical Menu):** This pattern is often used for more complex sites with lots of content. A vertical menu on the left or right side of the page can hold many categories and subcategories, making it a great option for e-commerce sites or online learning platforms. It allows for easy expansion and doesn't clutter the page.

3. **Dropdown Menus:** Dropdown menus are useful when you need to provide additional options without

overwhelming the user with too many visible links. They work well when there are multiple subcategories under a main heading. However, it's important not to overload dropdowns with too many items, as this can become cumbersome to navigate.

4. **Hamburger Menu:** Commonly used on mobile websites and apps, the hamburger menu hides the navigation behind a small icon (three horizontal lines). When clicked, the menu expands to show the available options. This helps save space on smaller screens but should be used thoughtfully, as it can hide important links from view.

5. **Breadcrumb Navigation:** Breadcrumbs are a secondary navigation pattern, often used in websites with deep hierarchies, such as e-commerce sites or blogs. They show users their current location within the site and provide an easy way to navigate back to higher-level pages. For example, on an online store, a breadcrumb might look like: Home > Electronics > Mobile Phones > Samsung.

6. **Footer Navigation:** Footers are often used to provide links to important sections of a website that might not need to be in the main navigation. Common footer links include contact information, privacy policies, terms of service, and social media links. Since footers are at the bottom of the page, they are often a fallback option for users looking for less urgent information.

7. **Mega Menus:** Mega menus are large dropdowns that display multiple options at once, often with subcategories, images, or additional links. They are typically used on e-commerce sites or sites with many content categories. For instance, a travel website might have a mega menu that lists holiday destinations, types of accommodation, travel guides, and deals all in one place.

When choosing a navigation pattern, it's essential to consider your users' needs and the type of content your site or app contains. A simple blog with a few categories will likely work well with a top navigation bar, while a complex e-commerce site with hundreds of products might benefit from a side navigation and breadcrumb combination. Always test your navigation design with real users to ensure that it works well and meets their needs.

25

Chapter 25: Taxonomy and Classification Systems

Introduction to Taxonomy and Classification Systems in UX Design

In the world of UX design, organizing information is one of the most crucial tasks. When users interact with a product, they need to easily find what they are looking for. This is where taxonomy and classification systems play an important role. Taxonomy, in simple terms, is the science of categorizing and classifying information. Just as a library organizes its books by genre, author, and subject, a well-structured website or application groups its content into meaningful categories to help users find what they need.

Understanding and implementing taxonomy is essential to creating a smooth, intuitive user experience. Whether you're building an e-commerce platform, a blog, or a government website, a clear, logical classification system helps users quickly navigate through your content. The right taxonomy ensures that information is easy to locate and retrieve, reducing user frustration and making their interaction with your product more enjoyable.

A key aspect of good taxonomy is that it is user-centered. The categories and labels should reflect how users think about and search for information, rather than how a business or organization internally views it. For example, if you are creating a recipe website, categorizing recipes by "vegetarian," "gluten-free," and "quick meals" might be more useful for users than categories like "chef specials" or "featured ingredients."

Types of Taxonomy in UX Design

There are different types of taxonomy used in UX design, and the right choice depends on the nature of the content, the target audience, and the overall goals of the product. The three most common types of taxonomy are:

1. **Hierarchical Taxonomy**: This is one of the most traditional and widely used systems of classification. In a hierarchical taxonomy, information is organized in a tree-like structure with parent categories and subcategories. For example, an online clothing store may have main categories like "Men," "Women," and "Kids." Under the "Women" category, there may be subcategories such as "Dresses," "Trousers," and "Tops." This method of organization helps users drill down into specific areas of interest and progressively

refine their search.

2. **Faceted Taxonomy**: Faceted taxonomy allows content to be classified in multiple ways. Instead of a strict hierarchy, users can filter or search content based on various attributes or facets. For instance, in an online store, users could filter products by size, colour, brand, price range, or material. Faceted taxonomies are particularly useful for large, complex datasets where users may have different criteria for finding what they need. It also provides more flexibility compared to hierarchical systems, as users can choose which attributes are most relevant to their search.

3. **Networked Taxonomy**: Networked taxonomy doesn't follow a strict hierarchy and is less structured than the previous two types. It allows for more fluid relationships between content elements. This approach is often used for social media platforms, knowledge management systems, or online communities where there may be multiple, overlapping connections between pieces of content. For example, in a social media network, a single post could be linked to multiple tags, categories, and user profiles.

Importance of Clear Labeling

An essential component of taxonomy is labeling. Labels are the words or phrases used to describe each category or facet within the system. Well-chosen labels make a taxonomy more effective by helping users understand what they are looking at. If labels are confusing or unclear, users may struggle to navigate through the site or application.

Labels should be clear, concise, and aligned with the users' mental models. A mental model refers to how users perceive and understand a particular domain of knowledge. For example, if you are designing a travel website, users may expect categories like "Flights," "Hotels," and "Car Hire," as this mirrors how people typically plan their trips. Using jargon or overly technical terms for labels can create confusion, so it's crucial to use language that your target audience will understand.

User-Centered Taxonomy Design

When designing a taxonomy, one of the best practices is to conduct user research. This helps you understand how your audience thinks about and organizes information. Card sorting is a common research method used for this purpose. In a card sorting exercise, users are asked to group different pieces of information into categories that make sense to them. By analysing the results, you can determine how users naturally organize content and which labels they prefer.

Another helpful technique is tree testing, which evaluates how well users can navigate through a hierarchical structure. In tree testing, users are given a task, such as finding a specific product or piece of information, and are then asked to navigate through the category tree to find it. This helps identify any points of confusion or where users may be getting lost.

Additionally, it's important to keep the taxonomy flexible and scalable. As the product grows and more content is added, the classification system should be able to accommodate these changes without becoming unwieldy or disorganized. Building in flexibility from the start allows for smoother transitions and updates as the system evolves.

Challenges in Building a Taxonomy

Creating an effective taxonomy is not without its challenges. One common issue is balancing the needs of different user groups. In many cases, the audience for a product may consist of diverse users who think about and categorize information in different ways. For instance, a health website may serve both medical professionals and the general public. Doctors may expect categories based on medical specialities, while everyday users might prefer categories like "Symptoms," "Conditions," and "Treatments." In such cases, a faceted taxonomy can help, offering different pathways for different user groups.

Another challenge is avoiding overcomplication. It can be tempting to create a highly detailed taxonomy with numerous categories and subcategories, but this can overwhelm users. A simpler, more streamlined system is often more effective, especially for users who want to find information quickly.

Finally, maintaining consistency is essential for a taxonomy to be effective. If similar items are categorized differently or if labels are inconsistent, users may struggle to understand the structure of the content. Regular reviews and updates are necessary to ensure that the taxonomy remains clear and logical over time.

Conclusion

In summary, taxonomy and classification systems are fundamental to good UX design. They allow users to navigate content more easily, find what they need quickly, and enjoy a more intuitive experience with the product. Whether you use a hierarchical, faceted, or networked taxonomy, the key is to stay focused on the user's needs and mental models. Clear labeling, user research, and a flexible approach to design are critical to building a successful taxonomy system. With a well-designed classification system, your product will be more user-friendly and efficient, helping both your users and your business achieve their goals.

26

Chapter 26: Designing for Searchability

26.1 Importance of Searchability in UX

In today's digital age, users expect to find information quickly and easily. Whether on a website, app, or digital product, one of the key features that enhance the user experience (UX) is effective search functionality. Searchability refers to the ease with which users can locate information or content within a digital environment. Designing for searchability is crucial because users often look for specific information, products, or answers rather than browsing or exploring.

When users can't find what they are searching for, they are likely to become frustrated, abandon the platform, or choose a competitor's product. In contrast, a well-designed search function improves user satisfaction, engagement, and retention. It can also contribute to achieving business goals, such as increased sales, lead generation, and user loyalty.

The significance of searchability goes beyond simple navigation. Users have different intentions when searching: some may know exactly what they want, while others might be looking for suggestions or broad information. Designing for these varied needs is a challenge that UX designers must address through thoughtful architecture, intuitive design, and clever use of technology.

26.2 Structuring Search for User Needs

Understanding user needs is the first step in creating an effective search experience. User research, personas, and journey mapping can provide insights into how and why users search, what they expect to find, and where they may encounter frustrations.

A search system should cater to different types of users. For example, some users may type very specific queries, while others may use vague terms. Some users might need suggestions as they type, or wish to filter their results based on certain criteria, such as price, category, or popularity.

An effective search design should consider the following elements:

- **Search Bar Placement**: The search bar should be highly visible and accessible on all pages. Users expect to find it at the top of the page or prominently within the navigation.

- **Autocomplete and Suggestions**: Implementing autocomplete or search suggestions helps guide users and speeds up the search process. It reduces errors and provides users with options they might not have considered.

- **Filters and Sorting**: After performing a search, users should be able to filter results based on relevant categories. For example, an e-commerce site may offer filters by brand, price range, or customer ratings.

- **Natural Language Processing (NLP)**: Modern search engines use NLP to interpret user queries. This helps to understand conversational search queries or ambiguous terms and produce more relevant results.

- **Mobile Search**: With the growing use of mobile devices, search functions should be optimised for small screens. This includes having a responsive design, easy-to-tap filters, and mobile-friendly layouts.

26.3 Search Result Pages

Search result pages play a key role in delivering the right information. Users want results that are both relevant and clear. The presentation of search results should make it easy for users to quickly scan and find what they are looking for.

The following principles should guide the design of search result pages:

- **Relevance and Ranking**: The most relevant results should be displayed first. This is usually based on algorithms that rank content by keywords, popularity, and user behaviour. Designers can assist this process by ensuring that content is well organised and tagged appropriately.

- **Snippets and Previews**: Providing snippets or previews of content can help users decide whether a particular result meets their needs. These snippets might include a brief summary, a thumbnail image, or key information, depending on the context.

- **Pagination or Infinite Scroll**: Search results can be displayed using pagination (where results are divided into separate pages) or infinite scrolling (where more results load as users scroll down). Each method has its pros and cons. Pagination can give a clearer sense of the amount of content available, while infinite scroll keeps users engaged without requiring them to click for more results.

- **Error Handling**: Sometimes users won't find what they're looking for. Designing for "no results" scenarios is just as important as designing for successful searches. Useful messages, alternative suggestions, or ways to refine the search can prevent user frustration.

26.4 Enhancing Search Experience with Personalisation

Personalisation is a powerful way to improve searchability. Tailoring search results based on a user's past behaviour, preferences, or location can make the search experience more relevant and efficient. For example, an online retailer might display products similar to those a user has previously browsed or purchased. Similarly, a news site could show articles related to topics the user has read about.

However, it's important to balance personalisation with privacy. Users should feel that the platform respects their data, and they should have control over what is personalised. Transparency in how personal data is used is crucial for maintaining user trust.

26.5 Analytics and Iteration

Search functionality should be continuously monitored and improved based on user feedback and behaviour. Analytics tools can track how users interact with the search feature, what they search for, and where they drop off. This data is invaluable for refining the search experience over time.

For example, if users frequently abandon the search process or cannot find what they need, it may indicate that the search algorithm needs improvement, the content needs better tagging, or the search interface needs to be simplified. Regularly iterating on the design based on real-world use ensures that the search function remains effective and meets user expectations.

26.6 Conclusion

Designing for searchability is an essential part of UX design, especially as users increasingly rely on search to navigate digital environments. By understanding user needs, crafting intuitive search interfaces, and leveraging technology like NLP and personalisation, UX designers can create a seamless search experience that meets both user and business goals. Ultimately, good search design empowers users to find what they need quickly and effortlessly, leading to higher satisfaction and engagement.

27

Chapter 27: The Role of Metadata in UX Design

Understanding Metadata: The Foundation of Digital Information

Metadata, often referred to as "data about data," plays a crucial role in organising and managing digital content. In its simplest form, metadata is information that describes other data. For example, in a photo file, metadata might include details such as the date the photo was taken, the camera used, or the location of the image. For a webpage, metadata could describe its title, author, creation date, and keywords.

In the context of UX design, metadata is often unseen by users but directly impacts how they interact with and find content. When metadata is correctly implemented, it helps users discover relevant information, navigate websites efficiently, and achieve their goals faster.

To understand the role of metadata, we can break it down into different categories:

1. **Descriptive Metadata** – This type of metadata helps describe an asset, such as a webpage or file. It includes details like title, author, keywords, and a brief description.

2. **Structural Metadata** – This type defines how data is structured. For example, it describes the relationships between different parts of a webpage or sections of a document.

3. **Administrative Metadata** – It contains information that helps manage resources, such as when a file was created, modified, or who has access to it.

Effective UX design considers how metadata improves accessibility, searchability, and the overall user experience. Without it, users may struggle to locate the information they need or understand the context of the content they're engaging with. Therefore, metadata acts as a silent yet powerful tool, ensuring digital systems work seamlessly for the end-user.

Why Metadata Matters in UX Design: The Hidden Power Behind Great Experiences

Metadata might not be visible on the surface of a website or app, but it is essential for creating an efficient and effective user experience. When used correctly, metadata helps users find what they need quickly and intuitively. As the amount of digital content continues to grow, the role of metadata in UX design becomes even more critical.

Here's why metadata is so important in UX design:

1. **Enhancing Searchability and Discoverability** One of the key roles of metadata in UX design is making content searchable and discoverable. For example, when users search for something on a website, they often rely on search engines that use metadata to index and retrieve relevant pages. Well-crafted metadata ensures that the right pages appear in response to specific queries, increasing the chances of users finding the information they need.

2. **Improving Navigation and Content Organisation** Metadata helps organise and structure content, making it easier for users to navigate complex websites or apps. In a large e-commerce platform, for example, metadata can categorise products by type, price, or brand, allowing users to filter and sort items based on their preferences. Without metadata, the sheer volume of content could overwhelm users, leading to frustration and poor experiences.

3. **Boosting SEO and Online Visibility** Metadata plays a significant role in search engine optimisation (SEO). Search engines like Google rely on metadata, such as meta titles, descriptions, and keywords, to understand what a webpage is about. Properly optimised metadata improves the visibility of websites, helping them rank higher in search results and attracting more users. For UX designers, this means balancing user needs with search engine requirements to ensure that content is not only engaging but also discoverable.

4. **Enhancing Accessibility for All Users** Metadata also supports accessibility, ensuring that digital content can be accessed and understood by all users, including those with disabilities. For example, metadata can be used to provide alternative text for images, helping visually impaired users who rely on screen readers to navigate websites. Similarly, metadata can help provide transcripts for audio and video content, making it accessible to those with hearing impairments.

5. **Context and Relevance** Metadata provides context to digital content, ensuring that users understand what they are viewing or interacting with. For example, in a blog post, metadata might include the author's name, publication date, and category, helping users understand whether the content is current and relevant to their needs. By providing this additional information, metadata helps users make informed decisions and ensures a smoother experience.

Best Practices for Incorporating Metadata in UX Design

Now that we understand the importance of metadata in UX design, how can we ensure we're using it effectively? The following best practices outline how designers can make the most of metadata to enhance user experiences.

1. **Prioritise User-Centred Metadata** The primary goal of UX design is to create a positive experience for the user, and the same should apply to metadata. It's essential to focus on what users need and expect when interacting with content.

   For example, when defining metadata for a blog post, consider what details the user would find most helpful. Metadata such as the post's date, topic, and author can provide valuable context for users, making the content easier to understand.

2. **Use Clear and Descriptive Language** Metadata should be written in clear and descriptive language. Avoid jargon or overly technical terms, as these may confuse both users and search engines. When crafting meta titles and descriptions for web pages, ensure they accurately reflect the content on the page and include key terms users are likely to search for. This improves both the searchability and usability of the content.

3. **Optimise for SEO Without Compromising User Experience** While optimising metadata for search engines is essential, it's important not to over-prioritise

SEO at the expense of the user experience. Keywords should be naturally integrated into metadata rather than forced, and the focus should always remain on providing valuable, relevant information to users. Meta descriptions, in particular, should be compelling and informative, encouraging users to click through to the content.

4. **Maintain Consistency Across Platforms** Metadata should be consistent across all digital platforms, ensuring a cohesive user experience. Whether users are accessing content via a website, mobile app, or another platform, they should receive the same level of information and clarity. This means maintaining consistent titles, descriptions, and keyword strategies across all touchpoints.

5. **Regularly Review and Update Metadata** As content evolves and user needs change, metadata must be reviewed and updated regularly. Outdated or incorrect metadata can negatively impact the user experience, leading to confusion and frustration. UX designers should regularly audit their metadata to ensure it remains relevant and accurate, making adjustments as necessary to improve the user experience.

6. **Leverage Metadata for Personalisation** Personalisation is becoming increasingly important in UX design, and metadata can help support this. By using metadata to understand user preferences and behaviour, designers can create more tailored experiences. For example,

metadata can be used to recommend related content based on a user's previous interactions, making the experience more personalised and engaging.

Conclusion

Metadata is often an overlooked but essential part of UX design. While it may not be visible to users, it plays a critical role in enhancing discoverability, improving navigation, boosting accessibility, and ensuring that content is relevant and well-organised. By following best practices and prioritising user needs, designers can leverage the power of metadata to create seamless, intuitive, and effective user experiences. In an increasingly complex digital landscape, the importance of metadata in UX design cannot be underestimated. It is the hidden framework that supports every interaction, guiding users to the right content at the right time and ensuring a smooth and satisfying experience.

28

Chapter 28: Effective Labeling and Terminology

When designing a user experience (UX), one of the most critical yet often overlooked aspects is how we label things and the terminology we use throughout a product. Labels, instructions, and terminology guide users through an interface, helping them make sense of what they see and how they should interact with it. If these elements are unclear, inconsistent, or confusing, users will struggle to complete tasks, potentially leading to frustration, errors, and abandonment of the product.

In this chapter, we'll explore how to create effective labels and use appropriate terminology. We will look at the importance of consistency, clarity, and context when choosing labels, as well as how to ensure they are easily understood by a wide range of users. A well-thought-out labelling system improves the usability of any digital product, whether it's a website, an app, or even physical devices with digital interfaces.

CHAPTER 28: EFFECTIVE LABELING AND TERMINOLOGY

The Role of Labels in UX Design

Labels serve a fundamental purpose in user interfaces. They describe elements, actions, and sections, enabling users to navigate and interact with a product efficiently. Without labels, users would be left guessing about the purpose of buttons, forms, menus, and other interactive elements.

In UX design, we use labels for various elements such as:

- **Navigation menus**: Labels guide users through the structure of a website or app, indicating where they will go when they click or tap a particular option.

- **Buttons and action items**: Labels on buttons tell users what will happen if they click it, like "Submit," "Cancel," or "Learn More."

- **Forms**: Labels for form fields ensure users know what information is required, such as "Name," "Email," or "Password."

Because of their crucial role in guiding users, labels must be intuitive and easy to understand.

Clarity Above All

When it comes to labeling, clarity is key. The labels we choose must be simple, straightforward, and self-explanatory. Users should not have to guess or interpret the meaning of a label – it should be obvious at first glance.

Consider the example of a button that deletes an item. If we label this button as "Remove," some users might not realise that clicking it will permanently delete something. A clearer label would be "Delete," because it directly communicates the action and leaves little room for misunderstanding.

The language used should also match the user's level of understanding. If your audience is made up of technical professionals, using industry jargon might be appropriate. However, if your users are the general public, simpler, everyday language is the better choice.

Here are a few tips for achieving clarity in labeling:

- **Use familiar words**: Use common, everyday language where possible. For example, instead of saying "Execute," say "Run" or "Start."

- **Be specific**: Avoid vague terms. Instead of saying "Click here," specify what the user is clicking for, like "Download File" or "View Details."

- **Avoid jargon**: Unless you are working with a highly technical or specialised user base, avoid using jargon that could confuse or alienate users.

Consistency is Key

Another essential rule in UX design is to maintain consistency in labeling. Consistency makes interfaces more predictable, which increases ease of use. When users see a familiar term used in the same way throughout a product, they can rely on their previous understanding to navigate more efficiently. Inconsistent labels, on the other hand, lead to confusion and errors.

For instance, if a shopping cart is labeled as "Cart" on one page but "Basket" on another, users might think these are two separate things, even though they serve the same purpose. Consistent terminology ensures that users always know what they are dealing with, no matter where they are in the product.

Here's how you can maintain consistency:

- **Create a style guide**: Document your labels and terms in a UX style guide, which should be referenced by all team members. This ensures everyone is using the same language across the product.

- **Stick to established patterns**: Don't reinvent the wheel. Use established design patterns and labels that users are already familiar with. For example, most users understand that a gear icon usually represents "Settings," so there's no need to label it differently.

Context Matters

Effective labeling also depends on the context in which it's used. Context influences how users interpret labels and how successful those labels are at conveying their intended meaning. A button labeled "Submit" in a form is clear because users understand they are submitting information. However, if that same button appeared on a random part of the page, the label alone might not provide enough context.

The way labels are presented should be tied to the user's current task and expectations. Consider the user's journey and make sure labels are placed where they make sense within that flow. For example, after filling out a registration form, the primary button should say something like "Sign Up" or "Create Account" rather than a generic term like "Submit," which doesn't convey the result of the action.

Using Descriptive Labels for Actions

Labels that accompany buttons or actions should clearly describe the expected result of that action. Users should know what will happen when they press a button or interact with an element. Vague terms such as "OK" or "Proceed" should be avoided when more descriptive options are available.

For instance, if users are confirming their subscription to a newsletter, the button should say "Subscribe" rather than something less specific like "Submit" or "Continue." Descriptive labels give users confidence that they know what will happen next, reducing the likelihood of errors or hesitation.

Testing and Feedback

It's vital to test labels and terminology with real users to ensure they are understood correctly. What seems clear to a designer or developer might be confusing to an average user. Usability testing allows you to identify any problematic labels and fix them before the product is released.

You can also gather feedback through surveys, interviews, or other research methods. Ask users if the labels were intuitive, and whether they encountered any points of confusion. Based on this feedback, you can make adjustments to improve clarity and usability.

Cultural Sensitivity and Localisation

When designing for a global audience, it's important to consider the cultural context in which your labels and terminology will be interpreted. Words that are clear and effective in one language or culture might not translate well to another.

For example, a label like "Home" might make sense to English-speaking users as a way to return to the main page, but in other languages, a more appropriate translation might be needed to convey the same concept. If you're designing a product for multiple regions or languages, it's essential to invest in proper localisation and translation to ensure labels remain effective across cultures.

Conclusion

Effective labeling and terminology are fundamental to a positive user experience. Clear, consistent, and context-aware labels ensure users can navigate your product effortlessly, while also reducing the chance of confusion or errors. By prioritising clarity, maintaining consistency, and considering cultural differences, you can create labels that guide users through your product in a seamless and intuitive way.

Always remember to test your labels with real users and be open to feedback. What might seem obvious to you as a designer may not be so straightforward for someone else. With thoughtful consideration and attention to detail, your labels and terminology can significantly enhance the overall user experience.

29

Chapter 29: The Importance of Content Hierarchy

Introduction to Content Hierarchy

Content hierarchy is one of the most important aspects of User Experience (UX) design. It refers to the way information is structured and prioritised on a webpage or interface. In essence, content hierarchy guides users to the most important pieces of information first and then lets them naturally explore deeper levels of content. Without a proper hierarchy, users might struggle to find the information they need, causing frustration and potentially abandoning the website or app.

Why is content hierarchy so important? In the modern digital age, people have shorter attention spans, and they want to access the right information quickly and efficiently. If users can't easily locate what they're looking for, they will likely leave and go somewhere else. A well-thought-out content hierarchy helps avoid this by creating a clear, logical flow of information.

At its core, content hierarchy ensures that the most important information is presented in a way that stands out, while secondary and tertiary content is still available but does not overpower the key message. This helps in creating a positive user experience by ensuring that users can navigate and digest information easily. This chapter will explore why content hierarchy matters in UX design, how to create effective hierarchies, and the principles that can guide designers in their work.

Part 1: Why Content Hierarchy Matters in UX Design

In UX design, the way content is organised can either make or break the user experience. Without a clear content hierarchy, users can become lost, overwhelmed, or frustrated. The importance of content hierarchy in UX design can be summarised in three key points: efficiency, clarity, and usability.

1. **Efficiency** Users often visit websites or use apps with a specific purpose in mind. Whether it's to purchase a product, find information, or complete a task, they expect to achieve their goal quickly. A good content hierarchy allows users to locate essential information effortlessly. By placing the most important content at the top or in the most visible areas, users can focus their attention where it's needed the most. This reduces the time they spend searching for information and

increases the likelihood of them completing their task.

For example, on an e-commerce website, users are often looking for product details, reviews, and prices. If these elements are buried within the page or spread out in a confusing way, users might become frustrated and leave. But when these elements are displayed in a logical order—price and product details near the top, with reviews or extra information following—it becomes easier for users to make a decision.

2. **Clarity** Content hierarchy helps in creating a clear and organised layout. When information is structured well, users can quickly grasp the message being conveyed. For instance, headings, subheadings, and body text are essential parts of content hierarchy. By using a distinct visual style for each, such as larger fonts for headings and smaller text for details, users can instantly understand which information is most important and which is supplementary.

A clear hierarchy also helps reduce cognitive load. When users don't have to think hard about where to find information, it leaves them with more mental energy to engage with the content itself. This is particularly important for mobile design, where space is limited, and users may only spend a few seconds scanning a page.

3. **Usability** Usability is one of the main goals of UX design. If a website or app isn't usable, it will fail its users. A well-structured content hierarchy is vital for usability

because it makes navigation intuitive and information easy to consume. If users can't quickly find what they need, they're more likely to abandon the experience altogether. By prioritising content logically and visually, designers help users navigate smoothly.

For example, consider a news website. Readers expect the most important stories, headlines, or breaking news to be highlighted at the top. Secondary stories should follow, and less urgent content, like opinion pieces or older articles, can appear lower down. This helps readers stay informed without feeling overwhelmed by too much content.

Part 2: How to Create an Effective Content Hierarchy

Designing an effective content hierarchy isn't just about placing information on a page. It requires a deep understanding of the user's needs, goals, and behaviour. Here are several strategies to create an effective content hierarchy:

1. **Understand User Goals** Before designing any content layout, it's essential to understand what users want to achieve. A user's goal will often dictate the hierarchy of information on a page. For example, if you're designing a recipe app, the most important information users want to see first might be the ingredients and cooking time. Secondary information, such as nutritional details,

might be useful but should not overpower the primary content.

Conducting user research can help identify which pieces of information are most important to users. Surveys, interviews, and usability testing are great methods to gather these insights. Once you understand user goals, you can prioritise content accordingly.

2. **Use Visual Weight** Visual weight refers to the prominence of different elements on a page. By giving certain pieces of content more visual weight, you can guide the user's eye towards the most critical information first. Several factors contribute to visual weight, including size, colour, contrast, and spacing.

- **Size**: Larger elements naturally draw more attention. This is why headings are often larger than body text.
- **Colour**: Bright or bold colours can make content stand out. Using contrasting colours for headings or buttons can direct users to take action.
- **Spacing**: Proper use of white space (or negative space) can make important content stand out by giving it room to breathe.

A combination of these visual techniques can create a clear hierarchy that guides users through the content in a logical order.

3. Hierarchy of Headings Headings and subheadings are powerful tools in creating a logical content structure. They allow users to quickly scan a page and locate specific sections of information. Each level of heading should be styled differently to reflect its importance. For instance, primary headings might be bold and large, while subheadings could be smaller but still stand out from the body text.

By providing a clear hierarchy of headings, you also help improve the accessibility of the content. Screen readers and other assistive technologies rely on heading structure to help users navigate through a webpage.

4. Use of Imagery and Icons Imagery and icons are often overlooked when it comes to content hierarchy, but they play an important role in UX design. Visual elements can complement text and make information more digestible. For instance, icons can help identify key actions, such as adding to a cart or downloading a file. Similarly, well-placed images can support or break up blocks of text, making the content easier to scan and understand.

However, it's important to use visuals thoughtfully. Too many images or icons can overwhelm users and take attention away from the primary content. Striking a balance between text and visual elements is key to creating a cohesive design.

Part 3: Principles of Good Content Hierarchy in UX

The principles of good content hierarchy are based on fundamental design concepts that ensure a seamless and intuitive user experience. These principles serve as guidelines for creating a logical and user-friendly content structure.

1. **Simplicity** Simplicity is crucial when designing content hierarchy. Overloading users with too much information can lead to confusion and frustration. Instead, focus on keeping the layout clean and uncluttered. Prioritise the most important information and remove unnecessary elements that could distract or overwhelm the user. Less is often more when it comes to UX design.

2. **Consistency** Consistency helps users become familiar with the structure of the content and navigate it more easily. This applies to both visual consistency (such as the same style of headings, buttons, and icons) and the consistency of information flow. If users expect a certain type of content to appear in a specific place, it's important to meet that expectation. For example, on an e-commerce site, product prices should consistently be placed near the top of each product page, so users know exactly where to look.

3. **Accessibility** Good content hierarchy should cater to all users, including those with disabilities. Designers need to ensure that the content is accessible to people using screen readers, as well as those with visual or cognitive

impairments. Structuring the content logically, using proper HTML tags, and ensuring high-contrast colours can all contribute to making a design more accessible.

4. **Mobile-Friendly Design** With a growing number of users accessing websites and apps via mobile devices, it's essential to design content hierarchies that are mobile-friendly. This means ensuring that the most important content is easily viewable and accessible on smaller screens. Mobile design also often requires a more simplified hierarchy, as there is less space to work with. Designers should focus on creating layouts that adapt well to various screen sizes, using responsive design techniques to maintain a clear hierarchy regardless of the device.

5. **Feedback and Iteration** Finally, good UX design, including content hierarchy, is never static. Designers should continually gather user feedback and iterate on their designs to improve usability. Conducting A/B testing or usability studies can help identify which aspects of the hierarchy are working well and which need improvement. By continually refining the design based on real user feedback, designers can ensure that the content hierarchy remains effective and user-friendly.

Conclusion

Content hierarchy is a fundamental aspect of UX design that plays a vital role in ensuring that users can navigate and consume information efficiently. By understanding user goals, using visual weight, and adhering to key design principles, designers can create clear and logical content structures. A good content hierarchy not only enhances usability but also contributes to a positive and enjoyable user experience. In the end, it

30

Chapter 30: Optimizing Information Architecture for Scalability

Introduction: Understanding Information Architecture and Scalability

Information architecture (IA) is a fundamental aspect of user experience (UX) design. It involves organising and structuring content in a way that helps users navigate websites or applications efficiently. As digital products evolve, grow, and change, scalability becomes a crucial factor to consider. Scalability refers to the ability of a system or structure to handle increased usage or content without losing performance or usability. When designing for scalability, it's important to anticipate future growth and ensure the IA can adapt and expand without causing confusion or frustration for users.

In this chapter, we'll explore how to optimise information architecture for scalability, focusing on strategies that help create a flexible, adaptable, and user-friendly structure that can accommodate both current needs and future changes. We'll discuss the principles of IA, the challenges of scaling digital products, and techniques to maintain clarity and usability even as content or user demands increase.

1. Principles of Information Architecture

Before we dive into scalability, it's essential to revisit the core principles of information architecture. These principles guide the process of organising and labelling content in a way that makes sense to users and supports easy navigation:

- **Hierarchy:** Organising information from general to specific helps users easily find what they're looking for. A clear hierarchy ensures that users can start at a broad level and drill down to more detailed content if needed.

- **Consistency:** Consistent labelling, structure, and design patterns make navigation more intuitive. Users shouldn't have to re-learn how to navigate the system every time they move from one section to another.

- **Findability:** Users must be able to quickly locate the information they need. This involves not only good organisation but also effective search functionality.

- **Clarity:** Labels and categories should be clear, concise, and descriptive. Ambiguous terminology or overly complex navigation paths can lead to confusion and frustration.

- **Flexibility:** The structure should be flexible enough to accommodate changes, such as adding new content or features, without disrupting the overall experience.

When planning for scalability, these principles remain at the forefront of the IA design process. However, we must also think about how the system will evolve over time and how to future-proof the architecture.

2. The Challenge of Scaling Digital Products

One of the most significant challenges in UX design is ensuring that a product's information architecture can scale effectively. As websites, apps, or platforms grow, they often face several common issues:

- **Content Overload:** As more content is added, the structure can become cluttered or overwhelming, making it harder for users to find what they need.

- **Navigation Complexity:** A growing site or app can lead to convoluted navigation paths, with too many clicks or confusing menus that make it difficult for users to move around efficiently.

- **Inconsistent Categorisation:** With the addition of new content or features, the categories or labels initially created may no longer make sense, leading to inconsistency.

- **Search Efficiency:** As content expands, search functionality needs to become more powerful and precise to help users filter through larger volumes of information.

If not addressed early, these challenges can result in a poor user experience, leading to frustration, drop-offs, or decreased engagement. To avoid these issues, it's essential to build a scalable IA from the start.

3. Strategies for Optimising Information Architecture for Scalability

Now that we understand the challenges, let's explore some effective strategies for optimising information architecture for scalability.

3.1. Modular Design: Building with Flexibility in Mind

A modular design approach breaks down the structure into smaller, reusable components or modules. Each module can be independently managed, updated, or expanded without affecting the entire system. For example, think of a website as a series of sections – the homepage, product pages, blog, contact, etc. Each of these sections can grow independently, allowing for more flexibility. This approach allows UX designers to plan for future content without overcomplicating the initial structure. It also makes it easier to add or remove sections without disrupting the overall user experience.

3.2. Scalability Through Hierarchical Structures

A well-defined hierarchy is crucial for scalability. By maintaining a clear top-level structure that branches into subcategories, you can accommodate future growth without compromising usability. As new content or sections are added, they can slot into the existing hierarchy without creating confusion. For instance, an e-commerce website might start with categories like "Men," "Women," and "Children." As the product catalogue expands, subcategories can be added (e.g., "Men's Shoes," "Women's Accessories") without disrupting the overall navigation. It's important to avoid over-complicating the hierarchy, as too many levels can lead to confusion. Instead, aim for a balance between breadth and depth in the structure, keeping the user's perspective in mind.

3.3. Card Sorting and User Research: Involving Users in IA Design

Card sorting is a valuable UX research method that involves users in the process of organising content. By asking users to group related items or categories, you can gain insights into how real people would expect to find information. This user-centred approach helps you design a structure that makes sense to your audience, reducing the likelihood of navigation issues as the site grows. Conducting user research and testing regularly will help you identify potential problems early on, allowing you to adjust the IA before it becomes too complex to fix easily.

3.4. Optimising Search Functionality

As content grows, the search function becomes increasingly important. A well-designed search system can help users find what they need quickly, even if they're unfamiliar with the navigation structure. For large-scale websites or apps, it's essential to incorporate advanced search features, such as filtering, predictive search, and faceted navigation. Faceted navigation allows users to refine their search results by applying filters, such as price range, category, or brand. This helps users narrow down large volumes of content to find exactly what they're looking for, which becomes increasingly important as the site or app grows.

3.5. Metadata and Taxonomy: Structuring Information Behind the Scenes

Metadata and taxonomy play a key role in scaling information architecture. Metadata is the data that describes other data, such as tags, categories, and keywords, which help organise and label content behind the scenes. A well-thought-out taxonomy ensures that content can be grouped and retrieved efficiently, even as the system grows. For instance, an online library might use metadata like "author," "publication year," and "genre" to categorise books. As more books are added, users can search and filter by these categories to quickly find the content they need. Properly managing metadata and taxonomy ensures that the system can handle large amounts of content without sacrificing usability.

3.6. Regular IA Audits: Ensuring Continuous Optimisation

As your digital product evolves, it's essential to conduct regular audits of the information architecture. This involves reviewing the existing structure, identifying areas that have become cluttered or outdated, and making adjustments where necessary. By regularly auditing the IA, you can catch issues early and ensure that the system remains scalable and user-friendly as it grows. It's also a good opportunity to assess user feedback and adjust the structure based on real-world usage patterns.

4. Conclusion: Building for the Future

Optimising information architecture for scalability is an essential part of creating a successful digital product. By focusing on flexibility, user involvement, and continuous improvement, you can build an IA that not only meets current needs but can also adapt to future growth. This ensures a seamless user experience, even as your website or app expands.

When designing for scalability, always keep the user at the forefront of your decision-making. A clear, consistent, and flexible IA will support your product's growth while ensuring that users can easily find the information they need, no matter how much content you add in the future. Ultimately, scalability is about planning for the long term, anticipating changes, and building a structure that can grow and evolve while maintaining clarity, usability, and efficiency.

IV

Interaction Design

Master the art of designing seamless interactions between users and interfaces.
Interaction design is about creating intuitive flows and responsive experiences. This section dives into wireframing, prototyping, microinteractions, and designing for multiple devices, ensuring that users interact effortlessly with your designs.

31

Chapter 31: Introduction to Interaction Design

What is Interaction Design?

Interaction Design, or IxD, is a crucial part of User Experience (UX) design that focuses on how users interact with digital products and services. It involves creating engaging and intuitive interfaces that allow users to achieve their goals effortlessly. When we think of interaction, we often imagine a conversation or exchange between two people. In the context of design, interaction refers to how users engage with a system, such as a website, an app, or even a physical device. Interaction design aims to make these exchanges smooth, efficient, and even enjoyable.

At the heart of interaction design is the relationship between a user and a product. The designer's role is to ensure that this relationship is functional and meaningful. Interaction design goes beyond aesthetics; it is about understanding user behaviour, anticipating needs, and creating interfaces that respond accordingly. It encompasses everything from the buttons users click to the way they navigate through content and the feedback they receive while doing so.

The Importance of Interaction Design

Good interaction design is essential because it impacts the overall user experience. If a user struggles to interact with a product, they are likely to feel frustrated, which can lead to abandoning the product altogether. On the other hand, smooth, intuitive interaction leads to satisfaction, increasing the chances that users will return and recommend the product to others.

The goal of interaction design is to create an experience that feels natural and seamless. Designers must consider how users will move through a system and what they need at each step. This requires empathy, as designers need to put themselves in the user's shoes and understand their goals, frustrations, and motivations. In essence, interaction design bridges the gap between technology and people. It ensures that the user doesn't have to struggle to understand how to use a product. Instead, the product adapts to the user's needs and provides a clear, logical path to their goal.

Key Principles of Interaction Design

There are several key principles that guide successful interaction design:

1. **Clarity**
   Clarity is the most important principle of interaction design. Users should always know where they are, what they can do, and what will happen when they take an action. Clear instructions, labels, and feedback help users to navigate the interface with ease.

2. **Feedback**
   Feedback tells users whether their actions have been successful or not. This can be as simple as a button changing colour when clicked, or as complex as a detailed error message. Feedback reassures users that the system is working as expected and reduces uncertainty.

3. **Consistency**
   Consistency means that the same actions should always lead to the same results. For example, if a user taps a button to submit a form, they should expect that all submit buttons across the site or app will behave the same way. Inconsistent interactions confuse users and lead to mistakes.

4. **Affordance**
   Affordance refers to the way design elements suggest their functionality. For example, a button should look

like it can be clicked, and a text box should look like it can be typed into. Good affordances help users understand what actions they can take without the need for instructions.

5. **Simplicity**
Simplicity is key in interaction design. The simpler an interface, the easier it is to use. Designers should focus on reducing unnecessary elements and distractions. Every component should have a purpose, and every interaction should be as straightforward as possible.

6. **Learnability**
Users should be able to quickly learn how to interact with a product. This means that even first-time users should be able to complete basic tasks without much difficulty. Clear instructions and a familiar layout can aid in learnability.

7. **Error Prevention and Recovery**
Interaction design should aim to prevent users from making mistakes, but it should also provide ways for users to recover when errors do occur. This can involve designing systems that provide clear error messages and offering solutions, such as undo buttons or step-by-step guidance.

Interaction Design in the Digital Age

As technology evolves, so does the field of interaction design. Modern digital products are becoming more complex, and users expect higher standards of usability and engagement. The rise of mobile devices, voice assistants, and augmented reality means that designers must consider new ways that users interact with products. Interaction design is no longer limited to clicking buttons or typing text; it now involves gestures, voice commands, and even eye movement.

In the digital age, interaction design must also account for accessibility. Designers need to ensure that their products can be used by everyone, including people with disabilities. This means creating interfaces that can be navigated with a keyboard, designing for screen readers, and ensuring that text is legible and colour choices are suitable for people with visual impairments. Designing for accessibility isn't just a legal or ethical responsibility; it also improves the overall user experience. When products are designed with accessibility in mind, they become easier to use for everyone, not just those with disabilities.

The Role of Interaction Designers

Interaction designers play a key role in the product development process. They work closely with other UX professionals, such as researchers and visual designers, to create user-friendly products. They are responsible for designing the flow of interactions, mapping out user journeys, and prototyping solutions.

A typical day for an interaction designer might involve sketching out wireframes, running usability tests, and iterating on designs based on user feedback. They must balance technical constraints, business goals, and user needs to create products that are both functional and enjoyable to use. Interaction designers use various tools, from basic paper sketches to advanced software like Sketch or Figma, to create prototypes and test their ideas. They often collaborate with developers to ensure that their designs are implemented correctly and function as intended.

Conclusion: Why Interaction Design Matters

Interaction design is a vital component of UX that directly influences how users feel when using a product. When done well, it can lead to products that are not only functional but delightful to use. The best interaction designs are often invisible—users don't notice them because they just work. They are intuitive, responsive, and seamless.

However, poor interaction design can frustrate users and drive them away from a product. It's important for designers to invest time and effort into understanding users' needs and testing their designs to ensure they deliver the best possible experience. In today's world, where digital products and services play a huge role in everyday life, mastering interaction design is essential for any designer. It's the key to creating products that users love, and it ensures that technology serves people, rather than the other way around.

32

Chapter 32: Designing User Flows

Introduction to User Flows

User flows are a key aspect of UX design, forming the blueprint of how users move through a product or website. A well-designed user flow guides users from one step to another smoothly, ensuring that their journey is efficient, intuitive, and aligned with their goals. At its core, a user flow is the path a user takes to complete a task, such as signing up for a newsletter, purchasing a product, or finding information.

In the early stages of product design, understanding user flows helps designers and developers map out how users will interact with the system. This insight ensures that users don't get lost or frustrated. The flow of the design should align with the user's natural thought process, making their experience as straightforward as possible.

The importance of user flows extends beyond just wireframes or prototypes. They help teams visualise how a user interacts with various screens or touchpoints, creating a clear plan of action for product development. Well-crafted user flows ultimately lead to more seamless designs, saving time and reducing the need for significant changes later in the project. **In this chapter, we'll explore three key parts of designing user flows:**

1. **Understanding the User's Journey**
2. **Mapping User Flows Effectively**
3. **Testing and Refining User Flows**

Part 1: Understanding the User's Journey

Before diving into the specifics of user flows, it's crucial to first understand the user's journey. This refers to the path a user takes from the moment they discover a product or service, through their experience of using it, to the completion of their goal. This journey can include various stages, from awareness and discovery, to learning and adoption, all the way to engagement and retention.

1.1 Defining User Personas

To create an effective user flow, it is important to have a clear understanding of who your users are. One way to achieve this is by creating *user personas.* A persona is a fictional representation of your typical user, based on real data and research. Personas highlight user needs, frustrations, goals,

and behaviour patterns.
Consider factors such as:

- **Demographics**: Age, occupation, location, and education level.
- **Motivations**: What does this user hope to achieve by using your product?
- **Pain Points**: What challenges do they face that your product can solve?
- **Goals**: What are their short-term and long-term objectives?

Having a clear picture of your users allows you to design flows that cater to their needs, ensuring a more personalised experience.

1.2 Identifying Key Touchpoints

A user's journey is often composed of multiple touchpoints where they interact with a product. These touchpoints could be the homepage, a product page, the checkout page, or even a customer support section. Identifying these critical points is essential to understanding how users navigate through your platform.

For example, in an e-commerce website, the touchpoints might include:

- Homepage or landing page.
- Search or product category page.
- Product detail page.

- Shopping cart or checkout page.
- Confirmation or thank-you page.

By knowing these, you can start crafting user flows that guide users seamlessly from one point to another. Each touchpoint should serve a purpose in helping the user achieve their goal.

1.3 Analysing User Intent

Once the touchpoints are identified, it's important to understand the user's intent at each stage of the journey. User intent refers to the motivation or reasoning behind each action the user takes.

For example:

- When a user visits a product page, their intent could be to compare products or gather information.
- When they reach the checkout, their intent is likely to complete a purchase.

Recognising the user's intent helps you create a smoother flow. For instance, providing users with product comparisons or offering quick payment options at the right moment reduces friction and encourages users to complete their tasks.

Part 2: Mapping User Flows Effectively

With a solid understanding of the user's journey, the next step is to map out the actual user flow. This is a visual representation of the steps a user will take to complete a specific task within your product.

2.1 Defining the Start and End Points

Every user flow has a starting point and an end goal. The starting point could be anything from opening an app, landing on a homepage, or clicking a promotional email. The end goal is what the user hopes to achieve, like signing up for a service, downloading an app, or completing a purchase. When mapping user flows, it's crucial to clearly define both the starting point and the end goal. This clarity ensures that each step in the user flow drives the user toward that final objective.

2.2 Breaking Down Each Step

Once you've defined the start and end points, it's time to break down the journey into smaller steps. Think of these steps as individual actions the user needs to take to reach their goal.

For example, for a user trying to purchase a product online, the steps might include:

1. Viewing the homepage.
2. Searching for a product.
3. Viewing the product details.
4. Adding the product to the cart.
5. Entering delivery information.
6. Completing the payment.

Each step should feel logical and guide the user naturally from one action to the next. Avoid overwhelming the user with too many choices or steps, as this can lead to frustration or confusion.

2.3 Creating Visual Flowcharts

A useful way to represent user flows is through flowcharts. These visual maps provide a clear overview of how users will navigate through the system. Flowcharts use shapes like boxes and arrows to represent different actions and decisions users may face along the way.

For example:

- **Boxes** can represent screens or actions (e.g., "Search Results Page" or "Enter Payment Details").
- **Arrows** show the direction in which the user moves based on their actions.

Flowcharts are beneficial because they give both designers and stakeholders a high-level view of how the system works, making it easier to spot potential issues or redundancies in the flow.

2.4 Considering Alternative Paths

In real life, users don't always follow a straight path. They may abandon a task, return to a previous screen, or even encounter errors. When designing user flows, it's essential to account for these alternative paths. Consider how users might backtrack or deviate from the expected path, and design solutions for these cases.

For example:

- What happens if a user clicks "Back" during checkout?
- What if they want to remove an item from their cart after they've added it?

Building in flexibility for alternative paths ensures that users don't get stuck or frustrated when things don't go exactly as planned.

Part 3: Testing and Refining User Flows

Designing a user flow is only half the battle. Once the flow is mapped out, it needs to be tested and refined to ensure it works in practice. Testing helps identify potential pain points and areas of confusion that might not be obvious during the design phase.

3.1 Usability Testing

Usability testing involves observing real users as they interact with your design. This process provides valuable insights into how users experience the flow and where they might struggle. During usability testing, you can ask users to complete specific tasks that reflect the user flows you've designed. For example, ask users to sign up for an account or complete a purchase. Observe where they encounter difficulties, and take note of any areas where they hesitate or become confused.

3.2 Collecting Feedback

In addition to usability testing, gathering feedback from users is another critical step. User feedback can help identify both obvious and subtle issues in the flow. Sometimes, users will provide solutions to problems you might not have considered.

You can collect feedback through:

- Surveys after a user completes a task.
- In-person interviews.
- Analytics to track user behaviour (e.g., where users drop off in the flow).

Feedback offers an external perspective, which is essential for improving the flow's overall effectiveness.

3.3 Iterating and Improving

After testing and gathering feedback, it's time to make improvements. Iterating on your design based on real user data ensures that you're making changes that will genuinely enhance the user experience. Sometimes, small tweaks can make a significant difference. For instance, simplifying the checkout process by removing unnecessary fields, or making buttons more prominent, can have a big impact on conversion rates. It's important to remember that user flows are not static. As your product evolves and user needs change, user flows should be continuously revisited and refined to ensure they stay relevant and effective.

3.4 Monitoring User Flows Over Time

Even after you've refined the user flow, monitoring its performance over time is crucial. Use tools like heatmaps, session recordings, or analytics dashboards to track how users move through the flow. If you notice any bottlenecks or a high abandonment rate at certain steps, it might be time to revisit and adjust the flow.

Conclusion

Designing user flows is a vital part of the UX design process, ensuring that users can navigate through a product smoothly and efficiently. By understanding the user's journey, mapping out flows carefully, and testing and refining the process, you can create a seamless experience that leads to better user satisfaction and higher conversion rates. The key to successful user flows is empathy—putting yourself in the user's shoes and designing a path that makes sense to them. With proper planning, testing, and iteration, user flows can become the backbone of an intuitive and enjoyable user experience.

33

Chapter 33: Wireframing: From Concept to Creation

1. What is Wireframing?

Wireframing is a crucial stage in the user experience (UX) design process. It's like drawing the blueprint of a building before construction begins. When an architect designs a building, they don't start with bricks and cement. Instead, they begin with a plan or sketch. In UX design, wireframes serve as that plan. They provide a basic outline of a digital product, like a website or app, showing its structure and layout without focusing on specific design details like colours, fonts, or images.

At its core, wireframing is about creating a simple, visual guide that maps out the different elements on a page and how they interact with one another. It includes things like navigation menus, buttons, content areas, and forms, but these are all displayed as boxes and lines rather than detailed designs. This makes wireframes fast to create and easy to update. The purpose is to focus on the functionality and structure of the design, ensuring that the user journey is clear before moving into more detailed design stages.

Wireframes are also essential for communication. They allow designers to share their ideas with clients, developers, and other stakeholders early in the process. This way, everyone can see the basic layout and structure of the project and provide feedback before more time and effort are invested. If changes are needed, it's much easier to modify a simple wireframe than to redesign a fully detailed mock-up.

There are different types of wireframes, ranging from low-fidelity to high-fidelity. Low-fidelity wireframes are the simplest and quickest to create. They often look like rough sketches, focusing only on the layout and structure. High-fidelity wireframes, on the other hand, include more details and may start to look like the final product but still lack colours, images, and advanced styling.

Why is Wireframing Important?

Wireframing serves several key purposes in UX design:

1. **Clarifies ideas early**: Wireframes help translate abstract ideas into something concrete. Designers can quickly visualise their thoughts and share them with others.

2. **User-focused design**: By concentrating on structure and functionality rather than aesthetics, wireframes

encourage designers to focus on the user's journey and how easy it is for them to navigate the product.

3. **Saves time and resources**: Early feedback from stakeholders can prevent costly changes later in the project. Wireframes allow teams to catch potential issues or misunderstandings before moving to more detailed design work.

4. **Facilitates collaboration**: Wireframes are easy to share and understand, making them a useful tool for communication between designers, developers, and clients.

2. The Wireframing Process: Step by Step

Creating a wireframe follows a simple but structured process. Below is an outline of the common steps taken to move from concept to creation.

1. Define the Project Goals

Before starting on a wireframe, it's essential to understand the project goals. What is the purpose of the website or app? What are the business objectives, and what are the users trying to achieve? For example, a retail website will have very different goals compared to a social media app. Defining clear goals will ensure that the wireframe aligns with the product's purpose.

2. Understand the User's Needs

UX design is centred around the user. It's important to consider who the users are, their needs, and how they will interact with the product. This is where research becomes vital. Understanding user behaviours, pain points, and expectations can inform the structure of the wireframe. For instance, a shopping website will need an easy way for users to search for products, view details, and make purchases.

3. Create User Flow Diagrams

Before jumping into the wireframe, it can be helpful to create a user flow diagram. This diagram maps out the different paths a user might take to complete a task on the site or app. For example, on an e-commerce website, the user flow might start with browsing products, moving to the shopping cart, then to checkout, and finally to payment. User flows help ensure that the wireframe includes all necessary pages and that navigation is smooth and logical.

4. Start with Sketches or Low-Fidelity Wireframes

Once the goals, user needs, and user flows are clear, it's time to start sketching. Many designers begin with rough, low-fidelity wireframes using pencil and paper or simple digital tools. At this stage, focus only on layout and functionality. For example, where will the logo go? How will users navigate between different sections? Where will buttons and forms be placed? Don't worry about colours or detailed styling yet.

Low-fidelity wireframes are quick to produce, which makes them perfect for exploring different layouts and ideas. It's common to try out a few different versions before deciding on the best option. Sharing these early wireframes with stakeholders for feedback can prevent future problems and ensure everyone is on the same page.

5. Move to High-Fidelity Wireframes

Once the basic layout has been agreed upon, it's time to move on to high-fidelity wireframes. These wireframes still avoid colour and advanced styling but include more detailed information about spacing, sizing, and the placement of interactive elements like buttons or forms. Some high-fidelity wireframes may even start to include simple placeholder text and images to give a clearer sense of the final design. High-fidelity wireframes are often created using digital tools like Sketch, Figma, or Adobe XD. These tools allow designers to create more polished wireframes and even simulate basic interactions, like what happens when a user clicks a button.

6. Test and Iterate

No design is perfect on the first try, which is why testing is a key part of the wireframing process. Showing the wireframes to users or stakeholders and gathering feedback can highlight areas that need improvement. Maybe a button isn't in the most intuitive place, or perhaps the navigation is confusing. By making changes and testing again, the design can be refined before moving to the more expensive stages of development.

3. Tools and Best Practices for Effective Wireframing

Wireframing has evolved with the availability of digital tools, which can streamline the process and make it easier to collaborate with teams. Additionally, there are some best practices that all UX designers should keep in mind when creating wireframes.

Popular Wireframing Tools

1. **Sketch**: This is one of the most popular tools among UX designers. Sketch is great for creating both wireframes and more detailed UI designs. It offers a range of plugins that make the design process more efficient.

2. **Figma**: Figma is another widely used tool for wireframing. One of its standout features is real-time collaboration, allowing teams to work together on the same wireframe simultaneously, even if they are in different locations.

3. **Adobe XD**: Adobe XD is part of the Adobe Creative Cloud suite and provides a robust platform for creating both wireframes and prototypes. It's known for its smooth integration with other Adobe tools like Photoshop and Illustrator.

4. **Balsamiq**: This tool is designed specifically for low-fidelity wireframes. Balsamiq's simple, sketch-like style makes it ideal for quickly drafting ideas and sharing them with clients or team members for feedback.

5. **Axure**: For more complex projects, Axure is a powerful tool that allows designers to create detailed wireframes with interactive elements. This can be particularly useful for projects where stakeholders need to see how certain features will behave.

Wireframing Best Practices

1. **Keep it Simple**: The purpose of a wireframe is to focus on layout and functionality. There's no need to include colours, images, or detailed styling at this stage. Keep everything simple and clean to ensure the structure is clear.

2. **Use Consistent Design Patterns**: Users expect consistency when interacting with digital products. For example, placing navigation menus in familiar locations, like the top or side of the page, makes the product easier to use. Following common design patterns can improve the user experience.

3. **Label Clearly**: Make sure all elements on your wireframe are labelled clearly. Buttons, forms, and content areas should all have simple, descriptive labels so that anyone looking at the wireframe understands what each element represents.

4. **Focus on Functionality**: While it can be tempting to think about design details early, wireframes should focus on functionality. Ensure that all key features, like navigation, buttons, and forms, are in the right place and easy for users to find.

5. **Be Open to Feedback**: Wireframes are a tool for exploration and iteration. Be open to feedback from stakeholders, clients, and users, and don't be afraid to make changes. The more feedback you gather early on, the fewer revisions will be needed later in the process.

6. **Test Early and Often**: Testing wireframes with real users can reveal important insights. Even if you're just showing them the wireframe on paper, getting their feedback can prevent bigger usability issues later on.

Conclusion

Wireframing is an essential part of UX design, acting as the bridge between concept and creation. It helps designers and stakeholders visualise the structure and functionality of a product before investing in detailed design work. By focusing on user needs, clear layouts, and simple design patterns, wireframes ensure that the end product is user-friendly and aligned with project goals. The process of creating wireframes, from low-fidelity sketches to high-fidelity digital drafts, is a collaborative and iterative journey, making it a cornerstone of effective UX design.

34

Chapter 34: Prototyping for Interaction

1. Understanding Prototyping in UX Design

Prototyping is an essential stage in the UX design process that helps designers create a visual and interactive representation of their ideas. It serves as a bridge between concept and reality, allowing designers to test and refine their ideas before moving into full development. A prototype can be as simple as a paper sketch or as complex as a fully functional digital model. The main purpose of prototyping is to explore different design options and assess how users interact with the product. By creating a prototype, designers can identify issues and make improvements based on user feedback.

Understanding the various types of prototypes is crucial. There are low-fidelity prototypes, which are quick and inexpensive to create. These include sketches and wireframes that focus on layout and functionality rather than detailed design. High-fidelity prototypes, on the other hand, resemble the final product more closely. They include interactive elements and visual details, which can be tested in a realistic environment. Choosing the right type of prototype depends on the stage of the design process and the specific goals of the project.

Prototyping also encourages collaboration among team members. Designers, developers, and stakeholders can come together to discuss ideas and make decisions based on tangible models rather than abstract concepts. This collaborative approach fosters a better understanding of user needs and helps ensure that the final product meets those needs effectively. In this way, prototyping is not just a tool for individual designers; it is a vital part of the overall design process that promotes teamwork and creativity.

2. The Importance of Interaction in Prototyping

Interaction is a key aspect of UX design that significantly impacts how users engage with a product. When creating prototypes, it is essential to focus on how users will interact with the design. This includes considering elements like navigation, responsiveness, and feedback. An interactive prototype allows users to simulate real interactions, giving designers valuable insights into usability and functionality. By observing how users navigate through the prototype, designers can identify potential obstacles and areas for improvement.

Creating interactive prototypes can involve various tools

and techniques. Popular prototyping tools, such as Figma, Sketch, and Adobe XD, enable designers to build interactive models that mimic the behaviour of the final product. These tools often allow for easy sharing and collaboration, making it simpler to gather feedback from users and stakeholders. Testing with interactive prototypes is crucial because it helps designers understand the flow of information and how different elements work together.

User testing during the prototyping phase provides a wealth of information. Designers can observe users as they interact with the prototype and gather their thoughts on the experience. This feedback is invaluable for making adjustments and ensuring that the final product is intuitive and user-friendly. Additionally, interactive prototypes can help uncover any misunderstandings about the design, allowing for clarification and refinement before development begins. The goal is to create a seamless experience that aligns with users' expectations and needs, which is why interaction is a fundamental component of effective prototyping.

3. Best Practices for Prototyping Interactions

To create effective prototypes for interaction, designers should follow several best practices. First, it is important to define clear objectives for the prototype. What specific interactions or features are being tested? Setting clear goals helps to guide the design process and ensures that the prototype focuses on relevant elements.

Next, it is essential to involve users early and often. User feedback is crucial in shaping the design and understanding how real users will interact with the product. This can involve conducting user testing sessions where participants can interact with the prototype and provide insights into their experiences. Recording these sessions can help designers identify patterns in user behaviour and address any issues that arise.

Another best practice is to iterate based on feedback. Prototyping is an ongoing process that benefits from continuous improvement. After testing, designers should review the feedback and make necessary changes to the prototype. This iterative approach helps to refine the design and ensures that the final product meets user expectations.

Moreover, designers should consider the overall context in which the product will be used. This means thinking about factors such as the user's environment, their goals, and any potential challenges they might face. By understanding the broader context, designers can create prototypes that provide a more accurate representation of the user experience. Finally, it's important to maintain a balance between detail and simplicity in the prototype. While it's essential to include interactive elements, overcomplicating the design can distract from the primary objectives.

In conclusion, prototyping for interaction is a vital aspect of UX design that enables designers to create user-centred products. By understanding the purpose of prototyping, focusing on interaction, and following best practices, designers can develop effective prototypes that lead to successful user experiences. This chapter has explored the essential elements of prototyping, providing a comprehensive guide for creating meaningful interactions that enhance the overall design process.

35

Chapter 35: Design Patterns in Interaction Design

Part 1: Understanding Design Patterns

Design patterns in interaction design are like templates that help designers solve common problems when creating user interfaces. Just as a blueprint guides builders in constructing a house, design patterns guide designers in crafting effective and user-friendly experiences. These patterns are based on tried-and-tested solutions, making them reliable and efficient.

At their core, design patterns help streamline the design process. They provide a shared language for designers, developers, and stakeholders, enabling everyone to communicate more effectively. For example, if a designer mentions a "modal window," the entire team understands it refers to a pop-up that requires users to interact with it before returning to the main content. This shared understanding reduces confusion and speeds up the design process.

Moreover, design patterns are not rigid rules. They are flexible guidelines that can be adapted to fit the unique context of a project. Designers can modify and mix these patterns to create innovative solutions tailored to specific user needs. For instance, a designer might take the idea of a "card layout" and combine it with a "carousel" to showcase products in an engaging way.

In summary, design patterns are essential tools in interaction design. They help designers create intuitive and user-friendly experiences by providing a solid foundation built on established practices. By understanding and using design patterns, designers can improve their workflow and produce better outcomes for users.

Part 2: Common Design Patterns in Interaction Design

There are several common design patterns in interaction design, each serving a specific purpose. Let's explore some of these patterns, along with examples of how they can be effectively used.

1. Navigation Menus
Navigation menus are essential for guiding users through a website or application. A well-structured navigation menu helps users find the information they need quickly. Common types of navigation include top navigation bars, side menus, and breadcrumb trails. For example, a top navigation bar on an e-commerce site might include links to categories such

as "Home," "Products," "About Us," and "Contact." This clear layout allows users to navigate with ease.

2. Forms

Forms are used to collect information from users. They can range from simple contact forms to complex registration forms. Good design patterns for forms include using clear labels, grouping related fields, and providing error messages that are easy to understand. For instance, if a user forgets to fill in their email address, a message like "Please enter a valid email address" helps guide them to correct the error without frustration.

3. Cards

Card layouts present information in a visually appealing way. Each card can contain an image, a title, a description, and a call to action. This design pattern is particularly useful for displaying products, articles, or any content that benefits from visual separation. For example, a recipe website might use cards to showcase various dishes, allowing users to easily scan and select their interests.

4. Modal Windows

Modal windows are pop-up dialogues that capture user attention. They are often used for notifications, confirmations, or additional information without navigating away from the current page. For example, when a user clicks "Delete," a modal might appear asking, "Are you sure you want to delete this item?" This pattern prevents accidental actions and ensures users make informed decisions.

5. Infinite Scroll

Infinite scroll allows users to continuously load content as they scroll down a page. This pattern is popular in social media and content-rich websites. For instance, on a news site, as users scroll down, more articles automatically appear, keeping them engaged without the need for pagination. However, it's essential to include a way for users to navigate back to the top or access other sections easily. These design patterns enhance user interaction and create a smoother experience. By incorporating these patterns thoughtfully, designers can ensure that users can navigate, input information, and engage with content effortlessly.

Part 3: The Importance of Context in Applying Design Patterns

While design patterns provide valuable guidelines, context plays a critical role in their application. Understanding the specific needs of the users and the goals of the project is crucial for successful interaction design. Here are some factors to consider when applying design patterns:

1. User Needs

Different users have different needs. A design pattern that works well for one audience may not be suitable for another. For example, a younger audience may prefer bold, vibrant designs, while an older audience might appreciate simplicity and clarity. Conducting user research helps identify the target audience and tailor the design accordingly.

2. Platform

The platform on which the design will be used also influences the choice of design patterns. Mobile devices require different patterns compared to desktop applications. For example, touch gestures are common on mobile, so patterns like swipe navigation may be more effective than traditional click-based methods.

3. Content Type

The type of content being presented also impacts the choice of design patterns. A photography website might benefit from large image galleries and sliders, while a news website might prioritise a clear layout with headlines and summaries. Understanding the content type helps designers select patterns that enhance the user experience.

4. Accessibility

Accessibility should always be a priority in design. Patterns must accommodate users with varying abilities, ensuring that everyone can interact with the interface. For instance, providing alternative text for images and ensuring proper colour contrast can make a significant difference for users with visual impairments.

5. Feedback and Iteration

Finally, feedback is vital in the design process. After implementing design patterns, it is essential to test them with real users. Gathering feedback can reveal what works and what needs improvement. Iteration allows designers to refine patterns based on user input, creating a more effective and user-friendly experience.

In conclusion, while design patterns offer valuable frameworks for interaction design, understanding the context in which they will be applied is crucial. By considering user needs, the platform, content type, accessibility, and feedback, designers can create tailored experiences that truly meet the needs of their users.

36

Chapter 36: Microinteractions: Small Details, Big Impact

Introduction to Microinteractions

Microinteractions are the small, often unnoticed details in the user experience that can make a significant difference in how users engage with a product. They are the tiny moments where users interact with a system or product, and while they may seem insignificant, they play a crucial role in shaping the overall experience. Microinteractions can be found in various places, such as the subtle animations when buttons are clicked, notifications that appear to confirm an action, or the changing of a toggle switch. These small interactions are designed to provide feedback, guide users, and enhance their emotional connection to a product.

Understanding microinteractions is essential for any UX designer because they can influence how users perceive a product's usability and enjoyment. When executed well, microinteractions can make users feel more in control and informed, ultimately leading to a more positive user experience. For example, consider a simple action like liking a post on social media. The quick animation of a heart filling up or a thumbs-up icon appearing serves as instant feedback, confirming that the action was successful. This feedback not only reassures users that their actions have been registered but also adds a layer of delight to the experience.

Additionally, well-designed microinteractions can enhance the aesthetic appeal of a product, making it feel more polished and engaging. As designers, we need to pay attention to these details because they contribute to the overall impression users have of our products. If users find microinteractions enjoyable and helpful, they are more likely to continue using the product and recommend it to others.

Types of Microinteractions

There are several types of microinteractions, each serving a different purpose in enhancing the user experience. One common type is **feedback microinteractions**, which provide users with information about the results of their actions. For instance, when a user submits a form, a brief message or visual cue may appear to confirm that their submission was successful.

This type of microinteraction is crucial for helping users understand the impact of their actions, especially in complex applications. Another type is **functional microinteractions**, which help users navigate a product more effectively. These include elements like progress indicators that show how far along a user is in a task, or animated transitions that guide users from one screen to another. Functional microinteractions can help reduce cognitive load by making it easier for users to understand where they are and what they need to do next.

Exploratory microinteractions allow users to discover features or content they might not have noticed otherwise. For example, a subtle animation that highlights a new feature when users first log in can encourage them to explore further. Finally, there are **social microinteractions**, which create a sense of community and connection among users.

These can include notifications that inform users when their friends have interacted with their content or when someone has commented on their post. Social microinteractions can foster engagement and encourage users to return to a product frequently. Each type of microinteraction plays a vital role in enhancing the overall user experience, and designers should consider how to incorporate them thoughtfully into their products.

Practical Tips for Implementing Microinteractions

When it comes to implementing microinteractions, there are several practical tips that designers can follow to ensure their effectiveness. First and foremost, it's essential to keep microinteractions simple and purposeful. Overly complex or distracting animations can detract from the user experience rather than enhance it. Designers should focus on creating clear, concise interactions that serve a specific purpose, whether that is providing feedback, guiding navigation, or encouraging exploration. Another important aspect is to ensure consistency in design and behaviour. Microinteractions should align with the overall design language of the product and behave in a predictable manner. For instance, if a button changes colour when hovered over, it should do so consistently across the entire product. This consistency helps build user familiarity and trust, making the product feel more intuitive and reliable.

Additionally, designers should consider the timing and duration of microinteractions. Microinteractions should occur at just the right moment, providing feedback or guidance without causing delays in the user experience. Animations should be smooth and quick, ideally lasting no longer than 200 milliseconds. This ensures that users receive feedback without feeling like the product is lagging or unresponsive. Finally, testing and iteration are critical to refining microinteractions. Designers should gather user feedback to understand how people interact with the product and identify any pain points.

By observing users in real-world scenarios, designers can discover areas for improvement and make adjustments to enhance the effectiveness of microinteractions. In conclusion, microinteractions may seem small, but they have the power to create a big impact on the user experience. By understanding their importance, recognising the different types, and implementing them thoughtfully, designers can elevate their products and create more engaging, user-friendly experiences.

37

Chapter 37: Gestures, Taps, and Clicks

Understanding Gestures

In today's digital age, gestures, taps, and clicks play a crucial role in how we interact with our devices. Understanding these interactions is vital for creating a user-friendly experience. Firstly, let's talk about gestures. Gestures are actions we perform on a touchscreen or touchpad. They can be as simple as swiping a finger across the screen or pinching to zoom in on an image. Gestures have become a natural way for people to communicate with their devices. For instance, swiping left or right can help users navigate through photos or apps quickly. As designers, we must ensure that the gestures we use are intuitive and easy to remember. It is essential to keep in mind that not all users are familiar with the same gestures. Some people might find gestures like a double-tap or long press confusing. Therefore, it is beneficial to include visual cues or tutorials that guide users on how to perform specific gestures. This can enhance their confidence and make the overall experience smoother.

The Importance of Taps

Next, we have taps, which are perhaps the most straightforward form of interaction. A tap is simply touching the screen once to select an item or open an app. It is crucial to design tap targets that are large enough to be easily tapped. If the targets are too small, users might accidentally hit the wrong item, leading to frustration. A good rule of thumb is to make tap targets at least 44 pixels wide. This helps accommodate users with different finger sizes and improves accessibility for those with limited dexterity. Moreover, it is essential to provide feedback when a tap is registered. This can be done through visual changes, such as highlighting the tapped item or providing a brief sound. Feedback reassures users that their action has been acknowledged, making the interaction feel more responsive. When designing taps, also consider the context in which users are tapping. For example, if they are using a device while walking, they may need larger buttons and clearer feedback to ensure they can interact without difficulty.

The Role of Clicks

Clicks are another critical aspect of interaction design, particularly for desktop users. Clicking is a fundamental action that involves pressing a mouse button to select or open something on the screen. Similar to taps, it is essential to ensure that clickable elements are easy to identify. Clear labels and intuitive icons help users understand what will happen when they click. Moreover, the placement of clickable elements matters significantly. For example, buttons should be located in areas where users expect to find them, such as at the bottom of a page or near related content. This familiarity helps users navigate more effectively. It's also vital to consider the different types of clicks, such as right-clicking for additional options or double-clicking to open files. Users should be aware of these options through visual cues or tooltips. Providing these hints can greatly enhance the user experience.

Considering User Context

Another important aspect of gestures, taps, and clicks is the role of context. Users are often in different environments when interacting with their devices. For instance, someone using a smartphone while commuting may not have the same level of attention as someone using a tablet at home. Understanding these contexts can guide the design of gestures, taps, and clicks. For mobile devices, it's essential to create interactions that are quick and efficient, allowing users to achieve their goals with minimal effort. This means prioritising the most important actions and making them easily accessible. On the other hand, desktop interactions may allow for more complex gestures and options since users can devote more time and attention. Therefore, understanding the context in which users operate will help tailor the interactions accordingly.

User Preferences and Flexibility

Moreover, it's worth noting that user preferences can vary widely. Some users may prefer gestures because they feel more natural and fluid, while others may favour taps and clicks because they are familiar with them. Therefore, providing multiple interaction options can enhance the user experience. For example, an app could allow users to either tap a button or swipe to access features. This flexibility accommodates different user preferences and helps create a more inclusive experience. Additionally, consider implementing settings that allow users to customize their interaction methods. Some users may benefit from larger buttons or simplified gestures, while others may want to use shortcuts or advanced gestures. This kind of personalisation enhances usability and empowers users to tailor their experiences to their liking.

Prioritising Accessibility

Accessibility is another key consideration when designing gestures, taps, and clicks. It is essential to ensure that all users, including those with disabilities, can interact with your design effectively. This can involve offering alternative methods of interaction, such as voice commands or keyboard shortcuts, for those who may have difficulty using touch screens or mice. Furthermore, providing clear instructions and feedback can greatly assist users with disabilities. For instance, adding screen reader compatibility or visual indicators can help guide users through the interactions. By prioritising accessibility, designers can create a more inclusive experience for all users.

Ensuring Consistency Across Platforms

Another factor to consider is the consistency of interactions across different platforms and devices. Users often switch between their smartphones, tablets, and desktops, so maintaining similar gestures, taps, and clicks across these platforms can enhance familiarity and reduce confusion. For example, if a user learns to swipe left to delete an email on their phone, they should ideally have a similar experience when using the same email service on their laptop. Consistency builds trust and improves usability, allowing users to transition seamlessly between devices. Designers should also be aware of the differences in operating systems, as they may have specific gestures and interactions that are expected by users. For instance, iOS devices may use different gestures compared to Android devices, and understanding these distinctions can help create a smoother user experience.

The Importance of Usability Testing

In addition to understanding how users interact with gestures, taps, and clicks, it is vital to test these interactions with real users. Conducting usability testing can provide valuable insights into how people engage with your design. Observing users as they navigate through tasks can highlight areas of confusion or frustration that may not be immediately apparent. Gathering feedback on their experiences can help identify any improvements needed. Additionally, testing can reveal whether certain gestures or taps are intuitive or if users require additional guidance. A/B testing different designs can also provide insights into which interactions are more effective. For example, comparing two different button sizes can help determine which one leads to more successful interactions. By prioritising user feedback and testing, designers can refine their interactions and create a more user-friendly experience.

Staying Updated with Trends and Innovations

Finally, let's not forget the importance of keeping up with trends and innovations in technology. As devices evolve, so do the ways in which we interact with them. New technologies, such as haptic feedback, can enhance the experience of gestures and taps by providing tactile responses. This adds another layer of engagement and can make interactions feel more satisfying. Additionally, advancements in artificial intelligence and machine learning can enable more intuitive gestures and personalized interactions. As designers, staying informed about these trends can help us create designs that are not only functional but also engaging and enjoyable for users. Embracing new technologies and understanding how they impact interactions can keep designs relevant and user-centered.

Conclusion: Creating Empowering Interactions

In conclusion, gestures, taps, and clicks are fundamental components of user experience design. By understanding the nuances of each interaction and considering the diverse needs of users, designers can create more intuitive and enjoyable experiences. Whether through simple taps, complex gestures, or precise clicks, the goal is to facilitate seamless interactions that empower users. By prioritising accessibility, consistency, and user feedback, we can create designs that resonate with a wide range of users. Ultimately, gestures, taps, and clicks shape how we connect with our devices and the digital world around us, making it essential for designers to approach these interactions with care and consideration.

38

Chapter 38: Designing for Different Devices (Mobile, Web, Tablets)

In today's world, users interact with digital content on various devices, including mobile phones, tablets, and desktop computers. Each of these devices offers a unique way to experience content, and understanding how to design for each one is essential for creating a great user experience. This chapter explores the key principles of UX design for mobile, web, and tablet devices, helping you to ensure that your designs are effective, accessible, and enjoyable across all platforms.

Understanding Device Differences

Before diving into the specifics of design, it's crucial to understand the differences between mobile devices, tablets, and desktops. Mobile phones are typically smaller and often used for quick interactions. Users may be on the move, and their attention spans can be shorter. Therefore, designs for mobile devices should prioritize simplicity and speed.

Tablets, on the other hand, offer a larger screen than mobile phones, making them suitable for both casual browsing and more involved tasks. Users may spend more time on tablets, so you can include slightly more content and interactive elements compared to mobile designs.

Desktops provide the largest screen space, allowing for complex layouts and detailed information. Users on desktops are often engaged in longer sessions, which means you can include more features and content. However, it's important to ensure that the experience is seamless and easy to navigate, regardless of screen size.

Responsive Design Principles

Responsive design is a key principle that allows your website or application to adapt to different screen sizes. By using flexible grids and layouts, designers can ensure that content is displayed appropriately on any device. When designing responsively, it's important to consider how elements like text, images, and buttons will resize and reposition. For instance, a navigation menu that works well on a desktop may need to transform into a hamburger menu on mobile devices to save space.

Using relative units like percentages instead of fixed pixel sizes can help achieve a responsive layout. This means that your design will automatically adjust to fit the user's screen, providing a better experience. Testing your designs on various devices is crucial to ensure they work as intended.

Emulating different screen sizes in design tools can also help you visualize how your content will appear.

Prioritizing Touch and Interaction

When designing for mobile and tablet devices, touch interaction becomes a significant factor. Users interact with these devices using their fingers, so it's vital to consider touch targets. Buttons and links should be large enough to tap easily without making mistakes. A common guideline is to ensure that touch targets are at least 44 x 44 pixels. This size reduces the chances of users accidentally tapping the wrong item.

Gestures, like swiping and pinching, can also enhance the user experience. For example, allowing users to swipe between images in a gallery or pinch to zoom on an image can make the interaction more intuitive. However, it's essential to provide clear feedback for touch actions, such as highlighting buttons when they are pressed or showing a loading spinner when content is being fetched.

Content Strategy Across Devices

Content is at the heart of any design, and how you present that content can vary significantly between devices. On mobile, it's important to prioritize essential information and present it clearly. Users may not want to scroll endlessly, so consider using vertical scrolling rather than horizontal. This approach allows users to navigate more easily on smaller screens.

On tablets, you can be a bit more flexible with the amount of content you display. Users may be more willing to read longer articles or view more images on a tablet. However, ensure that the content remains scannable. Use headings, bullet points, and images to break up text and keep users engaged.

For desktop designs, you can present more detailed content and use sidebars for additional information or links. However, keep in mind that users should still be able to navigate the site easily. Overloading the screen with too much information can overwhelm users, so balance content density with clarity.

Consistency in Design

Consistency is crucial across different devices. Users should be able to recognize your brand and its visual language, regardless of whether they are on a mobile phone, tablet, or desktop. This includes using consistent colours, fonts, and styles throughout your designs. Establish a design system or style guide to help maintain consistency across platforms. This way, your team can ensure that all design elements align with your brand's identity.

Additionally, consistent navigation helps users feel at ease when moving between devices. If a user starts their journey on a mobile device and later switches to a desktop, they should be able to find their way around easily. Keeping navigation elements in familiar locations, such as placing the menu at the top or using icons that represent the same actions, can enhance usability.

Performance Considerations

Performance is an essential aspect of UX design that can significantly impact user experience. Mobile devices often have slower internet connections than desktops, so it's essential to optimize your designs for performance. This means compressing images, minimizing code, and ensuring that your website loads quickly. Users are less likely to wait for a slow-loading site, which can lead to frustration and abandonment.

For tablets and desktops, while users may have better connectivity, it's still essential to focus on performance. Heavy animations and excessive graphics can slow down loading times, so always keep user experience in mind. Conducting performance tests across devices can help identify areas that need improvement, ensuring that users have a smooth and responsive experience.

Accessibility Across Devices

Accessibility should be a fundamental consideration in all your designs. Ensure that your designs are usable for people with disabilities, regardless of the device. This includes providing alternative text for images, using proper heading structures, and ensuring that all interactive elements can be navigated using a keyboard or screen reader.

Mobile and tablet devices may have different accessibility

features than desktops, so be sure to test your designs using various tools and devices. For example, many mobile devices have built-in screen readers that users rely on. Testing your designs for compatibility with these tools will help ensure that all users can access your content.

Final Thoughts

Designing for different devices requires careful consideration of how users interact with each platform. By understanding the unique characteristics of mobile phones, tablets, and desktops, you can create designs that are tailored to the needs of each user group. Emphasizing responsive design, touch interactions, consistent branding, and performance can significantly improve the user experience across devices. Always keep user needs at the forefront of your design process, and don't forget to test your designs on multiple devices to ensure that your work meets the highest standards of usability and accessibility.

By applying these principles, you can create engaging and effective user experiences that resonate with your audience, regardless of the device they choose to use. Remember, in a world where users are constantly switching between devices, your designs must be adaptable and user-friendly to capture their attention and keep them coming back for more.

39

Chapter 39: Feedback and Responsiveness in Interaction

The Importance of Feedback and Responsiveness

Feedback and responsiveness are essential elements in interaction design, serving as the backbone of user experience (UX). They play a crucial role in how users perceive and engage with digital products. Feedback is the information that users receive after performing an action, while responsiveness refers to how quickly and effectively a system reacts to user input. Together, these components shape the user's journey and can significantly influence their satisfaction and overall experience.

Immediate Feedback: A User Expectation

In any interactive system, users expect to see immediate feedback following their actions. For instance, when a user clicks a button, they anticipate a response, whether it's a visual change, a sound, or a notification. This instant feedback reassures users that their action has been recognised and understood by the system. Without proper feedback, users may feel confused or uncertain about whether their action has been successful. For example, if a user fills out a form and submits it, they should receive a confirmation message indicating that the submission was successful. Conversely, if there's an error, the user needs clear feedback about what went wrong and how to fix it.

Types of Feedback: Visual, Auditory, and More

Effective feedback can take many forms, including visual cues like colour changes, animations, or progress indicators. Visual cues should be intuitive and easy to understand. For example, changing a button from grey to blue after it has been clicked can indicate that the action has been recognised. Furthermore, animations can enhance the user experience by providing visual engagement while reinforcing the feedback. For instance, a spinning wheel can signal that the system is processing a request, giving users a sense of progress and reducing frustration. However, it's important to strike a balance. Overloading users with too much feedback can lead to confusion or frustration. Too many notifications or visual cues can clutter the interface, making it hard for users to focus on what matters most. Designers must be mindful of how much feedback they provide and ensure it is meaningful and relevant.

Timeliness of Feedback: Managing User Expectations

Additionally, feedback should be timely. Delayed responses can create anxiety and make users feel disconnected from the system. If a user clicks a button to send a message, they expect an almost instantaneous reaction. If the system takes too long to respond, users may think the action failed or become impatient, leading them to abandon their task. Therefore, it's essential for designers to create a system that not only responds quickly but also manages users' expectations by providing informative messages during any delays. This can be achieved through loading indicators, such as progress bars or spinners, that inform users that their action is being processed. This type of feedback fosters trust and encourages users to wait for the system to respond.

Consistency Across Devices: A Seamless Experience

Responsiveness also extends to the adaptability of the interface across various devices and screen sizes. In today's world, users interact with products on a myriad of devices, from desktops to smartphones. Ensuring that feedback mechanisms are consistent and effective across all platforms is vital. For instance, a notification that appears on a desktop should also be accessible on mobile devices. This consistency in responsiveness ensures users can seamlessly transition between devices without losing the context of their actions.

Accessibility Considerations: Inclusivity in Design

In addition to visual feedback, auditory feedback can also enhance the interaction experience. Sounds can provide immediate recognition of actions, such as a soft click when a button is pressed or a beep to indicate an error. However, designers must use sound judiciously. Not all users appreciate auditory feedback, and in some contexts, it may be disruptive. Therefore, it is essential to provide users with options to enable or disable sound effects according to their preferences. Moreover, feedback should also consider accessibility for users with disabilities. Providing text descriptions for visual elements can assist visually impaired users in understanding feedback through screen readers. Similarly, ensuring that auditory feedback is also available in visual form can cater to users who may be hard of hearing. The design of feedback systems should aim to be inclusive and cater to the diverse needs of users.

User Testing: The Key to Effective Design

Furthermore, user testing is critical in assessing the effectiveness of feedback and responsiveness. Observing how real users interact with a product can reveal insights that designers may overlook. For example, during usability testing, designers may notice that users struggle to understand a specific feedback mechanism. This can highlight areas for improvement and help designers create a more intuitive and responsive interaction. Continuous feedback from users should be integrated into the design process. This can involve surveys, focus groups, or usability tests where users provide input on their experiences. By actively engaging users in the design process, designers can refine feedback mechanisms to better meet their needs and expectations.

Tailoring Feedback: Addressing User Expertise

In addition, it's important to remember that users come with varying levels of expertise. Novice users may require more explicit and frequent feedback, while experienced users may prefer subtle cues. Designers should consider implementing a tiered feedback system that adjusts the amount and type of feedback based on the user's familiarity with the product. For instance, a first-time user might benefit from more detailed guidance and visual cues, while a returning user may appreciate a more streamlined experience with less intrusive feedback. This adaptive approach can enhance the user experience and promote a sense of mastery over time.

The Emotional Impact of Feedback

Another aspect to consider is the emotional impact of feedback. Positive feedback can enhance user satisfaction, while negative feedback can lead to frustration or disappointment. Therefore, when designing feedback for errors or unsuccessful actions, it's essential to frame it in a constructive manner. Instead of simply stating that an action has failed, provide users with clear and actionable steps to rectify the issue. This can empower users and help them feel more in control of their experience. For example, instead of displaying a generic error message, a system could provide specific guidance on how to fix the issue, such as "Please check your email address format." This approach transforms a negative experience into a learning opportunity, making users feel more engaged and satisfied.

Real-Time Feedback: Enhancing Interactions

Responsiveness also encompasses how a system handles user input in real time. For instance, when users are typing in a search box, the system should provide instant suggestions or corrections based on their input. This not only improves efficiency but also demonstrates that the system is actively engaged with the user. Real-time feedback can enhance the user experience by making interactions more dynamic and fluid. However, it's crucial to ensure that real-time feedback does not become overwhelming. Too many suggestions or changes can distract users from their primary task. Therefore, designers should aim for a balance between providing helpful suggestions and maintaining a clear, focused interface.

Conclusion: The Path to a Positive User Experience

In conclusion, feedback and responsiveness are fundamental to creating a positive user experience in interaction design. They foster trust, clarity, and satisfaction among users, ultimately guiding them toward their goals. Designers must prioritise clear, timely, and meaningful feedback while ensuring that the system responds quickly and effectively to user input. By incorporating auditory and visual feedback, considering accessibility, and engaging users in the design process, designers can create a responsive environment that caters to the diverse needs of users. Moreover, adapting feedback to the user's level of expertise and managing the emotional impact of feedback can enhance satisfaction and engagement. Ultimately, a thoughtful approach to feedback and responsiveness in interaction design can lead to a more intuitive, enjoyable, and effective user experience, ensuring that users feel valued and empowered throughout their journey.

40

Chapter 40: Error Handling in UX

Error handling is a crucial aspect of user experience (UX) design that often goes unnoticed until something goes wrong. When users interact with digital products, they expect things to work smoothly. However, errors are inevitable. Whether it's a typo in a form, a failed connection, or an unexpected crash, how these errors are communicated to users can make a significant difference in their overall experience. Effective error handling can enhance user satisfaction, reduce frustration, and ultimately foster a sense of trust in the product.

Understanding Errors

To design an effective error handling system, it's essential to first understand the different types of errors users may encounter. Errors can generally be categorized into two main types: user errors and system errors. User errors are mistakes made by users, such as entering incorrect information or forgetting a password. System errors, on the other hand, occur due to issues within the system, like server downtime or bugs in the code. Recognising these distinctions allows designers to tailor their responses accordingly.

Importance of Error Handling

The way errors are managed in a digital environment can significantly influence a user's perception of the product. If users encounter an error but are left confused or frustrated by a lack of guidance, they may abandon the task or, worse, the entire application. On the other hand, a well-handled error can turn a negative experience into a positive one. Effective error messages reassure users that the issue can be resolved and guide them on the next steps. This approach not only helps in retaining users but also enhances their confidence in using the product.

Best Practices for Error Handling

1. **Clarity and Simplicity**: Error messages should be clear and concise. Avoid technical jargon that may confuse users. Instead, use simple language that everyone can understand. For example, instead of saying "Input format is invalid," you could say, "Please enter your email address in the correct format."

2. **Visibility**: When an error occurs, it's essential that users are immediately aware of it. Error messages should be prominently displayed, ideally near the area where the error occurred. This visibility allows users to quickly identify and correct their mistakes.

3. **Constructive Feedback**: Instead of simply telling users what went wrong, provide constructive feedback. For example, if a password is too weak, instead of just stating "Password is weak," suggest how to create a stronger password by indicating the required characters, length, or types of symbols needed.

4. **Preventive Measures**: Wherever possible, design systems that prevent errors from occurring in the first place. This can include using input masks for fields like phone numbers or dates, which guide users to enter information in the correct format. Additionally, using real-time validation as users type can help catch errors before they submit a form.

5. **Graceful Recovery**: Provide users with a clear path to recover from errors. This could involve including a "try again" button or directing users back to the previous step. Making it easy to correct mistakes helps maintain a positive user experience even when errors happen.

6. **Empathy and Tone**: The tone of error messages should be empathetic. Users often feel frustrated or embarrassed when they make mistakes. Using a friendly and understanding tone can help ease those feelings. For instance, saying "Oops! Looks like something went wrong. Let's fix it together!" is far more reassuring than a cold, technical message.

7. **Help and Support Options**: Sometimes, users may require additional assistance to resolve their errors.

Including links to help articles, FAQs, or support contact information within the error message can empower users to find solutions quickly.

8. **Logging and Analytics**: On the backend, tracking errors and understanding their frequency can help designers and developers improve the product over time. Implementing logging mechanisms can provide insights into common user errors, allowing for targeted improvements in the user interface or functionality.

9. **Consistent Design**: Consistency in how errors are presented throughout the application is key. This includes using the same colour schemes for error messages, consistent positioning, and uniform language. Consistent design helps users learn what to expect and reinforces their understanding of how to navigate the application.

Testing and Iteration

Once error handling strategies are in place, it's vital to test them with real users. Usability testing can reveal how users react to errors and whether the provided solutions are effective. Observing users as they encounter errors and noting their reactions can provide valuable insights. Based on this feedback, designers should be ready to iterate and improve error messages and handling processes continuously.

Conclusion

Error handling is an integral part of user experience design that can make or break a user's interaction with a product. By prioritising clarity, visibility, empathy, and constructive feedback, designers can create a robust error handling system that not only addresses issues effectively but also enhances overall user satisfaction. In an age where users expect seamless experiences, effective error handling can turn potential frustrations into opportunities for positive engagement, fostering trust and loyalty among users.

V

Visual Design in UX

Create visually appealing and functional designs that enhance the user experience.
Explore how color, typography, imagery, and layout affect the user's perception and interaction with digital products. This section focuses on using visual design to communicate hierarchy, ensure accessibility, and create consistency across products.

41

Chapter 41: Visual Hierarchy in UX Design

Part 1: Understanding Visual Hierarchy

Visual hierarchy is a fundamental concept in user experience (UX) design. It refers to the arrangement of elements on a page to guide users' attention and help them understand the information presented. When users visit a website or use an app, they often look for cues to determine what is most important. Visual hierarchy helps create these cues by manipulating size, colour, contrast, and spacing.

At its core, visual hierarchy is about prioritising information. Designers use various techniques to highlight the most important elements, ensuring that users can easily find what they are looking for. For example, headings are typically larger than body text, making them more noticeable. Similarly, buttons may be coloured brightly to draw attention, while less important information is kept smaller and more muted.

The brain naturally processes information from top to bottom and left to right. Designers can take advantage of this by placing important elements where users are likely to look first. This principle is known as the "F-Pattern" and is based on how people typically scan a webpage. The most crucial content should be placed in the upper left corner, followed by the next level of information moving across the top and then down the page.

Understanding visual hierarchy is essential for creating effective UX design. It helps designers make informed decisions about how to present information, ensuring that users can quickly grasp the layout and purpose of a page. By carefully considering the arrangement of elements, designers can improve user engagement and satisfaction.

Part 2: Techniques for Establishing Visual Hierarchy

There are several techniques designers can use to establish visual hierarchy in their designs. One of the most effective methods is through size. Larger elements naturally attract more attention. For instance, a big, bold headline will stand out, guiding users to read it first. In contrast, smaller text can convey less important details, such as disclaimers or footnotes.

Another technique is colour. Bright, contrasting colours can make an element pop, drawing the user's eye. For example, using a vibrant colour for a call-to-action button, such as "Buy Now" or "Sign Up," can encourage users to take action. On the other hand, softer colours can be used for background elements to ensure they do not distract from the main content.

Contrast is also crucial in establishing hierarchy. When two elements have a significant contrast in lightness, darkness, or colour, the one that stands out more will catch the user's eye first. For instance, white text on a dark background will be more noticeable than grey text on a light background. This technique is particularly useful for highlighting important messages or warnings.

Spacing is another critical element in visual hierarchy. Adequate spacing between elements helps to create a sense of order and organisation. If elements are too close together, they may blend into one another, causing confusion. On the other hand, giving enough space between elements allows users to distinguish different sections easily. This is often referred to as "white space," and it is essential for creating a clean and readable layout.

Lastly, the use of typography plays a significant role in visual hierarchy. Different font sizes, weights, and styles can signal the importance of text. For example, using a bold font for headings and a regular font for body text helps users understand the structure of the information presented. Consistent use of typography throughout a design can enhance the overall user experience by providing clear cues about what to focus on.

Part 3: Applying Visual Hierarchy in Your Designs

To effectively apply visual hierarchy in your designs, start by mapping out the information you want to present. Identify the most important elements and consider how users will interact with your design. Ask yourself questions such as: What action do you want users to take? What information is crucial for them to see first?

Once you have a clear understanding of your goals, you can begin to implement the techniques discussed earlier. Use size to your advantage by making key elements larger. Apply colour strategically to draw attention to important buttons or messages. Ensure that there is enough contrast between elements to highlight critical information effectively.

Additionally, pay attention to spacing. Create clear sections within your design, making it easy for users to navigate and understand the information presented. Avoid clutter by ensuring that each element has room to breathe. A well-spaced layout feels more inviting and easier to use.

As you design, always consider the user's perspective. Test your designs with real users to see how they interact with your layout. Observe where their eyes are drawn and whether they can easily find the information they need. Use feedback to refine your designs and improve the overall user experience.

In conclusion, visual hierarchy is a powerful tool in UX design. By understanding how to guide users' attention through size, colour, contrast, spacing, and typography, you can create designs that are not only visually appealing but also functional and user-friendly. Applying these principles will help ensure that users have a positive experience and can easily navigate your website or app.

42

Chapter 42: Designing for Accessibility

Understanding Accessibility in Design

Accessibility in design is about making products and services usable for everyone, regardless of their abilities or disabilities. When we think of accessibility, we often consider people with visual, hearing, or mobility impairments. However, accessibility is broader; it also includes older adults, people with temporary injuries, and even those who might be in challenging environments. For instance, someone might be trying to use a mobile app while commuting or in bright sunlight. Good design should take all these situations into account.

To start, it is essential to understand the various disabilities that users may have. Visual impairments can range from complete blindness to partial sight, meaning that some users may rely on screen readers, while others may need larger text or high-contrast colours. Hearing impairments can include those who are deaf or hard of hearing. These users benefit from captions and transcripts for audio content. Physical disabilities can affect a user's ability to use a mouse or keyboard, making it crucial to ensure that all interactive elements are accessible through keyboard navigation or voice commands. Lastly, cognitive disabilities might affect how someone understands information or navigates a website, highlighting the need for clear language and simple layouts.

Designing for accessibility is not just about compliance with laws or guidelines; it is about creating a better experience for everyone. Inclusive design benefits all users, leading to improved usability, customer satisfaction, and brand loyalty. In a world that is increasingly digital, businesses must prioritise accessibility to reach a broader audience. This focus on accessibility also aligns with ethical practices in design, ensuring that everyone can access information and services equally.

Principles of Accessible Design

When designing for accessibility, several principles can guide your work. These principles help ensure that your designs are not only usable but also enjoyable for all users.

1. **Perceivable**: Information and user interface components must be presented to users in ways that they can perceive. For example, text alternatives should be provided for non-text content, such as images or videos. This way, screen readers can describe these

elements to users with visual impairments. Moreover, using sufficient colour contrast helps users with low vision distinguish between different elements on the page.

2. **Operable**: User interface components and navigation must be operable. This means that users should be able to navigate and use all functions without requiring fine motor skills. For instance, buttons should be large enough to be easily clicked or tapped, and all interactive elements should be accessible via keyboard shortcuts. This principle ensures that users with motor disabilities can interact with the content effectively.

3. **Understandable**: Information and the operation of the user interface must be understandable. This principle stresses the need for clear and simple language, avoiding jargon that may confuse users. Additionally, consistent navigation and predictable actions enhance user understanding. For example, if a user clicks on a button, they should expect to be taken to the next logical step in the process.

4. **Robust**: Content must be robust enough to be interpreted by a wide variety of user agents, including assistive technologies. This means using proper HTML markup and coding practices to ensure compatibility with various browsers and screen readers. Regular testing with different technologies can help identify any issues that may hinder accessibility.

By adhering to these principles, designers can create websites and applications that are accessible to all users, regardless of their abilities. It is crucial to remember that accessibility should not be an afterthought; it should be integrated into the design process from the very beginning. Early consideration of accessibility can save time and resources in the long run, avoiding the need for costly redesigns later on.

Practical Steps to Improve Accessibility

Implementing accessibility features in your designs does not have to be overwhelming. Here are some practical steps that you can take to improve accessibility in your work:

1. **Conduct User Research**: Engage with users who have different abilities during the research phase. Their feedback will provide valuable insights into their needs and preferences. You can conduct interviews, surveys, or usability tests with users who have disabilities to understand their experiences and challenges better.

2. **Use Accessibility Guidelines**: Familiarise yourself with established accessibility standards, such as the Web Content Accessibility Guidelines (WCAG). These guidelines offer clear criteria for making web content more accessible. By following these guidelines, you can ensure that your designs meet minimum accessibility requirements.

3. **Choose Accessible Colour Palettes**: When selecting colours for your designs, consider colour contrast and

accessibility. Tools like contrast checkers can help you determine if your colour combinations are suitable for users with visual impairments. Aim for a contrast ratio of at least 4.5:1 for normal text to ensure readability.

4. **Add Alt Text for Images**: Always include descriptive alt text for images, graphics, and other visual content. This text should convey the essential information contained in the image, allowing screen readers to provide context for users with visual impairments.

5. **Design Responsive Layouts**: Ensure that your designs work well on various devices and screen sizes. Responsive design allows users to access your content on mobile devices, tablets, and desktops without losing functionality or accessibility.

6. **Test with Assistive Technologies**: Regularly test your designs using assistive technologies such as screen readers, voice recognition software, and keyboard-only navigation. This testing will help you identify areas for improvement and ensure that your design works for all users.

7. **Provide Clear Instructions**: When designing forms or interactive elements, provide clear instructions and labels. Users with cognitive disabilities may struggle with vague prompts, so ensure that all forms and buttons are labelled clearly and are easy to understand.

8. **Seek Feedback and Iterate**: Once your design is imple-

mented, continue to seek feedback from users. Accessibility is an ongoing process, and regular updates and improvements will ensure that your designs remain usable for all. Encourage users to report any accessibility issues they encounter, and be open to making changes based on their input.

By incorporating these practical steps into your design process, you can create more accessible products that cater to the diverse needs of all users. Accessibility is not just about compliance; it is about fostering inclusivity and ensuring that everyone can enjoy the benefits of your designs. Embracing accessibility in your work will not only enhance the user experience but also contribute to a more equitable digital landscape.

43

Chapter 43: Color Theory in UX

Part 1: Understanding Color Basics

Colour is one of the most powerful tools in design, playing a crucial role in how users interact with digital products. At its core, colour theory explores how colours combine, contrast, and convey emotions. Understanding the basics of colour is essential for creating an effective user experience. Each colour has its own psychological effect, which can influence how users perceive information. For example, blue often represents trust and security, making it a popular choice for banking and technology websites. Green is associated with growth and health, often used in health-related applications.

Red, on the other hand, can evoke feelings of urgency or excitement, frequently used in sale promotions. Designers should also consider colour harmonies, which are combinations of colours that work well together. The most common colour harmonies are complementary, analogous, and triadic schemes. Complementary colours are opposite each other on the colour wheel and create high contrast, while analogous colours are next to each other, providing a harmonious look. Triadic schemes consist of three evenly spaced colours on the wheel, offering a vibrant palette. Understanding these basic principles of colour theory helps designers make informed choices that enhance the user experience.

Part 2: Applying Colour in User Interfaces

When it comes to applying colour in user interfaces, designers must think carefully about the context and purpose of their designs. One of the first steps is to create a colour palette that reflects the brand identity and resonates with the target audience. A well-defined palette not only helps maintain consistency across the design but also guides users through their journey. For instance, if a website aims to create a calming atmosphere, using soft blues and greens can promote relaxation. In contrast, a fitness app might benefit from bright, energising colours like orange and yellow to encourage motivation. It's also essential to consider accessibility when choosing colours. Some users may have visual impairments, such as colour blindness, which can make it challenging to distinguish between certain colours.

To accommodate these users, designers should ensure sufficient contrast between text and background colours. Tools are available to check colour contrast ratios, helping to create an inclusive experience for all users. Furthermore, using colour to create visual hierarchy can significantly improve usability. By applying bolder or brighter colours to important elements like buttons or calls to action, designers can draw users' attention where it is needed most. This thoughtful application of colour not only enhances aesthetics but also improves the overall functionality of the user interface.

Part 3: Trends and Best Practices in Colour Usage

Keeping up with trends and best practices in colour usage is vital for any UX designer. Colour trends evolve, influenced by cultural shifts, technology, and design innovations. Designers should be aware of current trends while ensuring their choices align with the brand and user needs. For example, in recent years, minimalistic designs with muted colour palettes have become popular, reflecting a desire for simplicity and clarity in user interfaces. However, this does not mean that bold colours should be disregarded.

Strategic use of vibrant colours can create visual interest and guide user behaviour. Additionally, designers should regularly test their colour choices with users to gather feedback and understand their perceptions. A/B testing different colour schemes can provide valuable insights into which combinations resonate best with the audience.

Moreover, documenting colour choices and their intended effects can help maintain consistency throughout the design process. As a designer's library of colour palettes grows, so does their understanding of how different colours can work together to create compelling and effective designs. Overall, mastering colour theory is an ongoing journey that requires experimentation, feedback, and an understanding of the audience, ultimately leading to a more engaging user experience.

44

Chapter 44: Typography in User Interfaces

Understanding Typography

Typography is more than just selecting fonts; it plays a crucial role in how users interact with digital interfaces. In user interfaces, typography is essential for ensuring that text is legible, accessible, and engaging. The choice of typeface can evoke different feelings and create a mood, influencing how users perceive the content and interact with it. For example, a sleek, modern sans-serif font can give a feeling of professionalism, while a playful, handwritten font can create a sense of fun and creativity.

When designing user interfaces, it is vital to choose typography that matches the overall brand identity and resonates with the target audience. A well-chosen typeface can enhance the user experience by making it easier for users to read and understand the information presented.

Therefore, understanding the different types of fonts—serif, sans-serif, script, and decorative—is essential for making informed decisions. Serif fonts, with their small lines or embellishments at the ends of letters, are often seen as traditional and can convey trustworthiness. In contrast, sans-serif fonts, which do not have these lines, are usually considered more modern and clean, making them suitable for digital interfaces.

In addition to choosing the right typeface, designers must also consider font size and weight. A larger font size improves readability, especially on smaller screens like smartphones, where users may struggle to read smaller text. Likewise, varying the weight of fonts—such as bold or light—can help emphasize important information and guide the user's attention to specific areas of the interface. This deliberate manipulation of typography allows designers to create a hierarchy of information, making it easier for users to navigate through content efficiently.

Readability and Legibility

While typography contributes to aesthetics, its primary role in user interfaces is to ensure readability and legibility. Readability refers to how easily a reader can understand the text, while legibility focuses on how easy it is to distinguish individual letters and words. Poor typography can lead to frustration and confusion, causing users to abandon a website or application.

To enhance readability, it is essential to choose appropriate line lengths. Lines that are too long can make it challenging for users to find the next line of text, while very short lines can interrupt the flow of reading. A good rule of thumb is to aim for line lengths between 50 to 75 characters. Line spacing, also known as leading, is another critical factor. Sufficient spacing between lines can improve readability by preventing the text from feeling cramped and helping users scan the content more easily.

Contrast is also crucial for legibility. Text should stand out against its background to ensure that users can read it without straining their eyes. High contrast between text and background colors can significantly enhance legibility, particularly for users with visual impairments. For instance, black text on a white background offers high contrast and is generally easier to read than grey text on a light grey background.

In addition to color contrast, the use of hierarchy through typography is vital. By varying font sizes, weights, and styles, designers can create a clear visual structure that guides users through the content. For example, headings should be larger and bolder than body text to signal their importance. This hierarchy helps users scan the page quickly, allowing them to find the information they need without feeling overwhelmed by a wall of text.

Best Practices for Typography in UI Design

To make the most of typography in user interfaces, designers should follow several best practices. Firstly, consistency is key. Using a limited number of typefaces throughout the interface helps create a cohesive look and feel. Typically, a combination of one or two fonts—one for headings and another for body text—is sufficient. This approach prevents visual clutter and allows users to focus on the content.

Another essential practice is to consider the context in which the typography will be used. Different devices and screen sizes can impact how text is displayed. For instance, text that looks perfect on a desktop monitor may appear too small on a mobile device. Therefore, designers should test their typography across various devices to ensure optimal readability and legibility.

In addition to testing across devices, it is beneficial to gather user feedback on typography choices. This feedback can provide valuable insights into how real users interact with the interface and which typography elements they find most effective. Understanding user preferences can help refine typography choices to create a better user experience.

Finally, accessibility should always be a top priority when designing typography for user interfaces. Ensuring that text is readable for users with visual impairments is crucial. This can include using sufficient contrast ratios, providing text alternatives for images, and ensuring that font sizes can be adjusted easily. By adhering to accessibility guidelines, designers can create inclusive interfaces that cater to a broader audience.

In conclusion, typography is a vital component of user interface design that impacts readability, legibility, and overall user experience. By understanding the different aspects of typography and following best practices, designers can create engaging and accessible interfaces that enhance the way users interact with digital content.

45

Chapter 45: Creating Consistent Visual Design Systems

Introduction to Visual Design Systems

In today's digital world, a strong visual design system is essential for creating user-friendly experiences. A visual design system is a collection of design standards and guidelines that help maintain consistency across all products and platforms. It includes components such as colours, typography, spacing, and imagery. By using a visual design system, designers can ensure that their work is cohesive, making it easier for users to navigate and understand the interface.

Consistency in design is not just about aesthetics; it enhances usability and helps build trust with users. When a product looks and behaves in a predictable manner, users feel more comfortable and confident using it. They can focus on their tasks rather than getting distracted by inconsistent elements.

This chapter will explore the key components of a visual design system, why they are important, and how to create one that enhances the user experience.

The Importance of Consistency in Design

Consistency is a cornerstone of effective design. When users encounter familiar elements, they can quickly grasp how to interact with a product. This familiarity reduces the learning curve and speeds up task completion. For instance, consider a website where buttons have the same colour and shape across different pages. When users recognise these buttons as actionable elements, they can navigate the site with confidence.

Moreover, consistency helps to convey brand identity. When users see the same colours, fonts, and styles consistently, they associate these elements with the brand. This recognition fosters loyalty and reinforces the brand's message. A well-defined visual design system ensures that all design elements work together harmoniously, presenting a unified image to users.

Key Components of a Visual Design System

A successful visual design system comprises several key components. These include colour, typography, iconography, imagery, spacing, and layout. Each of these elements plays a vital role in creating a cohesive user experience.

1. Colour

Colour is one of the most powerful tools in design. It can

evoke emotions, influence perceptions, and guide users' actions. A well-defined colour palette helps establish a strong brand identity. When choosing colours for your design system, consider the psychological impact of each colour. For instance, blue often conveys trust and reliability, while red can signal urgency or excitement.

A typical colour palette includes primary, secondary, and accent colours. Primary colours are the main colours used in the interface, while secondary colours support the primary ones. Accent colours can be used sparingly to draw attention to important elements, such as call-to-action buttons or notifications.

It's important to ensure good contrast between text and background colours for readability. Accessibility is also a crucial consideration when selecting colours. Ensure that your colour choices are distinguishable for users with colour vision deficiencies. Tools such as contrast checkers can help you evaluate whether your colour combinations meet accessibility standards.

2. Typography

Typography is another critical component of a visual design system. The choice of fonts can significantly impact the overall look and feel of a product. It can convey professionalism, playfulness, or creativity, depending on the style selected. A consistent typographic hierarchy helps users navigate content more easily, allowing them to distinguish between headings, subheadings, and body text.

When creating a typographic system, select a limited number

of fonts—usually one for headings and another for body text. Ensure that the chosen fonts complement each other. Additionally, define rules for font sizes, line heights, and letter spacing. These guidelines will help maintain visual harmony and readability across different devices and screen sizes.

Pay attention to font weights as well; using bold fonts for emphasis can help guide users' attention. However, avoid overusing different font styles, as this can create visual clutter and confusion.

3. Iconography

Icons are essential for conveying meaning quickly and effectively. They provide visual cues that help users understand the functionality of an interface. A consistent icon style reinforces your brand's identity and makes the interface more intuitive.

When developing your iconography, choose a specific style— whether it's flat, outlined, or 3D—and stick to it throughout the design. Consistency in size, stroke width, and colour will enhance the overall coherence of your design.

Ensure that icons are meaningful and easily recognisable. Icons should be universally understood, avoiding ambiguous symbols that may confuse users. Consider creating a library of standard icons for common actions (like search, settings, and home) to maintain consistency across all products.

4. Imagery

Imagery plays a crucial role in visual storytelling. The images used in your designs can evoke emotions, illustrate concepts, and provide context. When selecting images, consider how they align with your brand identity and message.

Establish guidelines for imagery, including style, tone, and composition. Decide whether you will use photographs, illustrations, or a combination of both. Ensure that the chosen imagery complements the overall design and supports the content rather than distracting from it.

Additionally, consider the use of imagery for accessibility. Provide descriptive alt text for images to ensure that users with visual impairments can understand the context of the visuals.

5. Spacing

Spacing is an often-overlooked aspect of design, yet it significantly affects the overall layout and usability. Proper spacing helps to create visual hierarchy, improve readability, and guide users through the interface.

Establish a consistent grid system to guide the placement of elements on the page. Define rules for margins, padding, and line spacing to ensure that elements are appropriately spaced apart. This will create a clean and organised look, making it easier for users to focus on the content.

Avoid cramming too many elements into a small space, as this can overwhelm users. Instead, allow for breathing room between elements to enhance clarity and understanding.

6. **Layout**

The layout of a design determines how users interact with content and navigate through the interface. A well-structured layout guides users' attention to the most important elements, ensuring a seamless experience.

Define a layout system that includes grid structures, alignment guidelines, and placement rules for various elements. Consistency in layout helps users predict where to find specific features, which enhances usability.

Consider creating templates for different types of pages or screens within your product. These templates will serve as a reference for maintaining consistency while allowing for flexibility in content presentation.

Documenting Your Design System

Once you have defined the key components of your visual design system, it's essential to document them thoroughly. Documentation serves as a reference for designers, developers, and stakeholders, ensuring that everyone is aligned and understands how to use the system effectively.

Create a design system guide that includes detailed descriptions of each component, usage guidelines, and examples. This guide should be easily accessible to all team members. Consider using a collaborative platform where the design system can be updated and maintained as the product evolves.

Regularly review and update your design system to ensure

it remains relevant and effective. As design trends and user preferences change, your system should adapt accordingly.

Implementing the Design System

Implementing a visual design system involves integrating the defined components into your product. This process requires collaboration between designers, developers, and product managers to ensure a smooth transition.

Start by applying the design system to new projects or features, gradually updating existing ones. Use prototyping tools to create mock-ups that showcase how the design system works in practice. Gather feedback from users and team members to identify areas for improvement.

Be prepared for some challenges during implementation. Existing products may have established designs that don't align with the new system. In these cases, it's crucial to prioritise updates based on user impact and business goals.

Testing and Iteration

Once the design system is implemented, it's important to test its effectiveness. Conduct usability testing to gather insights on how users interact with the new design elements. Pay attention to user feedback and observe any difficulties they may encounter.

Based on the testing results, be open to making adjustments. Iteration is a natural part of the design process, and user feedback is invaluable for refining your visual design system. Regularly revisit your system to ensure it continues to meet the needs of users and the goals of your product.

Conclusion

Creating a consistent visual design system is essential for delivering exceptional user experiences. By focusing on key components such as colour, typography, iconography, imagery, spacing, and layout, designers can establish a cohesive identity that enhances usability and builds trust with users. Documenting and implementing the design system effectively ensures that all team members are aligned and that the system evolves as needed.

Ultimately, a well-crafted visual design system not only improves the overall look and feel of a product but also contributes to its success in meeting user needs. Consistency in design fosters familiarity, enabling users to navigate interfaces confidently. As you embark on this journey of creating a visual design system, remember to keep the user at the forefront of your decisions. Their experience is the ultimate measure of success.

46

Chapter 46: Using Imagery and Icons Effectively

Understanding the Importance of Imagery and Icons

Imagery and icons play a crucial role in user experience (UX) design. They help convey information quickly and effectively. People are naturally visual learners. This means that we understand and remember visual content better than text. When users visit a website or use an app, they often scan the page rather than reading every word. This is where good imagery and icons come into play.

Imagery refers to any visual element, such as photographs, illustrations, or graphics. Icons are simplified images that represent a concept or action. Both elements should work together to enhance the user experience. They guide users, making it easier for them to navigate the interface and find the information they need.

Using effective imagery and icons can create an emotional connection with users. For example, a cheerful image can evoke feelings of happiness, while a professional photograph can instill trust and credibility. By selecting the right images, you can influence how users perceive your brand or product.

In addition, imagery and icons can improve usability. Well-chosen images can clarify instructions, show product features, or highlight key messages. Icons can replace text in some cases, saving space and making the interface cleaner. For instance, a shopping cart icon is universally recognised and helps users understand that they can add items to their cart without needing to read the word "cart."

The key is to use imagery and icons that are relevant to your content. Random images can confuse users or distract them from the main message. Therefore, it's important to select visuals that align with your brand and the purpose of your website or app.

Best Practices for Selecting and Using Imagery

When selecting imagery for your design, there are several best practices to keep in mind. First, consider the quality of the images. High-quality visuals are essential for a professional look. Blurry or pixelated images can harm your credibility. Always use images that are sharp, well-lit, and appropriately sized for your interface.

Next, think about the context in which the imagery will

be used. The images should support the overall message of your content. For instance, if you're designing a website for a luxury hotel, you should use elegant and sophisticated images that reflect the quality of the hotel. On the other hand, a website for a children's toy store would benefit from bright, playful images that appeal to both children and parents.

Diversity in imagery is also important. Representation matters, and using diverse images can help all users feel included. This applies to both people in the images and the types of scenarios being depicted. Avoid stereotypes and strive for authentic representation.

Moreover, consider the emotional impact of your imagery. Different colours, styles, and subjects can evoke various feelings. For example, warm colours often create a sense of comfort, while cooler colours may feel more professional. Choose imagery that aligns with the feelings you want to evoke in your users.

When using icons, simplicity is key. Icons should be easily recognisable and not overly complicated. They should also maintain a consistent style throughout your design. For example, if you use flat icons, stick to flat icons across the entire interface. This consistency helps create a cohesive experience for users.

Additionally, consider accessibility when designing with imagery and icons. Ensure that images have appropriate alt text for users with visual impairments. Icons should also be accompanied by text labels or tooltips to provide context.

This not only helps those with disabilities but also enhances the overall usability of your design.

Finally, don't forget about the relevance of imagery in relation to the content. Images should complement the text and not distract from it. For instance, if you are writing a blog post about healthy eating, an image of fresh vegetables can reinforce your message. However, a random picture of a dessert would not be relevant and could confuse users.

Creating a Cohesive Visual Language

Creating a cohesive visual language is essential for effective UX design. This means that all your visual elements, including imagery and icons, should work together harmoniously. A cohesive visual language helps users understand the relationship between different elements and navigate your site or app more easily.

To achieve this, start by developing a style guide for your imagery and icons. A style guide should outline the types of images and icons you will use, including their colours, styles, and sizes. This guide will serve as a reference for anyone working on the project, ensuring consistency across all design elements.

When creating icons, consider using a set of established design principles. Icons should have a clear meaning, and their function should be apparent to users. Using familiar symbols helps users feel comfortable navigating your interface. For instance, a magnifying glass icon typically represents a search function. Users instantly understand its purpose, which enhances usability.

Another important aspect of a cohesive visual language is colour harmony. Choose a colour palette that reflects your brand and complements your imagery. Using a consistent colour scheme throughout your site or app creates a unified look. When selecting colours, consider their psychological effects. Different colours can evoke different feelings, so choose a palette that aligns with your brand message.

Typography also plays a significant role in your visual language. Use fonts that are easy to read and align with your overall design style. For instance, a modern, clean font might be suitable for a tech company, while a playful font could work for a children's brand. Make sure your typography works well with your imagery and icons, as this contributes to a consistent user experience.

In addition, ensure that your imagery and icons are appropriately sized for your design. Consistency in size helps create a balanced layout and prevents visual clutter. Images and icons that are too large or too small can disrupt the user flow and make navigation challenging.

Finally, test your imagery and icons with real users. Gathering feedback can help you understand how well your visual elements are working. User testing can reveal whether your icons are easily understood, if your imagery resonates with your audience, and if your visual language is cohesive. Use this feedback to refine your designs and improve the overall user experience.

Conclusion

In conclusion, effectively using imagery and icons is vital for enhancing user experience in design. High-quality, relevant imagery can create emotional connections, clarify content, and improve usability. Icons should be simple, recognisable, and consistent, helping users navigate easily. A cohesive visual language ties all these elements together, ensuring a harmonious user experience.

By following best practices for selecting and using imagery and icons, you can create a visually appealing and user-friendly design. Remember to consider context, emotional impact, and diversity when choosing your visuals. Accessibility should also be a priority, making your design inclusive for all users.

Finally, invest time in creating a cohesive visual language that reflects your brand and supports your content. Testing your designs with real users can provide valuable insights, helping you refine your approach and enhance the overall user experience.

By mastering the use of imagery and icons, you will not only elevate the aesthetics of your design but also create a more effective and enjoyable experience for your users. Your careful attention to these elements will lead to a design that is not only visually appealing but also functional and user-centric.

47

Chapter 47: Designing for Brand and Identity

Understanding Brand Identity

Brand identity is how a company presents itself to the world and how it wants to be perceived by its customers. This includes everything from the logo and colour scheme to the tone of voice in its communications. In simple terms, brand identity is the personality of a brand and the message it sends out. When designing for brand identity, it is crucial to keep in mind the values and mission of the brand. Designers should start by understanding the core values that define the brand. For example, if a brand is focused on sustainability, the design should reflect that through the use of earthy colours and natural materials. Likewise, if a brand aims to project luxury, it may use sleek lines, elegant fonts, and a minimalist approach to convey sophistication.

Creating a strong brand identity also involves consistency.

All elements of design should work together to create a cohesive look. This means that logos, packaging, website design, and advertising materials should all share common visual themes. For instance, if a brand uses a specific shade of blue in its logo, that same shade should appear across all other brand materials. This not only makes the brand easily recognisable but also builds trust with the audience. When people see the same visual elements repeatedly, they are more likely to remember the brand and what it stands for.

Another important aspect of brand identity is storytelling. Every brand has a story to tell, whether it is about its origins, its founders, or its mission. Designers can use visual elements to help tell this story. For example, a brand that prides itself on its handmade products may choose to use images of artisans at work or showcase the crafting process. This gives customers a deeper understanding of the brand and creates an emotional connection. Additionally, the tone of voice used in communications—whether friendly, professional, or playful—should match the brand identity. A youthful, energetic brand will use a different language than a serious, corporate brand. By aligning the design and the tone of voice, the brand can create a unified identity that resonates with its target audience.

Designing for User Experience

Designing for brand identity is not just about how things look; it's also about how users interact with the brand. User experience (UX) plays a critical role in how customers perceive a brand. If a customer has a positive experience with a brand, they are more likely to return and recommend it to others. Conversely, a negative experience can damage a brand's reputation, no matter how good the design is. Therefore, it is essential to design with the user in mind. This begins with understanding who the target audience is. Designers should conduct research to understand their needs, preferences, and pain points. For example, if the target audience is busy professionals, the design should focus on efficiency and ease of use.

Once the target audience is identified, designers should focus on creating intuitive navigation. Users should be able to find what they are looking for without frustration. This can be achieved through clear menus, search functions, and well-organised content. If a website is cluttered or difficult to navigate, users may leave and seek information elsewhere. In contrast, a clean and straightforward design encourages users to explore and engage with the content. Additionally, designers should pay attention to mobile responsiveness. Many users access websites on their phones, so designs must adapt to different screen sizes. A seamless experience across devices reinforces brand identity and keeps users engaged.

Another crucial aspect of UX design is accessibility. Brands should ensure that their products and services are accessible to everyone, including people with disabilities. This can involve using colour contrasts that are easy to see, providing text alternatives for images, and ensuring that websites can be navigated using a keyboard. By considering accessibility, brands not only expand their reach but also show that they value all customers, enhancing their identity. Furthermore, the use of feedback mechanisms can improve user experience. Providing options for users to leave comments or reviews gives them a voice and helps the brand understand what works and what doesn't. This two-way communication strengthens the relationship between the brand and its customers.

Building Emotional Connections

A well-designed brand identity should evoke emotions and create connections with its audience. Emotions play a significant role in decision-making, and brands that successfully tap into customers' feelings are often more successful. Designers can evoke emotions through colour, imagery, typography, and overall aesthetics. For instance, warm colours like reds and oranges can evoke feelings of excitement and energy, while cool colours like blues and greens can create a sense of calm and trust. The right choice of colours can significantly impact how a brand is perceived.

Imagery is another powerful tool in design. Using images that reflect the brand's values and connect with the audience's aspirations can strengthen the emotional bond. For example, a fitness brand might use images of diverse individuals exercising together to promote a sense of community and inclusivity. Additionally, the use of typography should align with the brand identity. A playful, handwritten font might suit a children's toy brand, while a sleek, modern font would be more appropriate for a tech company. By carefully choosing design elements, brands can convey the right emotions and create a connection with their audience.

Moreover, storytelling can be further enhanced by using narratives that resonate with the audience. Whether through advertising campaigns, social media posts, or website content, sharing stories that highlight the brand's mission and values can foster emotional connections. People love to support brands that have a purpose or stand for something meaningful. For example, a company that focuses on environmental sustainability might share stories about its efforts to reduce waste or support local communities. These narratives humanise the brand and allow customers to feel like they are part of a larger mission.

In conclusion, designing for brand identity is a multi-faceted process that goes beyond aesthetics. It involves understanding the brand's core values, ensuring consistency across all touchpoints, and prioritising user experience. By creating a strong brand identity, designers can foster emotional connections and build lasting relationships with their audience. When customers feel connected to a brand, they are more likely to become loyal advocates. In today's competitive market, investing in brand identity design is essential for any business looking to stand out and succeed.

48

Chapter 48: Simplicity and Minimalism in UX Design

Understanding Simplicity in UX Design

Simplicity is a fundamental principle of user experience (UX) design. It means creating products that are easy to understand and use. When we think of simplicity, we often picture clean lines, clear layouts, and intuitive navigation. The goal is to reduce confusion and frustration for the user. A simple design focuses on the essentials, removing unnecessary elements that can distract or overwhelm users. By doing so, we allow users to accomplish their tasks more efficiently.

To achieve simplicity, designers must consider what information is crucial for the user. This involves understanding the target audience and their needs. For instance, if a user wants to book a flight, they do not need to see unrelated advertisements or complex navigation options. Instead, the design should highlight the booking process with clear steps and minimal distractions.

One key aspect of simplicity is consistency. When users encounter familiar patterns and layouts, they can navigate a website or app more easily. For example, if buttons are always located in the same position and follow the same style, users can quickly learn how to interact with the interface. This consistency builds trust and confidence, encouraging users to engage more deeply with the product.

Embracing Minimalism in UX Design

Minimalism is closely related to simplicity but takes it a step further. Minimalism in UX design focuses on stripping away the non-essential elements to create a clean and uncluttered experience. It is about using the least amount of design elements to achieve the maximum effect. The goal of minimalism is not just to make things look simple, but to enhance the overall user experience.

In a minimalist design, every element must serve a purpose. This includes typography, colour, imagery, and space. For example, a minimalist website might use a limited colour palette, perhaps only two or three colours. This can create a cohesive look and feel, making the content stand out more. White space, or negative space, is another critical element of minimalism. It allows users to breathe and prevents them from feeling overwhelmed by too much information at once.

Good minimalist design also emphasises functionality. For

instance, consider a mobile app that allows users to track their fitness goals. A minimalist approach would focus on the core functions, such as logging workouts and viewing progress, while removing unnecessary features that could complicate the user experience. By prioritising essential tasks, users can easily navigate the app and achieve their fitness objectives.

The Benefits of Simplicity and Minimalism

Implementing simplicity and minimalism in UX design offers numerous benefits. First and foremost, it improves usability. Users are more likely to enjoy their experience when they can easily find what they need without unnecessary distractions. This can lead to higher engagement rates, as users are more likely to return to a product that provides a seamless experience.

Additionally, simple and minimalist designs often load faster and perform better. When fewer elements are present, the design is typically less resource-intensive, which can lead to faster loading times. This is crucial in today's fast-paced world, where users expect immediate results. Slow loading times can result in frustration and may cause users to abandon a website or app altogether.

Moreover, simplicity and minimalism can enhance accessibility. A clear and straightforward design allows users of all abilities to interact with the product more effectively. For example, individuals with visual impairments may struggle with complex layouts or excessive text. By using larger fonts, high-contrast colours, and simplified navigation, designers can create a more inclusive experience for everyone.

Practical Tips for Achieving Simplicity and Minimalism

To incorporate simplicity and minimalism into your design process, consider the following practical tips:

1. **Prioritise Content**: Identify the most important information or actions for users and focus on presenting those elements clearly. Use headings, bullet points, and short paragraphs to make content digestible.
2. **Limit Colour Palette**: Choose a limited number of colours that align with your brand identity. This creates a harmonious look and allows users to focus on the content rather than being distracted by competing colours.
3. **Use White Space Wisely**: Embrace negative space to separate different elements and create a sense of balance. This not only enhances visual appeal but also improves readability.
4. **Simplify Navigation**: Ensure that users can easily find what they need by designing clear and intuitive navigation. Use familiar icons and labels, and avoid overloading menus with too many options.
5. **Iterate and Test**: Always seek feedback on your designs. Conduct user testing to see how real users interact with your product. This will help you identify areas that may

need simplification.
6. **Stay Updated**: UX design trends evolve, and it's essential to stay informed about the latest practices in simplicity and minimalism. Regularly review your designs and be open to making changes that enhance user experience.

Conclusion: The Power of Simplicity and Minimalism

In summary, simplicity and minimalism are powerful tools in UX design. They help create user-friendly experiences that prioritise clarity, efficiency, and enjoyment. By focusing on what truly matters and removing unnecessary distractions, designers can craft interfaces that not only look good but also serve their users effectively.

Ultimately, the aim of simplicity and minimalism is to enhance the overall user experience. When users can navigate a product with ease and accomplish their goals without frustration, they are more likely to develop a positive perception of the brand. In a world where users are bombarded with information and options, simplicity and minimalism stand out as effective strategies for creating meaningful and memorable interactions.

49

Chapter 49: The Role of White Space

Understanding White Space

White space, often referred to as negative space, is the area around and between elements of a design. It is not just an absence of content; rather, it is a crucial aspect of design that helps to enhance user experience. Many people mistakenly believe that white space is simply empty space that is wasted. However, it serves several important functions in design, particularly in user experience (UX) design. When used effectively, white space can create a clean and organized layout, making it easier for users to navigate and comprehend the content. It gives the eye a place to rest, helping to avoid overwhelming the user with too much information at once. This can be particularly important in digital designs, where screens can quickly become cluttered with text, images, and buttons. By strategically incorporating white space, designers can guide users' attention and highlight the most important elements of a page, such as calls to action or key information.

The Benefits of White Space in Design

The benefits of using white space in design are numerous. First and foremost, it improves readability. Text that is surrounded by ample white space is easier to read and understand. When users can easily process the information presented to them, they are more likely to engage with it. This is especially important for web pages and mobile applications where users often skim content rather than reading every word. Moreover, white space enhances the overall aesthetics of a design. A well-spaced layout appears more professional and polished, which can build trust and credibility with users. A visually appealing design can significantly enhance the user experience, encouraging users to spend more time on the page and explore its content. White space can also help establish a hierarchy within a design. By grouping related elements together and separating them from others with white space, designers can indicate the importance of each element. For instance, a large heading might be surrounded by more white space than body text, signalling to users that it is the primary focus of the page. This hierarchical approach makes it easier for users to navigate content and find what they are looking for quickly.

Practical Applications of White Space

In practical terms, applying white space effectively involves careful consideration of layout, spacing, and alignment. Designers should think about how elements relate to one another and use white space to create a balanced composition. This might mean increasing the margin around text blocks, spacing out images, or leaving more room between buttons. It's also important to be mindful of the overall design context; too much white space can make a design feel empty or disconnected, while too little can make it feel cluttered and overwhelming. Finding the right balance is key. Testing different layouts and gathering user feedback can help identify the most effective use of white space. Designers can use tools such as wireframes and mockups to experiment with different arrangements, allowing them to see how white space impacts user experience before the final design is implemented. Additionally, designers should consider the specific needs of their target audience. Different users may respond differently to white space, so understanding user preferences and behaviours can guide the design process. In conclusion, white space plays a vital role in UX design. It enhances readability, improves aesthetics, and helps establish a clear hierarchy of information. By incorporating white space thoughtfully and intentionally, designers can create more effective and engaging user experiences.

50

Chapter 50: Designing Engaging Call-to-Actions

Understanding the Importance of Call-to-Actions

Call-to-Actions, often abbreviated as CTAs, are vital elements in any design aimed at achieving specific goals. They guide users toward taking actions that are important for the success of a website, application, or marketing campaign. A CTA can be anything from a button that says "Buy Now" to a link that prompts users to "Sign Up for Our Newsletter." These actions help businesses increase sales, gather leads, and improve user engagement.

To create a successful CTA, it is essential to understand its purpose. A well-designed CTA does not just inform; it motivates users to act. It should create a sense of urgency and make users feel that they will gain something valuable by clicking it. This can be achieved by using action-oriented language, such as "Join Now" or "Get Started Today." Such phrases can trigger emotions and encourage users to proceed rather than hesitate.

Key Elements of an Effective CTA

Creating an engaging call-to-action involves several key elements that must be carefully considered. First, the placement of the CTA is crucial. It should be positioned where users are most likely to see it, such as above the fold or at the end of a compelling piece of content. Users should not have to scroll too much to find it. Additionally, the design of the CTA itself should stand out. Using contrasting colours can draw attention to the CTA, making it pop against the background of the webpage or app.

Next, the text of the CTA needs to be concise and clear. It should communicate the action users need to take and what they will receive in return. Avoid using jargon or overly complicated phrases. Instead, focus on clarity and simplicity. For instance, instead of saying "Initiate Your Free Trial," one could simply say "Start Your Free Trial." This approach is more user-friendly and encourages action.

Another important aspect is to include a sense of urgency. Phrases like "Limited Time Offer" or "Only a Few Left!" can compel users to act quickly, reducing the chances of them abandoning the site without taking action. However, it is essential to ensure that these claims are genuine and not misleading. Users appreciate honesty, and deceptive practices can harm trust and lead to negative experiences.

Creating Visual Appeal

Visual design plays a significant role in the effectiveness of a CTA. The use of shapes, colours, and fonts can all impact how users perceive a call-to-action. Rounded buttons, for example, are often seen as more inviting than square buttons. The colour of the button should also be carefully chosen; using colours that evoke specific emotions can influence user behaviour. For instance, red can create a sense of urgency, while blue can convey trustworthiness.

In addition to colour and shape, the size of the CTA is essential. It should be large enough to be easily clicked, especially on mobile devices, but not so large that it overwhelms other elements on the page. Finding the right balance is key. Always remember to test different designs to see which one performs better. A/B testing, where you compare two versions of a CTA, can provide valuable insights into what works best for your audience.

Crafting a Compelling Message

The message accompanying the CTA is equally important. It should reinforce the action you want users to take. For example, if the CTA is for a free trial, the surrounding text should highlight the benefits of signing up. Use bullet points to list key features, making it easy for users to digest the information quickly. This can help to alleviate any concerns they may have about taking action.

Social proof can also be an effective way to increase the credibility of your CTA. Including testimonials, user reviews, or statistics can help reassure users that they are making the right choice. For example, stating "Join over 10,000 satisfied customers!" can provide the extra nudge that some users need to click the button.

Testing and Optimising Your CTAs

Once your CTA is live, the work is not done. It is crucial to continually test and optimise your CTAs to ensure they remain effective. Monitor metrics such as click-through rates (CTR) to gauge how well your CTAs are performing. If you notice low engagement, consider revising the copy, adjusting the placement, or even experimenting with different colours and designs.

Feedback from users can also provide valuable insights. Consider conducting user testing sessions to see how real users interact with your CTAs. Their responses can highlight areas for improvement that you may not have considered. Remember, what works for one audience may not work for another, so understanding your users is key to success.

Conclusion

Designing engaging call-to-actions is a critical aspect of user experience design. By understanding their importance and carefully considering elements such as placement, design, messaging, and testing, you can create CTAs that effectively motivate users to take action. Keep in mind that the ultimate goal of a CTA is not just to get clicks but to enhance the overall user experience and drive meaningful interactions.

As you continue to develop your skills in UX design, always remember that each CTA is an opportunity to connect with users. A well-crafted CTA can lead to increased engagement, conversions, and ultimately, the success of your digital product. By following these guidelines and continually refining your approach, you can ensure that your call-to-actions are not just seen but are also compelling enough to drive users to act.

VI

Usability Testing and Iteration

Refine your designs through feedback and continuous improvement.
Usability testing is essential for validating design decisions. This section covers testing methods, analyzing results, A/B testing, and the iterative process of refining and improving designs based on user feedback and performance metrics.

51

Chapter 51: Usability Testing and Iteration

Understanding Usability Testing

Usability testing is an important part of the user experience (UX) design process. It helps designers understand how real users interact with a product, such as a website or an app. The goal of usability testing is to find out if users can easily use the product to achieve their goals. In simple terms, usability means how easy and enjoyable it is for users to use something. When we talk about usability testing, we refer to observing users as they complete tasks on the product. This can be done in various ways, but the main idea is to see where users struggle and what can be improved.

Typically, usability testing involves a small group of users who represent the target audience. These users are asked to perform specific tasks while observers take notes and record any difficulties they encounter. It is crucial to set clear objectives before conducting usability tests. These objectives guide the testing process and help in analysing the results later. For example, if a website has a new feature, the test might focus on how easily users can find and use that feature. By watching users, designers can gather valuable insights about how people think and behave. This information is incredibly useful in identifying pain points—those moments when users feel frustrated or confused.

There are different methods of usability testing. One common method is moderated testing, where a facilitator guides users through the tasks. The facilitator can ask questions and provide help if users get stuck. This approach allows for deeper understanding because the facilitator can probe further into users' thoughts and feelings. Another method is unmoderated testing, where users complete tasks on their own, often in their own environment. This method can provide more natural feedback because users are in a comfortable setting. Both methods have their advantages, and the choice between them often depends on the goals of the study and the resources available. Once usability testing is completed, the next step is analysing the results.

This analysis often involves looking for patterns in user behaviour and identifying common issues. Designers can use this information to prioritise changes and improvements. For example, if many users struggled to find a button, it may need to be made more visible or easier to access. On the other hand, if only a few users had trouble, the design might not need significant changes. Overall, usability testing is a crucial step in creating products that meet users' needs.

It helps designers ensure that their solutions are not just innovative but also functional and user-friendly.

The Importance of Iteration

Iteration is a key concept in the UX design process. After conducting usability testing, designers must be willing to make changes based on the feedback they receive. This is where iteration comes into play. The idea behind iteration is simple: design, test, learn, and improve. Each cycle of this process helps to refine the product further. When designers make changes based on user feedback, they create a new version of the product. This new version is then tested again to see if the changes were effective. The cycle continues until the product meets user needs and expectations. This iterative process is vital because it allows designers to respond to real-world usage rather than relying solely on assumptions. It helps avoid the trap of creating a product based on what designers think users want, rather than what they actually need. Each round of testing brings new insights, leading to better designs over time.

Another reason iteration is important is that user needs can change. A product that works well today may not be suitable tomorrow as technology and user behaviours evolve. For example, consider a mobile app designed for fitness tracking. As new fitness trends emerge or as users become more health-conscious, the app may need to adapt to stay relevant. Iteration allows designers to stay in tune with these changes and keep their products aligned with user expectations. Feedback from usability tests often uncovers unexpected user behaviours. Sometimes users may interact with a product in ways that designers did not anticipate. This feedback can lead to significant changes in design. The beauty of iteration is that it embraces these unexpected insights and uses them to enhance the overall user experience.

Incorporating user feedback into design is not just about making changes; it is about fostering a mindset of continuous improvement. Teams should encourage a culture where feedback is welcomed and seen as an opportunity for growth. This positive attitude towards feedback can lead to more innovative solutions and a better understanding of user needs. Furthermore, iteration does not always mean making large changes. Sometimes, small tweaks can lead to significant improvements. For example, changing the colour of a button or adjusting the text for clarity can make a huge difference in usability. Iteration also helps in validating design decisions. Each test can confirm whether a design choice is effective or needs further adjustment. This ongoing evaluation leads to more confident design decisions, ensuring that the final product is well-aligned with user expectations.

Best Practices for Usability Testing and Iteration

To make the most of usability testing and iteration, there are some best practices to consider. First, it is essential to plan usability tests carefully. This includes defining clear goals and selecting the right participants who represent the target audience. A diverse group of users can provide a broader range of insights. Secondly, ensure that tests are conducted in a comfortable environment. Users should feel at ease to express their thoughts openly. The facilitator's role is crucial in this context, as they should create a supportive atmosphere that encourages honest feedback. Another best practice is to keep testing sessions short and focused. This helps maintain users' attention and ensures that the testing process is efficient. Each session should have a specific set of tasks to avoid overwhelming participants.

After gathering feedback, prioritise changes based on their impact on usability. Not every piece of feedback will carry the same weight. Some issues may need immediate attention, while others can be addressed in future iterations. It is also important to communicate the findings clearly with the entire design team. Sharing insights from usability testing fosters collaboration and ensures that everyone is on the same page regarding user needs. This can lead to more cohesive design decisions and a shared understanding of the project goals.

In addition to traditional usability testing, consider using remote testing tools. These tools can facilitate gathering feedback from users who are not physically present, which can widen the pool of participants. Online testing allows designers to reach a larger and more diverse audience, providing a broader perspective on usability issues. Furthermore, keep an open mind when it comes to iteration. Be prepared to challenge existing design assumptions and consider new ideas. Sometimes, a radical change may be necessary to address user needs effectively. This openness to change can lead to innovative solutions that enhance the overall user experience.

Lastly, always document the testing process and the changes made during iterations. This documentation can be a valuable reference for future projects and can help teams understand the evolution of the design. By maintaining a clear record of what was tested, what feedback was received, and what changes were made, teams can learn from their experiences and improve their processes over time.

In conclusion, usability testing and iteration are crucial components of the UX design process. They provide the framework for creating user-friendly products that meet the needs of real users. By understanding usability testing, embracing iteration, and following best practices, designers can significantly enhance the overall user experience. Remember, the goal is not just to create a product that looks good but one that users can easily navigate and enjoy. Continuous improvement through usability testing and iteration will lead to successful design outcomes that truly resonate with users.

52

Chapter 52: Different Types of Usability Tests

Usability testing is an essential part of the user experience (UX) design process. It helps designers and developers understand how real users interact with a product or service. By observing users in action, designers can identify issues and improve the overall experience. There are several types of usability tests, each serving a different purpose and offering unique insights. In this chapter, we will explore the main types of usability tests: **Moderated vs. Unmoderated Testing**, **Remote vs. In-Person Testing**, and **Qualitative vs. Quantitative Testing**.

Moderated vs. Unmoderated Testing

The first distinction we need to consider is between moderated and unmoderated usability testing.

Moderated Testing involves a facilitator, usually a UX researcher or designer, who guides the participants through the test. This type of testing is often conducted in a controlled environment, such as a usability lab or a dedicated testing room. The moderator is there to provide instructions, ask follow-up questions, and observe the participants closely. This interaction allows the facilitator to gain deeper insights into the participants' thoughts and feelings as they navigate the product. Moderated testing is particularly useful for understanding complex tasks or when the researcher needs to clarify certain aspects of the test.

For instance, if a participant struggles with a specific feature, the moderator can ask questions to uncover the reasons behind the confusion. This approach is excellent for gaining qualitative insights into user behaviour and attitudes.

On the other hand, **Unmoderated Testing** does not involve a facilitator during the test. Participants complete the tasks on their own, often using their devices in their own environments. This type of testing can be more convenient for users, as they can participate at their own pace and choose the time that works best for them. Unmoderated tests are typically conducted using online platforms that provide the tasks and collect data automatically.

While unmoderated testing may lack the depth of interaction seen in moderated tests, it can reach a larger number of participants more quickly and at a lower cost. This makes it a popular choice for quick feedback on design changes or for testing prototypes early in the design process. Each type of testing has its advantages and drawbacks, and the choice between them often depends on the goals of the study and the resources available.

Remote vs. In-Person Testing

Another important distinction in usability testing is between remote and in-person testing.

In-Person Testing takes place when participants meet the researchers face-to-face in a controlled environment, such as a lab or an office. This setting allows for real-time observation of user interactions, enabling researchers to take notes and ask immediate questions. In-person testing can foster a more personal connection between the participant and the moderator, which may help participants feel more comfortable sharing their thoughts. However, scheduling can be challenging, and it may limit the number of participants, especially if they are not local.

In-person testing is often beneficial for complex products that require deeper exploration, as researchers can use follow-up questions to delve into specific issues that arise during the test. For example, if a user encounters difficulties with a particular feature, the moderator can ask for clarification to better understand the problem.

On the other hand, **Remote Testing** occurs when participants complete tasks from their own locations, using their own devices. This type of testing has become increasingly popular due to its flexibility and ability to reach a broader audience. Participants can be located anywhere, making it easier to gather diverse user feedback. Remote testing can take two forms: moderated remote testing, where a facilitator guides the session through video conferencing, and unmoderated remote testing, where participants complete tasks independently without a facilitator present.

Remote testing can provide valuable insights, especially for global products, as it allows researchers to observe how users interact with a product in their own environments. It can also save time and resources, as there is no need for travel or physical setups. However, remote testing can pose challenges, such as technical issues and a lack of direct interaction between the facilitator and the participant. Choosing between remote and in-person testing often depends on the specific needs of the project, the target audience, and the resources available.

Qualitative vs. Quantitative Testing

Finally, it's essential to understand the difference between qualitative and quantitative usability testing.

Qualitative Testing focuses on understanding the reasons behind user behaviours and experiences. This approach often involves open-ended questions, interviews, and observational methods that provide rich, descriptive data. Qualitative testing helps researchers explore users' thoughts, feelings, and motivations, allowing for a deeper understanding of how they interact with a product. For example, during a qualitative test, participants may be asked to describe their experience using a website, providing insights into what they liked, what frustrated them, and what improvements they would suggest.

This type of testing is particularly useful for uncovering issues that might not be immediately obvious through numbers alone. It can highlight areas where users feel confused or dissatisfied, offering valuable context for design decisions. However, qualitative data can be subjective and may not represent the broader user base, making it essential to use this type of testing in conjunction with other methods.

In contrast, **Quantitative Testing** focuses on numerical data and statistical analysis. This type of testing involves structured tasks and closed-ended questions, enabling researchers to collect measurable data. For example, a quantitative test may ask participants to complete specific tasks while recording the time taken, the number of errors made, and the success rate.

This data can be analysed to identify patterns and trends, providing insights into the overall performance of a product. Quantitative testing is useful for benchmarking performance, tracking changes over time, and making data-driven decisions. However, it often lacks the depth of understanding that qualitative testing offers, as it focuses more on what users did rather than why they did it.

In conclusion, usability testing is a crucial component of the UX design process. By understanding the different types of usability tests—moderated vs. unmoderated, remote vs. in-person, and qualitative vs. quantitative—designers and researchers can select the most appropriate methods for their specific goals. Each type of usability test offers unique insights, and using a combination of methods can lead to a more comprehensive understanding of user needs and preferences. By prioritising usability testing, designers can create products that not only meet user expectations but also provide enjoyable and meaningful experiences.

53

Chapter 53: How to Conduct Usability Testing

1. Understanding Usability Testing

Usability testing is an essential part of the user experience (UX) design process. It helps designers and developers understand how real users interact with a product. The main goal is to identify any problems users might encounter while using the product and to gather feedback on its overall usability. This testing can be applied to websites, applications, and any digital products. By observing users as they complete tasks, designers can discover areas where the user experience can be improved.

Usability testing typically involves selecting a group of users who represent the target audience for the product. These users are given specific tasks to complete while using the product. During this process, observers note how easily the users can complete the tasks, where they struggle, and any confusion they may express. It's important to create a comfortable environment for the participants, as this encourages them to share their thoughts openly. The findings from usability testing can lead to significant enhancements in the product, ensuring that it meets the needs of users effectively.

2. Planning and Preparing for Usability Testing

To conduct effective usability testing, thorough planning is crucial. Start by defining the goals of the testing. What do you want to learn? Are you testing a specific feature, the overall navigation, or the layout of the product? Clear objectives will guide the entire process.

Next, you need to select the right participants. Aim for a diverse group that reflects your target users. The number of participants can vary, but five to ten users are often enough to identify most usability issues. It's beneficial to conduct testing in stages, especially if you're working on a large project. Early testing can help catch issues before they become ingrained in the design.

Once you have your participants, prepare a test plan. This should outline the tasks users will complete during the test and the methods you will use to observe and record their behaviour. A mix of quantitative and qualitative data can provide a comprehensive understanding of user interactions. Consider using tools such as screen recorders or note-taking applications to document the sessions. Also, think about the environment where testing will take place. Ideally, it should be quiet and free from distractions to help participants focus on the tasks at hand.

Finally, ensure that all participants understand the purpose of the testing. Explain that the goal is to evaluate the product, not their abilities. This can help reduce any anxiety they may feel and lead to more honest feedback.

3. Conducting the Usability Testing Session

When the usability testing session begins, welcome the participants and remind them of the testing goals. Encourage them to think aloud as they complete their tasks. This verbal feedback is invaluable, as it reveals their thought processes and any frustrations they may experience.

As the observer, take careful notes, but also be attentive to the participants' non-verbal cues, such as body language or facial expressions. These can indicate confusion or frustration that they may not express verbally. Try to remain neutral and avoid leading participants in any way. It's essential to let them interact with the product naturally. If they encounter difficulties, ask follow-up questions to understand their thought process and identify where improvements can be made.

After the testing session, hold a debriefing discussion with the participants. Ask them about their overall impressions of the product, what they liked, and what they found challenging. This qualitative feedback can highlight areas for improvement that you might not have observed during the testing.

Once all testing sessions are complete, analyse the data you've collected. Look for patterns in user behaviour and identify common problems. Prioritise these issues based on their frequency and severity. Finally, prepare a report that summarises the findings and provides recommendations for improvements. Share this report with the design and development teams, as it will guide the next steps in refining the product.

In conclusion, usability testing is a vital process in UX design. It helps ensure that products are user-friendly and meet the needs of the audience. By following a structured approach to planning, preparing, and conducting usability tests, designers can gather valuable insights that lead to improved user experiences. Embracing this practice not only enhances the usability of products but also fosters a user-centred design culture within the organisation.

54

Chapter 54: Analyzing Usability Test Results

Introduction to Usability Testing

Usability testing is a vital part of the user experience (UX) design process. It helps designers understand how real users interact with their products. By observing users as they complete tasks, designers can identify any issues that may arise. This chapter focuses on analyzing the results of usability tests to improve the overall user experience.

What is Usability Testing?

Usability testing involves gathering real users to complete tasks on a product, such as a website or an application. During the test, observers note how easily users can accomplish their tasks. This process often includes asking users to think aloud as they work. Their comments provide valuable insights into their thought processes and frustrations. By the end of the test, the designers have a clearer picture of what works well and what doesn't.

The Importance of Analyzing Results

After conducting usability tests, the next step is to analyze the results. This analysis is crucial because it helps designers make informed decisions about the design. By carefully examining the data collected during the tests, designers can identify patterns and trends in user behaviour. This understanding can guide necessary changes to enhance the usability of the product.

Types of Usability Data

Usability tests generate both qualitative and quantitative data.

1. **Qualitative Data**: This type of data includes users' thoughts, feelings, and opinions about the product. It often comes from observation and feedback gathered during the tests. For instance, if several users express frustration over a confusing navigation menu, this feedback highlights a potential area for improvement.
2. **Quantitative Data**: This data involves measurable statistics, such as the time it takes to complete a task or the number of errors made. For example, if users take an average of 10 minutes to find a specific piece of information, this time can indicate whether the design is effective or not.

Gathering Data from Usability Tests

During usability testing, various methods are used to collect data. Common techniques include:

- **Observations**: Observers note how users interact with the product. They look for patterns in behaviour, such as where users struggle or succeed.
- **Surveys and Questionnaires**: After the test, users may be asked to complete a survey. These questions can cover aspects like satisfaction and ease of use. The feedback helps gauge users' overall impressions.
- **Session Recordings**: Many usability tests are recorded for later review. These recordings allow designers to revisit user interactions and understand the context of specific actions.

Organising the Results

Once data is gathered, it is essential to organise it for analysis. This process may involve creating charts or tables to highlight key findings. For example, if many users struggled with a specific task, it can be helpful to create a visual representation to demonstrate the extent of the issue.

Identifying Usability Issues

Analyzing the results requires identifying usability issues. Common problems may include:

- **Navigation Confusion**: If users cannot find their way around the site, it indicates a need for clearer navigation. Look for patterns where users hesitate or abandon tasks.

- **Complex Tasks**: Tasks that take longer than expected or cause frustration may need simplification. By examining the time taken for each task, designers can determine which ones require a redesign.
- **Error Patterns**: If users frequently make the same errors, this pattern can signal a design flaw. Understanding why users struggle can guide changes to improve usability.

Prioritising Usability Issues

Once usability issues are identified, the next step is prioritising them. Not all problems are equally important. Designers should consider the impact of each issue on the overall user experience. High-priority issues are those that significantly hinder usability and need immediate attention. For example, if many users fail to complete a task due to a critical error, this issue should be addressed first.

Collaborating with Stakeholders

After analysing the results, it is important to collaborate with stakeholders, such as team members and clients. Sharing the findings allows everyone involved to understand the usability issues. By presenting the data clearly, designers can help stakeholders see the importance of making necessary changes. Engaging in open discussions can also lead to additional insights and solutions.

Creating an Action Plan

Following the analysis and discussions, the next step is creating an action plan. This plan outlines the changes that need to be made to improve usability. It should include specific tasks, responsible team members, and timelines for completion. For example, if navigation confusion is a priority, the action plan may involve redesigning the menu structure and conducting further tests to ensure effectiveness.

Conducting Follow-Up Tests

Once changes have been implemented, conducting follow-up usability tests is essential. These tests assess whether the changes have improved the user experience. Comparing the results from the initial tests with the follow-up tests can help determine the effectiveness of the changes. If users are still struggling, further adjustments may be needed.

Continuous Improvement

Usability testing and analysis should not be viewed as a one-time process. Instead, it should be part of a continuous improvement cycle. As user needs evolve, so too should the product. Regularly conducting usability tests and analyzing the results ensures that the design remains user-centred. It helps identify new usability issues that may arise as features are added or changed.

Conclusion

Analyzing usability test results is a critical step in the UX design process. By understanding both qualitative and quantitative data, designers can identify and prioritise usability issues. Collaborating with stakeholders and creating action plans help ensure necessary changes are made. Continuous testing and improvement allow designers to create products that truly meet users' needs, leading to better overall experiences.

55

Chapter 55: A/B Testing for UX

Understanding A/B Testing

A/B testing, also known as split testing, is a method used to compare two versions of a webpage or app to determine which one performs better. The idea is simple: you create two different versions of a design element, such as a button, a headline, or an entire webpage, and then you show these versions to different users. By analysing how users interact with each version, you can identify which one leads to better outcomes, such as higher conversion rates, increased engagement, or improved user satisfaction.

The process of A/B testing starts with a hypothesis. For example, you might believe that changing the colour of a call-to-action button from blue to green will increase the number of users clicking on it. This hypothesis leads you to create two versions: one with the blue button and one with the green button. Once you have your versions, you direct half of your users to the blue button and half to the green button. After gathering data, you can see which version performed better and make informed decisions about future design changes.

The Importance of A/B Testing in UX Design

A/B testing is crucial in UX design because it allows designers to make data-driven decisions rather than relying solely on intuition or guesswork. User experience is subjective, and what works for one group of users may not work for another. By conducting A/B tests, you gain insights into how actual users interact with your designs, helping you create a more effective user experience.

One of the primary benefits of A/B testing is that it reduces the risk of making changes that could negatively impact user experience. Instead of implementing a significant redesign based on assumptions, A/B testing enables you to test small changes incrementally. This approach is less disruptive and allows you to refine your design based on real user feedback.

Moreover, A/B testing can lead to improved business outcomes. For instance, if a simple change to your website leads to a 10% increase in conversion rates, this can have a significant impact on your bottom line. A/B testing helps you understand what resonates with your audience, ensuring that your designs not only look good but also achieve their intended goals.

Setting Up an A/B Test

Setting up an A/B test involves several steps, and it is essential to follow a structured approach to ensure reliable results. First, define your objectives. What do you want to achieve with the test? This could be increasing click-through rates, reducing bounce rates, or improving the time users spend on your site.

Next, identify the element you want to test. This could be anything from the colour of a button to the wording of a headline. Once you have chosen your variable, create two versions of your design: the control (the original version) and the variant (the new version). Make sure that the only difference between the two versions is the element you are testing. This ensures that any changes in user behaviour can be attributed to that specific element.

After creating your test versions, you need to determine your audience. It is important to have a sufficient sample size to ensure that your results are statistically significant. If your sample size is too small, your results may not be reliable. You can use tools like Google Analytics or dedicated A/B testing software to help with this.

Once everything is set up, launch your A/B test and monitor the results. It is important to run the test long enough to gather sufficient data, but not so long that external factors could skew your results. After the test concludes, analyse the data to see which version performed better and draw conclusions based on the findings.

Analyzing A/B Test Results

After running an A/B test, the next step is to analyse the results. Start by looking at the key metrics you defined before the test. For instance, if you were testing a new button colour, focus on metrics like click-through rates, conversion rates, and user engagement levels.

Statistical significance is also crucial in this stage. You want to determine whether the observed differences between the control and variant versions are statistically significant. This means that the results are likely due to the changes made rather than random chance. Many online tools provide statistical analysis to help you understand your results better.

In addition to quantitative data, qualitative feedback can provide valuable insights. User surveys, feedback forms, or user interviews can help you understand why one version performed better than the other. This information can guide your design decisions moving forward.

It is essential to keep in mind that A/B testing is not a one-time process. User behaviour can change over time due to various factors, such as market trends or new technology. Regularly conducting A/B tests can help you stay aligned with user expectations and preferences.

Common Mistakes in A/B Testing

While A/B testing is a powerful tool, there are common pitfalls that designers should avoid. One common mistake is testing too many variables at once. When you change multiple elements in a single test, it becomes challenging to determine which specific change affected user behaviour. It is best to isolate one variable at a time for accurate results.

Another mistake is not allowing enough time for the test to run. Short tests may lead to inconclusive results. It is crucial to allow the test to gather sufficient data to make informed decisions. Similarly, be wary of changing the test conditions midway through. If you alter the test parameters after it has begun, you risk compromising the integrity of your results.

Additionally, relying solely on statistical significance without considering practical significance can lead to misguided decisions. A change may show statistical significance but may not have a meaningful impact on user experience or business goals. Always consider the broader context when interpreting your results.

Best Practices for A/B Testing

To maximise the effectiveness of your A/B tests, consider following these best practices. First, start with a clear hypothesis. A well-defined hypothesis sets a solid foundation for the testing process and helps focus your efforts. Ensure that your test aligns with your overall UX goals and objectives.

Second, test changes that are meaningful to your users. Small, insignificant changes may not lead to any substantial improvement in user experience. Focus on elements that can make a real difference, such as major call-to-action buttons or important content areas.

Third, ensure your sample size is large enough to produce reliable results. Use statistical tools to calculate the appropriate sample size before starting the test. This ensures that your findings are representative of your user base.

Fourth, document your tests and results thoroughly. Keeping a record of your hypotheses, tests, and outcomes can help you learn from past experiences and guide future A/B testing efforts. This documentation can also be valuable for sharing insights with your team or stakeholders.

Finally, embrace a culture of testing. A/B testing should not be viewed as a one-off task but as an integral part of the design process. Encourage your team to continuously experiment and seek opportunities for improvement.

Conclusion

A/B testing is an essential practice in UX design that enables designers to make informed decisions based on user behaviour. By systematically comparing different design elements, you can enhance user experiences and achieve better business outcomes. With a clear understanding of how to set up, run, and analyse A/B tests, as well as the common pitfalls and best practices to keep in mind, you can harness the power of A/B testing to create designs that truly resonate with users. Embracing A/B testing as part of your design process not only improves the quality of your work but also fosters a deeper connection with your audience.

56

Chapter 56: The Role of Analytics in UX Iteration

In the world of User Experience (UX) design, analytics play a vital role in shaping and improving the way users interact with products and services. Understanding user behaviour is key to creating an effective design that meets the needs of the audience. Analytics help designers and product teams gather data on how users engage with their websites or applications. This data provides insights into what works well and what needs improvement, allowing for an informed approach to iteration.

Analytics tools can track various metrics, including page views, click-through rates, bounce rates, and user paths. These metrics help identify patterns in user behaviour, revealing areas where users may struggle or drop off. For instance, if a particular page on a website has a high bounce rate, it indicates that users are leaving that page quickly, which could suggest that the content is not engaging or the layout is confusing. By analysing these patterns, designers can pinpoint specific problems and develop solutions to enhance the user experience.

Another critical aspect of analytics is A/B testing, where two versions of a webpage or app are compared to see which one performs better. This method allows designers to test different designs, features, or content in a controlled way. By analysing user responses to each version, teams can make data-driven decisions about which design to implement. For example, a simple change in the colour of a button or the wording of a call-to-action can significantly impact user engagement. Therefore, A/B testing becomes a powerful tool in the iterative design process, enabling constant improvement based on actual user behaviour.

User feedback is also essential for analytics in UX iteration. While analytics provide quantitative data, user feedback offers qualitative insights that can explain why users behave the way they do. Surveys, interviews, and usability testing can help gather this feedback. For instance, if users are dropping off at a specific point in a process, asking them why can provide valuable information that analytics alone may not reveal. Combining analytics with user feedback allows designers to develop a more comprehensive understanding of the user experience, leading to more effective iterations.

Moreover, it is important to consider the context in which users interact with a product. Analytics can reveal trends based on factors such as time of day, device used, or location. Understanding these contexts can inform design decisions. For example, if analytics show that mobile users are having difficulty completing a task, designers may prioritise creating a more streamlined mobile experience. This data-driven approach ensures that designs cater to the specific needs of different user groups, enhancing the overall experience.

As the digital landscape continues to evolve, so do user expectations. Regularly analysing user behaviour through analytics is crucial to staying relevant and competitive. UX designers must continually iterate on their designs based on the insights gained from analytics. This ongoing process not only improves user satisfaction but also drives business success. By keeping a close eye on analytics, designers can identify new opportunities for innovation and refine their products to meet changing user needs.

In conclusion, analytics play a critical role in UX iteration. By providing valuable data on user behaviour, A/B testing, user feedback, and context analysis, analytics empower designers to make informed decisions. This iterative process helps create a more user-centred design, ultimately leading to a better overall experience. In a world where user expectations are constantly changing, leveraging analytics is essential for creating successful products that resonate with users. As designers embrace the power of analytics, they can ensure that their designs not only meet but exceed user expectations, fostering loyalty and satisfaction.

57

Chapter 57: Iterative Design: Continuous Improvement

Understanding Iterative Design

Iterative design is a fundamental approach in user experience (UX) design that focuses on continuous improvement. It is a cycle that allows designers to create better products through repeated iterations. Instead of trying to get everything perfect on the first attempt, designers create a basic version of a product, test it, learn from user feedback, and make improvements. This cycle repeats itself until the product meets user needs effectively. The main idea behind iterative design is that each version of the product can be better than the last, allowing designers to learn and adapt to user preferences and behaviours. This method encourages flexibility and responsiveness, which are crucial in creating user-centered designs. By incorporating user feedback at every stage, designers can ensure that the end product is not only functional but also enjoyable to use.

The Benefits of Iterative Design

There are several benefits to using iterative design in UX. Firstly, it reduces the risk of failure. When designers invest time in testing and refining their designs through iterations, they can identify and fix problems early on. This early detection can save time and resources in the long run. Secondly, iterative design leads to higher user satisfaction. By actively involving users in the design process, their preferences and needs are taken into account. This leads to a product that feels tailored to their expectations, making them more likely to enjoy using it. Additionally, iterative design fosters collaboration among team members. Designers, developers, and stakeholders can work together closely during each iteration, sharing insights and suggestions. This collaborative spirit not only enhances the design process but also ensures that all voices are heard, leading to a more well-rounded final product. Lastly, the iterative process encourages innovation. As designers experiment with different ideas and solutions during each iteration, they may stumble upon creative breakthroughs that can enhance the overall user experience.

The Iterative Design Process

The iterative design process consists of several key stages that help guide designers through the cycle of improvement. The first stage is planning, where designers define the goals and objectives of the project. They identify the target audience, the problems the design aims to solve, and the key features to include. This stage sets the foundation for the design process and ensures that everyone is aligned on the project's vision.

The second stage is prototyping, where designers create a basic version of the product. This can be a low-fidelity prototype, such as paper sketches or wireframes, or a high-fidelity prototype that closely resembles the final product. The goal is to create something tangible that can be tested with users. Once the prototype is ready, the next stage is testing. Designers conduct usability tests to gather feedback from users as they interact with the prototype. Observing users in real-time provides valuable insights into their behaviour, preferences, and pain points. This feedback is crucial for understanding what works and what doesn't in the design.

After testing, designers move to the analysis stage. They review the feedback collected and identify patterns or common issues. This analysis helps them understand the strengths and weaknesses of the design, guiding them on what changes to make in the next iteration. The final stage is iteration, where designers implement the necessary changes based on user feedback and analysis. They refine the prototype, add new features, or simplify existing ones to enhance the overall user experience.

This cycle continues, with designers repeating the process of planning, prototyping, testing, analyzing, and iterating until they achieve a product that meets user needs effectively.

User Feedback and Its Importance

User feedback is a vital component of the iterative design process. It provides designers with insights that they may not have considered, highlighting areas for improvement that are crucial for success. Engaging with users during the testing phase allows designers to observe how real people interact with their designs. This first-hand experience can reveal usability issues, confusing elements, or features that are not as useful as initially thought. It's essential for designers to create a welcoming environment during testing so that users feel comfortable sharing their thoughts and opinions. This open communication fosters a sense of collaboration and encourages honest feedback.

Collecting feedback can be done through various methods, such as surveys, interviews, and usability testing sessions. Surveys can provide quantitative data, allowing designers to identify trends in user preferences. In contrast, interviews offer qualitative insights, giving designers a deeper understanding of user experiences and emotions. Usability testing sessions, where users perform specific tasks using the prototype, provide direct observations that can guide design decisions.

It's crucial for designers to analyse the feedback collected carefully. Not all user suggestions will be feasible or beneficial to implement, so it's essential to prioritise changes based on the impact they will have on the user experience. Designers should look for common themes in the feedback and focus on addressing the most critical issues first. By prioritising user feedback, designers can create a product that is genuinely user-centred and responsive to the needs of their audience.

Challenges in Iterative Design

While iterative design offers numerous benefits, it is not without its challenges. One common challenge is managing time and resources effectively. The iterative process requires multiple cycles of design, testing, and refinement, which can be time-consuming. Teams must balance the need for thorough testing and analysis with project deadlines and resource constraints. To overcome this challenge, designers can set clear goals for each iteration and focus on the most critical aspects of the design. By prioritising essential features and functionality, designers can streamline the process and ensure they make meaningful improvements without compromising the project timeline.

Another challenge in iterative design is handling conflicting feedback. When conducting usability tests, it is not uncommon for different users to provide varying opinions on the same aspect of the design. This can create confusion for designers trying to determine which feedback to act upon. To address this issue, designers should look for patterns in the feedback rather than focusing on individual opinions. They can also consult with team members and stakeholders to gain a broader perspective on the feedback received. By engaging in discussions and weighing the pros and cons of each piece of feedback, designers can make informed decisions on how to proceed.

Lastly, the iterative process can sometimes lead to "design by committee," where too many voices contribute to the design decisions. While collaboration is essential, it can also result in a diluted vision if not managed carefully. To prevent this, designers should establish clear design principles and guidelines that align with the project goals. By keeping the team focused on these guiding principles, they can ensure that the final design remains cohesive and user-centred, even as it evolves through multiple iterations.

Case Studies of Successful Iterative Design

Many successful products have been created using the iterative design process. One well-known example is the development of the iPhone. Apple used iterative design to refine the user interface and features of the iPhone based on user feedback and usability testing. Each new version of the iPhone introduced improvements that enhanced the user experience, leading to its widespread popularity and success.

Another example is the social media platform Facebook. The team behind Facebook continuously iterates on the platform, making changes based on user feedback and data analysis. They regularly test new features with select user groups before rolling them out to the entire user base. This iterative approach has allowed Facebook to remain relevant and responsive to the needs of its users over time.

In the realm of web design, the website Airbnb has also

benefitted from iterative design. The team at Airbnb frequently tests different design elements and layouts to determine what resonates most with their users. By collecting data on user interactions and conducting A/B testing, they can make informed decisions about design changes that lead to improved user engagement and satisfaction.

These case studies demonstrate the power of iterative design in creating successful products that evolve over time. By continually learning from user feedback and making adjustments, these companies have been able to stay ahead of the competition and provide exceptional user experiences.

Conclusion: Embracing Continuous Improvement

In conclusion, iterative design is a powerful approach that fosters continuous improvement in UX design. By embracing the cycle of planning, prototyping, testing, analysing, and iterating, designers can create products that truly meet the needs of their users. The benefits of iterative design, such as reducing the risk of failure, enhancing user satisfaction, promoting collaboration, and encouraging innovation, make it an essential strategy for any designer.

However, designers must also be mindful of the challenges associated with this process, including managing time and resources, handling conflicting feedback, and avoiding design by committee. By setting clear goals, prioritising user feedback, and adhering to guiding principles, designers can navigate these challenges effectively.

Ultimately, the key to successful iterative design lies in a commitment to learning and adapting. By valuing user feedback and continuously refining designs, designers can create products that not only meet but exceed user expectations. As the field of UX design continues to evolve, embracing the principles of iterative design will be crucial for creating exceptional user experiences that stand the test of time.

58

Chapter 58: Balancing Data-Driven and Intuitive Design Decisions

Understanding Data-Driven Design

In the world of user experience (UX) design, data-driven design refers to making decisions based on concrete evidence gathered from various sources. This evidence often comes from user analytics, feedback, surveys, A/B testing, and heat maps. The primary goal is to understand how users interact with a product, which features they use most, and where they encounter difficulties. By analysing this data, designers can identify patterns and trends that inform their decisions.

For example, let's consider an e-commerce website. Through data analysis, the design team may discover that users frequently abandon their shopping carts at a specific point in the checkout process. This information can guide them to investigate that stage further. They might find that the payment options are unclear or that there are unexpected charges appearing, leading to user frustration. By making changes based on this data, such as clarifying payment information or simplifying the process, the team can potentially reduce cart abandonment and improve overall user satisfaction.

However, while data is valuable, it is essential to remember that it does not tell the whole story. Data points represent user behaviour but do not always capture the reasons behind those actions. This is where intuitive design comes into play.

The Role of Intuitive Design

Intuitive design relies on the designer's instincts and understanding of human behaviour, psychology, and design principles. It focuses on creating a seamless user experience based on what feels right for the user, even if there is no data to support the decision. Intuitive design can be particularly effective when entering uncharted territory, such as developing a new product or feature where user behaviour is unknown.

Take the example of a new mobile application that introduces a novel way to interact with content. At first, there may not be enough data available to guide the design choices. In this case, designers rely on their knowledge of similar applications, trends in user interfaces, and user psychology. They might implement features that seem logical based on how people typically navigate and interact with digital products. This intuitive approach can foster creativity and innovation, allowing designers to explore possibilities that data alone might not suggest.

Intuition also plays a crucial role in understanding the emotional aspect of user experience. While data can tell you what users did, it often cannot convey how they felt during the interaction. Designers must consider user emotions and motivations to create a holistic experience. For instance, a brightly coloured button may seem effective based on data, but if it does not align with the brand's tone or the emotional state of the user, it could lead to confusion or frustration.

Striking a Balance

To create an effective UX, designers must find a balance between data-driven decisions and intuitive design. Relying solely on data can lead to a rigid design approach that may overlook the human aspect of interaction. Conversely, relying only on intuition can result in designs that are disconnected from user needs and preferences.

One way to strike this balance is by using an iterative design process. In this approach, designers can create prototypes based on intuitive ideas, then test them with real users to gather data on their effectiveness. By observing how users interact with the design and collecting feedback, designers can make informed adjustments that align with both user needs and their original vision. This process allows for a continuous cycle of improvement, ensuring that the final product is both user-friendly and innovative.

Moreover, fostering a collaborative environment where team

members from different disciplines, such as UX research, psychology, and visual design, come together can enhance this balance. By sharing insights and perspectives, the team can make more informed decisions that blend data and intuition. Designers should encourage open discussions about findings and instincts, creating an atmosphere where everyone feels valued and heard.

Practical Tips for Balancing Data and Intuition

1. **Use Data as a Guide, Not a Rulebook**: While data is essential, it should not dictate every decision. Instead, treat it as a guide that provides insights into user behaviour. Combine these insights with your understanding of design principles and user psychology to inform your choices.

2. **Trust Your Instincts**: Designers often have a good sense of what will work based on their experience and understanding of users. Don't ignore your instincts, especially when data is scarce or when venturing into new design territory.

3. **Test and Validate**: Whenever you make design decisions based on intuition, follow up with user testing to gather data on how effective those decisions are. This validation process can help you refine your design and ensure it meets user needs.

4. **Create User Personas**: Develop detailed user personas based on both qualitative and quantitative research.

These personas can guide your intuitive decisions by providing a clear picture of who your users are and what they need.

5. **Foster a Culture of Experimentation**: Encourage your team to experiment with both data-driven and intuitive approaches. This mindset can lead to innovative solutions and a deeper understanding of user behaviour.

6. **Stay Open to Change**: Be prepared to adjust your designs as you gather new data. The balance between data and intuition is not static; it evolves as user needs and technology change.

Conclusion

In conclusion, balancing data-driven and intuitive design decisions is crucial for creating effective user experiences. By understanding the strengths and limitations of both approaches, designers can make informed choices that resonate with users. Data provides valuable insights into user behaviour, while intuition fosters creativity and emotional connection. By finding the right balance, designers can create innovative, user-centred products that not only meet user needs but also enhance overall satisfaction. As you continue your journey in UX design, remember that both data and intuition are valuable tools in your design toolkit. Embrace the interplay between them to create meaningful experiences that delight users.

59

Chapter 59: The Importance of Feedback Loops

Understanding Feedback Loops

Feedback loops are an essential part of user experience (UX) design. They allow designers to gather information about how users interact with a product, system, or service. Essentially, a feedback loop is a process where the output of a system is circled back and used as input. In the context of UX design, this means that the experiences and opinions of users are collected, analysed, and then used to improve the design. This process can help designers make informed decisions and create products that truly meet the needs of their users. In today's fast-paced digital world, users have high expectations and demand seamless experiences. When they encounter difficulties or frustrations, their feedback is crucial for identifying and rectifying these issues. By establishing effective feedback loops, designers can gain valuable insights into user behaviours and preferences, allowing them to adapt and enhance the design iteratively.

This ensures that the final product not only satisfies user needs but also delights them. Feedback loops are not just beneficial; they are necessary. They allow for continuous improvement, keeping products relevant in an ever-changing market. Users might not always voice their opinions directly; however, their actions, such as how long they stay on a page or where they click, can speak volumes. By closely monitoring user interactions, designers can develop a deeper understanding of the user journey. This understanding can guide adjustments that make a real difference, whether it is simplifying navigation, enhancing accessibility, or tailoring content to specific user segments.

The Role of User Testing and Surveys

One of the most common methods of creating feedback loops in UX design is through user testing and surveys. User testing involves observing real users as they interact with a product. Designers can see firsthand where users struggle, what they enjoy, and where they might feel confused. This direct observation is invaluable, as it provides context to the data that designers collect.

Additionally, surveys and questionnaires can be employed to gather user opinions after they have used a product. These tools can be designed to ask specific questions about functionality, aesthetics, and overall satisfaction. By combining quantitative data from surveys with qualitative insights from user testing, designers can create a comprehensive picture of the user experience. This dual approach allows for identifying patterns and trends in user behaviour, leading to informed design decisions. Another important aspect of feedback loops is their role in prioritising improvements. Designers often have a long list of potential changes they would like to implement.

However, feedback helps to pinpoint which issues are most pressing for users. By focusing on the areas that matter most to the users, designers can ensure that their efforts lead to meaningful improvements. Regularly integrating feedback into the design process also helps build trust with users. When they see that their suggestions are taken seriously and result in actual changes, they are more likely to continue engaging with the product. This ongoing relationship between users and designers creates a community of collaboration, where users feel valued and designers feel motivated to create better experiences.

Creating a Culture of Continuous Improvement

Finally, feedback loops contribute to a culture of continuous improvement within teams and organisations. By making feedback a central part of the design process, teams can cultivate an environment where learning and adaptation are encouraged. This culture fosters creativity, as team members are more likely to share their ideas and seek innovative solutions when they know their input will be valued. Additionally, regular feedback sessions can help identify training needs within the team. If certain design principles or methodologies are not well understood, feedback can highlight areas for professional development. This focus on growth not only enhances the skills of individual team members but also elevates the quality of the work produced.

Moreover, creating a structured process for collecting and analysing feedback can lead to more consistent results. By standardising how feedback is gathered and implemented, teams can avoid inconsistencies that may arise from ad-hoc approaches. This consistency helps ensure that all team members are on the same page regarding user needs and expectations. Importantly, feedback loops should not be seen as a one-off task but as an ongoing commitment. Technology and user behaviours are constantly evolving, and what works well today might not be effective tomorrow. By embracing the concept of feedback loops, teams can remain agile and responsive to change.

This adaptability is crucial in a competitive market where user preferences can shift rapidly. Ultimately, the importance of feedback loops in UX design cannot be overstated. They empower designers to create user-centred products that resonate with their audience, driving satisfaction and loyalty. By prioritising feedback, organisations can cultivate a culture of continuous improvement that benefits both users and designers alike. As the digital landscape continues to evolve, embracing feedback loops will be essential for staying ahead of the curve and delivering exceptional user experiences.

VII

UX Design in Practice

*Apply UX design principles in real-world settings and stay ahead of industry trends.
This section covers the practical aspects of working in UX, including agile processes, collaboration with developers, and ethical design. It also looks at emerging trends like AI, inclusive design, and designing beyond screens, preparing you for the future of UX.*

60

Chapter 60: Agile UX and Working in Sprints

Understanding Agile UX

Agile UX is an approach that blends user experience design with agile development. This method is all about being flexible and responsive to change, which is essential in today's fast-paced digital world. Agile methodologies, originally designed for software development, emphasise iterative progress, teamwork, and constant feedback. When applied to UX design, it allows designers to adapt their work based on user feedback, ensuring that the final product meets the needs of its users effectively. The goal is to create a user experience that is not only functional but also enjoyable.

Agile UX focuses on collaboration between team members, including designers, developers, and product managers. By working closely together, they can share insights and make decisions quickly. This collaboration is vital in a digital landscape where user preferences can shift rapidly. An agile approach encourages teams to conduct regular meetings, often called stand-ups, to discuss progress, challenges, and plans for the next steps. These brief check-ins help keep everyone aligned and informed, ensuring that the project stays on track.

The Importance of Sprints

Sprints are at the heart of agile methodologies. A sprint is a set period during which specific work has to be completed and made ready for review. In UX design, sprints usually last between one and four weeks. Each sprint begins with a planning session where the team decides what work to prioritise based on user feedback and project goals. This helps to break down the project into manageable pieces, making it easier to focus on specific tasks without becoming overwhelmed.

During a sprint, the team collaborates closely to design, develop, and test their work. This includes creating wireframes, prototypes, and user testing. By the end of each sprint, the team presents their work to stakeholders and gathers feedback. This iterative process allows the team to learn and adapt their designs based on what users truly want and need. It helps ensure that the product is user-centred, resulting in a better overall experience.

Collaborating and Testing in Sprints

Collaboration and testing are crucial in Agile UX. Each sprint provides an opportunity for designers and developers to work together, share ideas, and iterate on their designs. This collaborative environment fosters creativity and innovation, as team members can bounce ideas off one another and build on each other's strengths.

User testing is another critical component of the sprint process. At the end of each sprint, the team should conduct user testing sessions to gather feedback on their designs. This could involve showing prototypes to real users and observing how they interact with the product. By understanding user behaviour and preferences, designers can make informed decisions about necessary changes. This continuous cycle of designing, testing, and refining ensures that the end product resonates with users and meets their expectations.

Embracing Change

One of the key principles of agile UX is embracing change. In traditional design processes, changes late in the development cycle can be costly and time-consuming. However, in agile UX, changes are expected and welcomed throughout the project. By allowing for adjustments based on user feedback, teams can create a more effective and user-friendly product.

Adopting an agile mindset also means being open to experimenting with new ideas and approaches. Designers should feel empowered to explore different solutions and learn from both successes and failures. This culture of experimentation not only enhances creativity but also leads to more innovative solutions that better serve users.

Conclusion

In summary, Agile UX and working in sprints offer a powerful framework for creating user-centred designs. By embracing collaboration, testing, and adaptability, teams can ensure that their products meet the ever-changing needs of users. The iterative nature of agile methodologies allows designers to continuously improve their work, resulting in a more effective and enjoyable user experience. As you apply these principles, remember that the ultimate goal is to create designs that not only function well but also delight users. With a focus on agility, collaboration, and user feedback, you can navigate the complexities of UX design and deliver exceptional results.

61

Chapter 61: Collaboration Between UX and Development

Understanding Each Other's Roles

In the world of product design, User Experience (UX) designers and developers play essential roles in creating successful digital products. Understanding these roles helps foster collaboration between the two teams.

UX designers focus on how users interact with a product. They conduct research to understand users' needs and behaviours. They create wireframes and prototypes to visualize the user journey. Their main goal is to design a product that is easy to use, enjoyable, and meets the users' needs. On the other hand, developers are responsible for building the product. They write the code that makes the designs come to life. Developers ensure that the product works properly and can handle different tasks without issues.

To work well together, both teams need to understand what the other does. UX designers should have a basic understanding of coding and the technical constraints developers face. This understanding helps designers create realistic designs that developers can implement. Similarly, developers should learn about user-centred design principles. This knowledge allows them to appreciate the importance of the user experience and consider it while building the product.

Having regular meetings and open lines of communication helps bridge the gap between UX designers and developers. By discussing challenges, sharing ideas, and providing feedback, both teams can align their goals and work towards a common objective: creating a successful product that users will love.

The Importance of Early Involvement

One of the best ways to ensure collaboration between UX and development is to involve both teams early in the project. When UX designers and developers work together from the beginning, they can share ideas and insights that lead to a better product.

Involving developers early allows them to provide input on the feasibility of design ideas. They can identify potential technical challenges and suggest alternatives that may work better. For example, a designer might create a complex interaction that seems user-friendly, but a developer may point out that it would be challenging to implement with the current technology. By working together, they can find a balance between innovative design and technical practicality.

Moreover, when developers understand the user's perspective from the start, they can build features that enhance the overall experience. They can suggest technical solutions that improve usability or performance, ensuring that the final product not only looks good but functions well.

Regular collaborative sessions, such as brainstorming meetings and design reviews, can help both teams share knowledge and build trust. When both UX and development teams feel heard and valued, they are more likely to collaborate effectively and contribute to the project's success.

Continuous Feedback and Iteration

Collaboration doesn't end once the initial design and development phases are complete. Continuous feedback and iteration are crucial for refining the product and improving the user experience.

After the product is launched, UX designers should gather user feedback to understand how well the design meets users' needs. This feedback can come from surveys, user testing, or analysing usage data. Designers can then share these insights with developers to make necessary adjustments.

Developers should also provide feedback on any technical limitations they encounter while building the product. This information is valuable for UX designers, as it can lead to improvements in future designs. For example, if a certain feature is too slow to load, designers might consider redesigning it to enhance performance.

The collaboration between UX and development is an ongoing process. By working together throughout the product lifecycle, both teams can create a better user experience. This partnership not only leads to a successful product but also strengthens the relationship between the two teams, fostering a culture of teamwork and shared responsibility.

62

Chapter 62: Working with Stakeholders

Understanding Stakeholders

In the world of User Experience (UX) design, working with stakeholders is a crucial aspect of the design process. Stakeholders are people or groups who have an interest in the project. They can include clients, users, managers, developers, and even investors. Each stakeholder brings their own perspective and expectations, which can influence the direction of the project. Therefore, it is essential to understand who these stakeholders are and what they want.

To begin with, it is vital to identify all the stakeholders involved in a project. This can be done through a stakeholder analysis. A stakeholder analysis is a process where you list all the people who have a say in the project and categorise them based on their level of influence and interest. For example, the project manager might have a high level of influence but a lower level of interest in specific user features. In contrast, end-users may have a high interest in usability but less influence over the overall project direction. Understanding these dynamics helps in prioritising communication and addressing concerns appropriately.

Once you have identified the stakeholders, the next step is to understand their needs and expectations. This can be done through interviews, surveys, or workshops. During these sessions, ask open-ended questions to encourage discussion. For instance, instead of asking, "Do you like this feature?" you could ask, "What do you think about this feature, and how does it meet your needs?" This approach allows stakeholders to express their thoughts and concerns in more detail.

In addition, keep in mind that stakeholders may have differing opinions. It is important to facilitate discussions and encourage collaboration among them. Sometimes, stakeholders might have conflicting ideas about the project's goals or direction. Your role as a UX designer is to mediate these discussions and help find common ground. This can involve creating visual aids, like wireframes or mockups, to help illustrate ideas and get feedback. This visual representation can help stakeholders understand the design better and contribute more effectively to the conversation.

Communication Strategies

Effective communication is key to successful collaboration with stakeholders. Good communication helps ensure that everyone is on the same page and that their expectations are managed. Regular updates and clear reporting are crucial elements of this process. This means sharing information about the project's progress, addressing any issues, and celebrating milestones together.

Using simple and clear language is essential when communicating with stakeholders. Technical jargon or overly complex explanations can lead to misunderstandings and confusion. Instead, aim to explain design concepts in straightforward terms. For example, if you are discussing a user flow, describe it as a "step-by-step guide on how users will navigate through the site." This way, stakeholders from non-technical backgrounds can grasp the concepts easily.

Another effective communication strategy is to utilise different formats for updates. Some stakeholders may prefer written reports, while others may appreciate visual presentations. Consider using tools like presentations, infographics, or even short video updates to convey your message. This variety can help keep stakeholders engaged and informed, catering to different preferences for receiving information.

Furthermore, be open to feedback. Encourage stakeholders to voice their opinions and suggestions, and be willing to adapt your designs based on their input. Create a safe space for discussions where everyone feels comfortable sharing their thoughts. Active listening is essential here. When a stakeholder shares their feedback, ensure that you acknowledge their concerns and clarify any misunderstandings. This shows that you value their input and are willing to incorporate it into your design process.

Lastly, consider setting up regular meetings or touchpoints throughout the project. These sessions can be used to review progress, discuss any challenges, and plan next steps. By maintaining an open line of communication, you can build trust with stakeholders, making them feel more involved and invested in the project.

Building Relationships

Building strong relationships with stakeholders is vital for the success of any UX design project. Trust and rapport can lead to better collaboration and a more positive working environment. To build these relationships, start by being transparent and honest in your interactions. Share both the successes and the challenges you encounter along the way. This openness can foster a sense of partnership and mutual respect among the team.

Show genuine interest in your stakeholders' opinions and experiences. Take the time to understand their backgrounds, roles, and how they relate to the project. When stakeholders feel valued and understood, they are more likely to engage positively with the design process. For instance, you could ask questions about their experiences with similar projects or their expectations for the outcome. This engagement not only helps you learn but also demonstrates that you care about their input.

Additionally, be proactive in seeking feedback throughout the project. Instead of waiting for formal reviews, ask for informal input as the design evolves. This practice helps catch potential issues early on and ensures that stakeholders remain engaged. For example, sharing early sketches or prototypes and inviting feedback can lead to valuable insights that enhance the design.

Remember to celebrate successes together, no matter how small. Recognising achievements boosts morale and strengthens relationships. Whether it's completing a significant milestone or receiving positive user feedback, sharing these moments with stakeholders helps reinforce their connection to the project.

Finally, be patient and understanding. Working with diverse stakeholders can be challenging, as they may have different priorities and working styles. Approach conflicts or disagreements with empathy, aiming to understand their perspectives rather than simply defending your position. By fostering an atmosphere of collaboration and respect, you can build lasting relationships that contribute positively to the project and to the UX design process as a whole.

63

Chapter 63: Design Handoff: From Design to Development

Understanding Design Handoff

Design handoff is a crucial process in the development of any product, particularly in digital design. It refers to the stage where designers transfer their work to developers, ensuring that the vision for the product is realised in the final product. This transition can be complex, as it requires clear communication and collaboration between designers and developers. The design handoff process should not be an afterthought but an integral part of the design lifecycle. A smooth handoff helps ensure that the final product aligns with the initial design, maintains the intended user experience, and meets business goals.

Designers create visually appealing and user-friendly designs, but if these designs are not communicated effectively, the end result can differ significantly from what was envisioned. Misunderstandings about design specifications, user interactions, and functionalities can lead to delays and increased costs. Therefore, establishing a clear, systematic process for design handoff is essential for successful collaboration between teams. This chapter will explore the key aspects of design handoff, the tools and techniques that can facilitate this process, and the importance of maintaining a good relationship between designers and developers.

Preparing for the Handoff

Before the handoff can occur, designers need to ensure that their designs are comprehensive and ready for development. This preparation includes several key steps:

Documentation
One of the most important aspects of preparing for a design handoff is thorough documentation. This documentation should include detailed specifications for each design element, including dimensions, spacing, colours, fonts, and other design properties. Documentation should also describe how each element should behave in different states, such as hover, click, and disabled states. This level of detail helps developers understand the design intent and reduces the likelihood of misinterpretation.

Additionally, designers should document user flows and interactions. This can include creating user journey maps that outline how a user will navigate through the product and interact with different elements. Clear documentation ensures that developers have a complete understanding of the design and can implement it accurately.

Design Systems

Using a design system can greatly enhance the handoff process. A design system is a collection of reusable components, guidelines, and best practices that ensure consistency across a product. By leveraging a design system, designers can create components that developers can easily implement. This reduces the need for developers to guess how elements should look or behave, as they can refer to the established guidelines.

A design system also facilitates collaboration between designers and developers, as it provides a shared language and understanding of design elements. Both teams can refer to the same resources, making it easier to align their visions and expectations.

Prototyping

Prototyping is another essential step in preparing for the design handoff. Creating interactive prototypes allows designers to demonstrate how the product should function and respond to user interactions. These prototypes can be used to showcase the design in action, helping developers better understand how the product should behave.

Prototypes can also be tested with users to gather feedback before development begins. This feedback can help identify potential issues early on, ensuring that the final product is user-friendly and effective. By involving users in the prototyping stage, designers can gather valuable insights that can be communicated to developers during the handoff.

The Handoff Process

Once the preparation is complete, the actual handoff process can begin. This stage is critical, as it is when designers and developers collaborate closely to ensure a successful transition from design to development.

Communication

Effective communication is paramount during the handoff process. Designers and developers should meet to discuss the design in detail, addressing any questions or concerns that may arise. This meeting should provide an opportunity for both parties to clarify expectations and ensure everyone is on the same page.

During this meeting, designers should present their documentation and prototypes, highlighting key aspects of the design. They should explain the rationale behind design choices and how those choices align with user needs and business goals. Developers should be encouraged to ask questions and provide feedback, as their insights can help refine the design and improve its feasibility.

Collaboration Tools

Using collaboration tools can streamline the handoff process and improve communication between teams. Tools such as Figma, Sketch, or Adobe XD allow designers to share their designs with developers in real time. These platforms often include features that enable developers to inspect design elements, view specifications, and access assets needed for development.

In addition to design tools, project management tools like Trello or Jira can help track the progress of the development process. These tools allow teams to assign tasks, set deadlines, and monitor progress, ensuring that everyone stays aligned and informed throughout the development phase.

Overcoming Challenges

Despite the best efforts to prepare and communicate, challenges can still arise during the design handoff. Understanding these challenges and finding ways to overcome them is essential for a successful outcome.

Misinterpretation

One of the most common challenges in design handoff is misinterpretation of design specifications. Developers may misinterpret design elements, leading to discrepancies between the final product and the original design. To mitigate this risk, designers should be available for clarification during the development process. Establishing an open line of communication can help address any misunderstandings quickly.

Designers should also encourage developers to ask questions whenever they are unsure about a design element. This approach fosters a collaborative atmosphere where both teams can work together to solve problems and ensure that the final product meets the design intent.

Time Constraints

Time constraints can also pose a challenge during the design handoff. Developers often work under tight deadlines, which can lead to rushed decisions and compromises in quality. To address this, it is essential to allocate sufficient time for the handoff process. Proper planning should include buffer time for any unforeseen issues that may arise.

Additionally, teams can adopt agile methodologies to help streamline the development process. By breaking the project into smaller, manageable tasks, teams can make steady progress while allowing for flexibility in response to changes or challenges.

Maintaining Quality Assurance

Quality assurance (QA) is a crucial step in the design handoff process. Once the development team has implemented the design, it is essential to conduct thorough testing to ensure that the final product aligns with the original design and meets user expectations.

Testing the Product

QA testing should involve various methods, including user testing, functional testing, and performance testing. User testing allows real users to interact with the product, providing valuable feedback on usability and functionality. This feedback can help identify areas for improvement and ensure that the product meets user needs.

Functional testing focuses on ensuring that all features work as intended. This includes testing user interactions, form submissions, and any other functionalities outlined in the design specifications. Performance testing evaluates how the product performs under various conditions, such as high traffic or low bandwidth.

Iterative Feedback
An iterative feedback loop is essential for maintaining quality throughout the development process. After testing, designers and developers should collaborate to address any issues that arise. This may involve making adjustments to the design or resolving technical challenges encountered during development.

Regular check-ins and feedback sessions help ensure that the project remains on track and aligned with the design intent. Encouraging an open and constructive feedback culture fosters a collaborative environment where teams can work together to achieve the best possible outcome.

Conclusion

The design handoff process is a critical stage in the development of any product. By understanding the importance of effective communication, thorough preparation, and collaboration, designers and developers can work together to ensure a successful transition from design to development. Overcoming challenges, maintaining quality assurance, and fostering a collaborative environment are essential for creating a product that meets user needs and achieves business goals.
By establishing a systematic approach to design handoff, teams can enhance their workflow and create products that resonate with users. Ultimately, a successful design handoff not only improves the quality of the final product but also strengthens the relationship between designers and developers, leading to more efficient and effective collaboration in

future projects.

64

Chapter 64: UX Writing: Crafting the Perfect Microcopy

Understanding Microcopy

Microcopy refers to the small bits of text you see in digital products, like buttons, error messages, and labels. Although these snippets may seem minor, they have a significant impact on the overall user experience (UX). Good microcopy guides users, eases their journey, and builds trust. In contrast, poor microcopy can confuse users, lead to mistakes, and ultimately frustrate them.

Microcopy is not just about being concise; it is about being clear and helpful. For instance, instead of using "Submit" on a button, consider using "Sign Up Now" if the action is related to registering for a service. This type of microcopy is direct and sets clear expectations for the user.

Additionally, microcopy can be playful or friendly, reflecting the tone of your brand. For example, instead of a stern "Error," you might say, "Oops! Something went wrong." This light-hearted approach can ease user frustration and make the interaction feel more human.

The Importance of Context

Context plays a crucial role in effective microcopy. The words you choose should fit the situation and the user's mindset. For example, if a user is filling out a form and leaves a required field blank, the error message should explain clearly what is wrong. Instead of saying, "Field required," try, "Please enter your email address to continue." This microcopy not only identifies the problem but also guides the user toward the solution.

Moreover, consider the user's journey when crafting microcopy. The language should match their expectations at each stage of interaction. If a user is in a relaxed, casual context, a friendly tone might work best. Conversely, in a professional setting, a more formal tone could be appropriate. Always tailor your words to fit the situation and your audience.

Best Practices for Crafting Microcopy

1. **Be Clear and Concise**: Clarity is key. Users should instantly understand what action they need to take. Use simple language and avoid jargon. For example, instead of saying "Authenticate your account," use "Log in" or "Sign in." These terms are straightforward and widely

understood.

2. **Use Active Voice**: Active voice is more engaging than passive voice. Instead of saying "Your password must be changed," say "Change your password." This not only makes the instruction clear but also encourages action.

3. **Be Positive and Encouraging**: A positive tone can make a big difference in user experience. Instead of saying, "You cannot access this feature," try, "This feature is coming soon! Stay tuned." This type of language fosters anticipation and keeps users engaged rather than disappointed.

4. **Utilise Familiar Language**: Use words that are familiar to your users. This creates a sense of comfort and relatability. For instance, if your target audience consists of young adults, incorporating slang or trendy phrases might resonate well. Always consider who your audience is and what language they relate to.

5. **Test and Iterate**: Like any aspect of design, microcopy should be tested. Gather feedback from real users to see if they understand your messages. A/B testing different versions can reveal what resonates most. Use this data to refine and improve your microcopy continuously.

Microcopy in Action

To illustrate the impact of microcopy, let's consider a typical scenario: a user attempting to reset their password.

- **Step 1: The Button**: Instead of a generic "Submit," use "Send Reset Link." This communicates exactly what will happen when the user clicks it.

- **Step 2: Confirmation Message**: After clicking the button, the user should see a confirmation message. A simple, reassuring message like "Check your email for the link to reset your password" guides the user through the next steps.

- **Step 3: Error Message**: If the email entered is not linked to an account, instead of a vague error, use "We couldn't find that email address. Please try again or create a new account." This not only informs the user of the issue but also offers a clear next step.

- **Step 4: Final Confirmation**: Once the user successfully resets their password, a message like "Your password has been successfully reset! You can now log in." gives them confidence that the action has been completed.

Each step in this process relies on microcopy to facilitate smooth navigation and prevent confusion.

The Role of Tone and Voice

Tone and voice are critical components of microcopy. The tone reflects the attitude of the brand, while the voice is the consistent personality behind the words. Together, they help establish a connection with the user.

For example, a financial institution might adopt a formal and trustworthy tone, using phrases like "For your security, please verify your identity." In contrast, a social media platform could use a more casual tone, saying, "Let's get you back in!"

The choice of tone should align with your brand's identity and the audience's expectations. It's essential to maintain this consistency throughout the user experience to build familiarity and trust.

Embracing Inclusivity in Microcopy

Inclusivity is increasingly important in UX writing. Your microcopy should be considerate of diverse audiences, ensuring that everyone feels welcome. Use gender-neutral language, avoid stereotypes, and be mindful of cultural differences.

For instance, instead of addressing users as "guys," opt for "everyone" or "friends." This small change can create a more inclusive environment. Additionally, ensure that your language is straightforward and avoids idioms or cultural references that might not be understood by all users.

Testing microcopy with diverse groups can help identify potential issues and ensure that your language is respectful and inclusive. This not only enhances the user experience but also reflects positively on your brand.

The Future of Microcopy in UX Design

As technology continues to evolve, so does the role of microcopy in UX design. With the rise of voice interfaces, chatbots, and artificial intelligence, the way we communicate with users is changing.

For voice interfaces, microcopy must be adapted for auditory consumption. This means crafting messages that are easy to understand when spoken and heard. Similarly, with chatbots, the microcopy should create a friendly, engaging interaction that feels natural for the user.

Incorporating machine learning can help personalise microcopy based on user behaviour. For example, if a user frequently makes the same mistake, the system could adapt the language to provide more specific guidance, enhancing the user experience.

The future will likely see an increased emphasis on context-aware microcopy, where messages adapt based on user actions and preferences. This will require a deeper understanding of user behaviour and the ability to analyse data effectively.

Conclusion: The Power of Microcopy

In conclusion, microcopy may be small, but its impact on UX design is immense. By focusing on clarity, tone, and context, you can create messages that guide and empower users. Good microcopy builds trust and enhances user satisfaction, while poor microcopy can lead to confusion and frustration.

Remember, microcopy is an ongoing process. Testing, gathering feedback, and iterating are essential to refining your approach. As technology evolves, so should your microcopy. Embrace the changes and continue to adapt to meet the needs of your users.

By investing time and effort into crafting the perfect microcopy, you contribute to creating a more enjoyable and seamless experience for your users, ultimately leading to a more successful product.

65

Chapter 65: Ethics in UX Design

Understanding Ethical Principles in UX Design

Ethics in UX design is about making choices that are not just good for business but also respectful and fair to users. As designers, we hold a responsibility to create experiences that consider the needs, feelings, and rights of users. This means that we should not deceive users or manipulate them into making choices they do not want to make. A key ethical principle is honesty. When users interact with a website or app, they should clearly understand what they are doing, how their data is being used, and what to expect from the experience. For instance, if a service collects personal information, it should be transparent about what information is being collected and why. This builds trust between the user and the designer.

Another important principle is accessibility. Designers must ensure that their products can be used by everyone, including people with disabilities. This means considering things like colour contrast, font size, and alternative text for images so that users with visual impairments can navigate easily. Ethical design also includes considering the cultural background of users. A design that works in one culture may not work in another. Therefore, it is crucial to research and understand the values, behaviours, and expectations of different user groups.

In essence, ethical UX design seeks to empower users. This means giving them control over their experience and ensuring that they have the tools and information they need to make informed decisions. By embracing ethical principles, designers can create positive experiences that respect users and promote fairness in the digital world.

The Role of Data Privacy and User Consent

Data privacy is a significant concern in UX design today. Users often share their personal information without fully understanding the implications. As designers, we have a responsibility to protect user data and ensure that it is handled with care. This begins with obtaining informed consent. Users should have the option to agree to share their data in a clear and straightforward manner. This means avoiding complex jargon and making sure that users understand what they are consenting to.

In addition to consent, it is essential to design with data security in mind. This means implementing strong security measures to protect user data from breaches or unauthorised access. Designers should also consider how long to retain user data and when to delete it. Respecting user privacy is not just a legal requirement; it is also an ethical obligation. When users feel that their privacy is respected, they are more likely to trust the platform and engage with it positively.

Moreover, designers should be aware of the potential consequences of their design choices. For instance, using dark patterns—design techniques that trick users into making choices they might not otherwise make—is unethical. These patterns can undermine user trust and lead to negative experiences. By prioritising ethical practices in data privacy, designers can foster a sense of security and trust, ensuring that users feel safe and respected throughout their interaction with the product.

Building Inclusive and Responsible Designs

Inclusivity is a crucial aspect of ethical UX design. It is essential to create products that are usable by a diverse range of people, regardless of their age, gender, race, or abilities. Inclusive design considers the unique needs of different user groups, ensuring that everyone has access to the same experiences. This can involve conducting user research with diverse groups and testing designs with real users from various backgrounds.

Responsible design goes hand in hand with inclusivity. Designers must think about the impact of their products on society and the environment. This includes considering how a product might be misused or how it might contribute to social issues, such as spreading misinformation or contributing to addiction. For instance, social media platforms have faced criticism for their role in spreading false information. Designers can take steps to create features that promote healthy user behaviour, such as limiting screen time or providing users with tools to report harmful content.

In summary, building ethical UX design involves a commitment to inclusivity and responsibility. By creating designs that cater to a broad audience and considering the societal impact of those designs, we can contribute to a digital world that is fair and respectful. This not only benefits users but also enhances the reputation of designers and their organisations. In the long run, ethical UX design leads to better products, happier users, and a more positive impact on society.

66

Chapter 66: The Future of UX Design

1. Emerging Technologies and Their Impact on UX

The future of user experience (UX) design is being shaped by a range of exciting new technologies. One major technology is artificial intelligence (AI). AI can help create smarter, more personalized experiences for users. For instance, AI can analyze user behaviour and preferences, allowing websites and apps to adapt their content and features to meet individual needs. This means that as you use an app or a website, it will learn from your actions and suggest things that are more relevant to you.

Another technology that is changing UX design is virtual reality (VR) and augmented reality (AR). These tools offer immersive experiences that can change the way people interact with digital products. For example, in e-commerce, customers can use AR to see how a piece of furniture might look in their home before buying it. This not only makes shopping more engaging but also helps users make better decisions. As VR and AR technology continue to develop, UX designers will need to create intuitive interfaces that allow users to navigate these new environments easily.

Additionally, voice user interfaces (VUIs) are becoming increasingly popular. Devices like smart speakers and virtual assistants allow users to interact with technology using their voices instead of a keyboard or touchscreen. This shift presents both challenges and opportunities for UX designers. They need to think about how to create seamless voice interactions that feel natural and provide users with the information they need quickly and effectively.

In summary, emerging technologies such as AI, VR, AR, and VUIs are significantly impacting UX design. Designers will need to adapt to these changes, ensuring that the experiences they create are not only user-friendly but also take advantage of these innovative tools.

2. The Evolving Role of UX Designers

As technology evolves, so does the role of the UX designer. In the past, UX designers focused mainly on the visual aspects of a product, such as layout and colour schemes. However, the future will see designers taking on a much broader range of responsibilities. They will need to understand not just design principles but also how technology works and how it can be used to improve user experiences.

CHAPTER 66: THE FUTURE OF UX DESIGN

One important aspect of this evolution is collaboration. UX designers will need to work closely with other professionals, such as developers, marketers, and product managers. By collaborating with these teams, designers can ensure that their ideas are implemented effectively and that the final product meets the needs of users. This teamwork will also help designers stay updated on the latest trends and technologies, enabling them to create more innovative and effective designs.

Furthermore, UX designers will increasingly need to focus on accessibility. As more people use digital products, it is crucial to design experiences that everyone can enjoy, including those with disabilities. This means considering factors such as screen readers, colour contrast, and easy navigation. By prioritizing accessibility, designers can create inclusive experiences that allow all users to engage with digital content.

In addition to technical skills, UX designers will also need strong soft skills. Empathy will become even more vital as designers strive to understand their users' needs and challenges. By putting themselves in the users' shoes, designers can create solutions that truly address their pain points. This focus on empathy will lead to better designs and improved user satisfaction.

In conclusion, the role of UX designers is evolving to encompass a wider range of skills and responsibilities. Collaboration, accessibility, and empathy will be key areas of focus as designers work to create meaningful and effective user experiences in the future.

3. The Importance of Continuous Learning and Adaptation

In a rapidly changing field like UX design, continuous learning is essential for success. As new technologies, tools, and methodologies emerge, designers must stay informed and adapt their skills accordingly. This commitment to lifelong learning will ensure that designers remain relevant and can create the best possible experiences for users.

One way to keep up with industry trends is by attending conferences and workshops. These events provide valuable opportunities to learn from experts, share ideas with peers, and discover new tools and techniques. Online courses and webinars are also excellent resources for gaining new skills and knowledge at your own pace. By engaging with these educational opportunities, designers can stay ahead of the curve and incorporate the latest trends into their work.

Networking is another important aspect of continuous learning. By connecting with other professionals in the UX field, designers can exchange insights, experiences, and advice. This exchange of ideas can lead to new collaborations and innovative projects. Additionally, following industry blogs and social media accounts can help designers stay updated on the latest news and trends in UX design.

Adaptation is equally important as learning. The ability

to pivot and adjust to new information or changing circumstances will be crucial for designers in the future. For example, if a new technology becomes popular, designers should be ready to incorporate it into their work, even if it means stepping outside their comfort zones. This flexibility will enable designers to create experiences that are not only current but also forward-thinking.

In summary, continuous learning and adaptation will be vital for UX designers in the future. By staying informed about industry trends, networking with peers, and being open to change, designers can ensure they are well-equipped to meet the challenges and opportunities that lie ahead.

67

Chapter 67: AI and Machine Learning in UX

In recent years, artificial intelligence (AI) and machine learning (ML) have become significant players in the field of user experience (UX) design. As technology continues to advance, designers and developers are increasingly looking to AI and ML to enhance how users interact with digital products. These technologies allow for a more personalised and engaging experience, transforming the way users engage with websites and applications.

AI and ML can analyse vast amounts of data much faster than a human can. This means that they can learn from user behaviour, preferences, and feedback to improve the overall experience. For instance, an e-commerce website can use AI to recommend products based on a user's past purchases and browsing history. This personal touch not only makes the shopping experience more enjoyable for the user but also increases the chances of conversion for the business.

One of the most exciting aspects of AI in UX design is its ability to adapt in real-time. Machine learning algorithms can learn from user interactions as they happen, allowing them to make immediate adjustments to the user interface (UI) or content presented. For example, if a user spends a lot of time looking at a specific category of products, the site can adjust its layout to highlight similar products or content, making it easier for the user to find what they are interested in. This level of personalisation creates a more engaging experience and keeps users coming back.

Additionally, AI can help in identifying usability issues before they become significant problems. By analysing user interactions, AI can pinpoint areas where users may struggle, such as confusing navigation or unclear calls to action. Designers can then use this data to make informed decisions about how to improve the interface. This proactive approach to design ensures that the user experience is constantly evolving and improving.

However, integrating AI and ML into UX design does not come without its challenges. One major concern is the ethical implications of using these technologies. For instance, data privacy is a significant issue when it comes to collecting and analysing user data. Users are becoming more aware of how their information is being used, and many are hesitant to share personal details with websites and applications. Designers must strike a balance between personalisation and privacy, ensuring that users feel comfortable with how their data is handled.

Another challenge is the potential for bias in AI algorithms. If the data used to train these systems is not diverse, it can lead to biased outcomes that may not reflect the preferences of all users. This could result in a user experience that is tailored only to a specific group, excluding others. Designers must ensure that the data used for training AI is representative of the broader user base to avoid such pitfalls.

Furthermore, as AI becomes more integrated into UX design, there is a concern that it may lead to a loss of the human touch. While AI can analyse data and make recommendations, it cannot replicate the empathy and understanding that a human designer brings to the table. Designers must remember that UX is not just about functionality; it is also about connecting with users on an emotional level. Therefore, while leveraging AI, designers should not lose sight of the importance of human creativity and insight.

Looking ahead, the future of AI and machine learning in UX design appears promising. As these technologies continue to evolve, they will offer even more opportunities for enhancing user experiences. For example, advancements in natural language processing (NLP) are making it easier for users to interact with systems through voice commands and chatbots. This opens up new avenues for creating more intuitive and user-friendly interfaces.

Moreover, as AI becomes more sophisticated, it can be used to create more immersive experiences. For instance, virtual reality (VR) and augmented reality (AR) applications can incorporate AI to adapt to user interactions in real-time, creating a dynamic and engaging environment. This could revolutionise industries such as gaming, education, and training, offering users experiences that are both interactive and personalised.

In summary, AI and machine learning are transforming the landscape of UX design, offering opportunities for personalisation, efficiency, and improvement. However, designers must navigate the challenges of data privacy, bias, and the loss of human touch to ensure that they create meaningful and inclusive user experiences. By balancing the capabilities of AI with the empathy and creativity of human designers, the future of UX holds great potential for creating experiences that resonate with users on multiple levels.

Chapter 68: How AI Fits into the UX Process

Artificial Intelligence is no longer a separate tool used occasionally in design—it is becoming embedded across the entire UX process. Rather than replacing designers, AI acts as a co-pilot, supporting decision-making, accelerating workflows, and expanding the range of ideas that can be explored.

The UX process itself does not fundamentally change. It still follows a human-centred structure: understanding users, defining problems, ideating solutions, designing experiences, testing them, and continuously improving. What AI changes is the *speed, scale, and depth* at which each of these stages can operate.

1. Understand Users & Context

At the start of any UX process, the goal is to understand user needs, behaviours, and the environment in which a product exists. Traditionally, this involves interviews, surveys, and observational research.

AI enhances this stage by working through large volumes of data quickly. It can analyse research transcripts, detect patterns across feedback, and identify recurring themes that may not be immediately visible to a human researcher. It can also summarise interviews and highlight sentiment, making early-stage research synthesis faster and more structured.

However, while AI can process information at scale, it does not replace empathy. Understanding *why* users behave the way they do still requires human interpretation.

2. Define Problems

Once research is collected, the next step is to define the right problems to solve. This involves synthesising insights, identifying pain points, and framing opportunities.

AI supports this by clustering similar issues, prioritising user problems, and suggesting possible root causes based on patterns in the data. It can also benchmark findings against market trends or competitor products, giving teams a broader perspective.

At this stage, AI helps reduce ambiguity—but it is still up to the designer to decide which problems are worth solving and why.

3. Ideate Solutions

Ideation is where creativity expands. Designers explore different directions, generate concepts, and consider multiple ways to solve a problem.

AI is particularly strong here. It can rapidly generate ideas, suggest variations, and help overcome creative blocks. Instead of producing one solution, designers can generate many and compare them. AI can also combine concepts and propose features based on user needs.

This stage highlights one of the most important shifts in working with AI: value comes from *breadth of exploration*, not depth of a single idea.

4. Design Solutions

In the design phase, ideas are turned into tangible outputs— wireframes, UI layouts, and interaction patterns.
AI can generate UI options, suggest layouts, automate repetitive design tasks, and even assist with accessibility improvements. It can also propose microcopy and help create components within a design system.

Rather than replacing the designer, AI speeds up execution and allows more time for refinement and decision-making.

5. Test & Validate

Testing ensures that designs actually work for users. This includes usability testing, feedback collection, and performance analysis.

AI can assist by analysing test results, identifying usability issues, and predicting user behaviour patterns. It can also speed up A/B testing and summarise large volumes of feedback into actionable insights.

While AI can highlight problems, it cannot fully understand human frustration or satisfaction—this still requires human judgment.

6. Implement & Iterate

Once designs are validated, they move into development and continuous improvement.

AI supports this phase by monitoring user behaviour, detecting friction points, and recommending improvements. It can help personalise experiences, analyse product performance, and continuously learn from new data.

This creates a feedback loop where products are constantly evolving rather than remaining static after launch.

AI as a Copilot Throughout

Across all stages, AI plays a consistent role: it increases speed, handles scale, and supports synthesis.

It helps teams:

- Save time on repetitive work
- Make more data-driven decisions
- Explore a wider range of ideas
- Improve overall user experience quality

However, AI does not replace critical thinking, creativity, or responsibility. It does not understand users in a human sense, and it cannot make strategic decisions on its own.

Key Insight

The UX process remains human-centred, but AI changes *how* it is executed.

It shifts design from:

- Linear → iterative
- Slow exploration → rapid variation
- Single solutions → multiple directions

Most importantly, it reinforces the role of the designer—not as someone who produces outputs, but as someone who **guides, filters, and refines them**.

Connection to AI Behaviour in Design

This aligns directly with how AI behaves in creative workflows:

- AI does not improve significantly by "thinking longer"
- It improves through **iteration, variation, and feedback loops**
- Multiple fast outputs are more valuable than one slow response

In UX terms, this means:

- Generate many ideas → not one perfect idea
- Compare outputs → don't trust a single result
- Use human judgment → to decide what actually works

Final Takeaway

AI is not a designer.

It is a **system for accelerating exploration**.
The real value comes from the combination:

- AI provides **speed and scale**
- Humans provide **direction and judgment**

Together, they create a new UX workflow—one that is faster, more iterative, and more expansive, but still fundamentally human at its core.

69

Chapter 69: How AI Thinks

Artificial Intelligence systems like large language models do not think in the way humans do. They do not understand meaning, form opinions, or reason with intent. Instead, they operate by recognising patterns in data and predicting what comes next.

At its core, AI "thinking" is a step-by-step process of turning language into numbers, analysing patterns, and generating responses one piece at a time.

1. You Ask a Question

The process begins with an input—usually a question or instruction written in natural language.

For example: *"Why is the sky blue?"*

To a human, this is a meaningful question. To an AI system, it is simply text that needs to be processed and translated into a format it can work with.

2. Text is Tokenised

The input text is broken down into smaller pieces called *tokens*.

Tokens are not always whole words—they can be parts of words, full words, or even punctuation. For example:

- "Why"
- "is"
- "the"
- "sky"
- "blue"
- "?"

This step allows the model to handle language in manageable units.

3. Tokens Become Numbers

Each token is then converted into a numerical representation.

These numbers act as identifiers that the model can process. At this stage, the original sentence is no longer treated as language—it becomes a sequence of numbers that represent patterns and relationships.

4. The Model Processes the Input

These numbers are passed through a neural network—a system made up of many layers that have learned patterns from vast amounts of data.

The model does not "look up" answers. Instead, it analyses the relationships between tokens based on what it has learned during training.

It builds a representation of the context, meaning it considers how each word relates to the others in the sentence.

5. The Model Calculates Probabilities

Once the input is processed, the model predicts the probability of possible next tokens.

For example, after the phrase:
"The sky is blue because…"
The model evaluates possible next words such as:

- "of"
- "light"
- "scattering"

Each option is assigned a probability based on patterns learned from data.

6. The Most Likely Token is Chosen

The model selects the next token based on these probabilities.

In many cases, it chooses the most likely option, though sometimes a small amount of randomness is introduced to make responses more natural and less repetitive.

This is why AI responses can vary slightly even when given the same prompt.

7. The Process Repeats

After selecting one token, it is added to the response.

Then the model repeats the process:

- Re-evaluates the updated sentence
- Predicts the next token
- Selects the most likely option

This continues step by step until a complete answer is formed.

What Happens Inside the Model (Simplified)

While the process appears simple from the outside, internally it involves several key behaviours:

Understanding Context

The model considers all previous tokens to build a contextual understanding of the input. This allows it to maintain coherence across a sentence or paragraph.

Finding Patterns

It relies on patterns learned from massive datasets. For example, it recognises that scientific questions often lead to explanatory answers.

Predicting Probabilities

For every step, the model calculates the likelihood of every possible next token. This is not a single guess—it is a distribution of possibilities.

Generating and Iterating

The model generates one token at a time, continuously updating its context and refining the response as it progresses.

Final Output

The final response is not generated all at once. It is built gradually, word by word, until the answer is complete.

For example:
  "because of Rayleigh scattering."
  This sentence is the result of many small predictions, not a single act of reasoning.

Key Insight

AI does not think—it predicts.

It does not:

- Understand meaning like a human
- Form intentions or beliefs
- Know whether something is true

Instead, it:

- Recognises patterns
- Calculates probabilities
- Generates responses step by step

In Short

AI builds answers one token at a time.
  Word by word.
  Step by step.

Connection to UX and Design

Understanding how AI "thinks" is essential when using it in UX or UI workflows.
  Because:

- AI outputs are based on probability, not certainty
- It can sound confident even when incorrect
- It may produce similar or repetitive ideas

- Small prompt changes can lead to very different results

This is why designers must:

- Treat AI outputs as **starting points, not final answers**
- Use **iteration and refinement**
- Apply **human judgment and validation**

Final Takeaway

AI is not an intelligent decision-maker.
It is a **pattern prediction system**.
The quality of its output depends on:

- The input you give it
- The way you guide it
- The decisions you make afterward

In other words, AI does not replace thinking.
It changes how thinking is done.

70

Chapter 70: How AI Creates an Image

Modern AI image generation may feel instant, but behind every result is a structured process that transforms randomness into meaning. Most image generation systems today use a method known as *diffusion*, where an image is gradually built step by step, guided by a text prompt.

Rather than "drawing" like a human, AI starts with noise—pure randomness—and refines it until it becomes a clear, recognisable image.

1. You Provide a Prompt

Every image begins with a prompt. This is a description of what you want the AI to create, such as *"a serene mountain lake at sunrise, photorealistic."*

The prompt acts as direction, not instruction. It doesn't tell the AI exactly how to draw the image—it guides the type of result the system should aim for.

2. Text Becomes Meaning (Embedding)

The AI cannot understand text in a human way, so it converts your prompt into a numerical representation called an *embedding*.
This embedding captures the meaning, relationships, and context of your words. For example, "sunrise," "mountain," and "lake" become mathematical signals that guide the visual outcome.

At this stage, the system is not creating an image yet—it is defining what the image should represent.

3. The Process Starts with Noise

Instead of beginning with a blank canvas, the AI starts with random visual noise—essentially a field of static.

This might seem counterintuitive, but it allows the model to gradually shape an image from nothing, rather than trying to construct it all at once.

4. Denoising: Building the Image Step by Step

The core of the process is *denoising*. The AI repeatedly looks at the noisy image and removes small amounts of noise in each step.

At every stage:

- The model examines the current image

- It compares it to the meaning of your prompt
- It predicts what part of the image is "noise"
- It removes a small portion of that noise

This process repeats dozens or even hundreds of times.

Early steps are very rough and unclear. As the steps continue, shapes begin to form, details emerge, and the image becomes more structured. By the final steps, most of the noise has been removed, leaving a clean and coherent image.

5. The Final Image

After many iterations, the result is a detailed image that aligns with the original prompt.
What started as randomness has been shaped into something meaningful—guided entirely by patterns the AI has learned during training.

What Happens Inside Each Step (Simplified)

Each denoising step follows a consistent loop:

1. The model looks at the current noisy image
2. It considers the meaning of the prompt
3. It predicts the noise within the image
4. It removes a small portion of that noise
5. The process repeats

With each cycle, the image becomes slightly clearer until the final result is reached.

Why This Process Works

During training, the AI learns from millions of images and their descriptions. It doesn't memorise images—it learns patterns of how visual elements relate to words.
Over time, it becomes capable of reversing the process:

- Instead of adding noise (as in training), it removes it
- Instead of breaking images down, it builds them up

This is why the system can generate entirely new images that still feel realistic and aligned with your prompt.

Key Ideas

- AI starts with noise, not a blank canvas
- The prompt guides the process at every step
- Images are built gradually, not instantly
- Quality improves through repeated refinement
- The process is iterative, not linear

In Short

AI turns randomness into meaning.
   Step by step.
   Pixel by pixel.

Connection to UX and Design Workflows

This process mirrors how AI behaves in UX and UI design:

- It does not produce perfect results instantly
- It improves through iteration and refinement
- Multiple passes lead to better outcomes than a single attempt

Just like image generation:

- Early outputs are rough
- Mid stages explore structure
- Final stages refine detail

This reinforces a key principle across AI workflows:

AI is not about getting it right the first time—it's about guiding it toward the right result over time.

71

Chapter 71: How AI Creates a Website Design

From your request to a complete website layout

1. You Describe What You Want

"Design a modern landing page for a fitness app. Clean look, motivated tone, blue and white colors."

- You provide a prompt, examples, or preferences.

2. AI Understands the Goal & Context

- Identify purpose: landing page
- Target audience: fitness enthusiasts
- Key needs: motivation, trust, easy navigation
- Style preferences: modern, clean, blue & white

3. AI Gathers Inspiration & Patterns

- Looks at high-quality websites
- Learns layout patterns, colours, typography, components
- Understands visual hierarchy and structure

4. AI Plans the Structure

- Defines layout sections:
- Logo / Navigation
- Hero section
- Features
- Testimonials
- CTA (Call to Action)
- Footer
- Chooses best information flow

5. AI Chooses Visual Design Elements

- Colours
- Typography
- UI components (buttons, inputs, cards)
- Images and icons

AI selects elements that match the brand and goal.

6. AI Composes the Design

- Arranges all elements into a balanced layout
- Ensures responsiveness (desktop, tablet, mobile)
- Builds a cohesive visual design

7. You Review & Refine

- Review the design
- Request changes
- AI updates the design

Repeat until satisfied

What Happens Inside the AI (Simplified)

1. Understand

- Converts prompt into a structured design brief
- Defines:
- Audience
- Goal
- Style
- Content

2. Retrieve Knowledge

- Searches training data for relevant design patterns
- Finds what works for similar problems

3. Generate Layout Options

- Creates multiple layout variations
- Explores different structures quickly

4. Score & Select

Evaluates designs based on:

- User experience
- Clarity of hierarchy
- Visual balance
- Aesthetic quality
- Goal effectiveness

Selects best option (or combination)

5. Add Visual Details

- Applies colours, fonts, spacing
- Adds imagery and micro-details
- Turns layout into polished UI

6. Iterate

- Improves design through feedback loops

Final Output

Design Result

- Clean, modern, ready to build
- Clear hierarchy
- Consistent design system
- Mobile-friendly
- Goal-focused

Behind the Scenes (Code Output)

AI can convert the design into code:

```html
<header class="header"></header>
<section class="hero"></section>
<section class="features"></section>
<section class="testimonials"></section>
<section class="cta"></section>
<footer class="footer"></footer>
```

- HTML (structure)
- CSS (styling)
- JS (interactions)
- Responsive layout

In Short

AI:

- Understands your goal
- Learns from design patterns
- Plans structure
- Chooses visuals
- Builds the design
- Improves it with feedback

From prompt → to fully designed website

72

Chapter 72: Designing for Inclusivity and Diversity

Understanding Inclusivity in Design

In today's world, inclusivity is more than just a buzzword; it is a fundamental principle in design. Designing for inclusivity means creating products and services that everyone can use, regardless of their background, abilities, or circumstances. This concept encompasses a wide range of factors, including physical disabilities, cultural backgrounds, gender identities, and age.

When we think about inclusivity, it is important to remember that everyone has unique needs. For instance, a person with a visual impairment may rely on screen readers, while an elderly person might struggle with tiny fonts. Designers must consider these differences and strive to create solutions that accommodate as many users as possible.

By embracing inclusivity, designers not only improve user experience but also widen their audience. Products that cater to a diverse range of users can tap into new markets, enhancing business success. Moreover, an inclusive design process fosters empathy and understanding among teams, leading to better collaboration and innovation.

The Importance of Diversity in Design

Diversity in design refers to the variety of perspectives that come from individuals with different experiences, backgrounds, and identities. A diverse team can bring fresh ideas and innovative solutions, as people from varied backgrounds can approach problems differently.

When creating a product, having diverse voices in the design process can help identify potential barriers that might be overlooked by a homogenous group. For example, a team comprising individuals from various ethnic backgrounds can better address cultural sensitivities in a design. This practice not only leads to better products but also helps build trust with users, as they see their identities reflected in the designs.

Moreover, diversity in design can improve accessibility. Different users have unique needs, and having a range of perspectives allows for a more holistic understanding of these needs. When diverse teams collaborate, they are more likely to challenge biases and assumptions, resulting in products that are user-friendly for everyone.

Principles of Inclusive Design

To create inclusive designs, it is essential to follow certain principles. Here are some key guidelines that can help ensure your designs are accessible to all:

1. **Start with Research**: Understanding the needs of diverse users begins with thorough research. Conduct surveys, interviews, and usability tests with individuals from various backgrounds. This will help you gather insights into their specific challenges and preferences.

2. **Emphasise Flexibility**: Design solutions that allow users to customise their experience. For example, providing options for adjusting text size, contrast, or layout can help meet the needs of different users. Flexibility ensures that everyone can interact with your product in a way that suits them.

3. **Prioritise Clarity**: Clear communication is vital in inclusive design. Use straightforward language and avoid jargon. When presenting information, ensure that it is easy to read and understand. Simple instructions and intuitive navigation help all users, especially those who may not be familiar with technology.

4. **Incorporate Accessibility Standards**: Familiarise yourself with accessibility standards, such as the Web Content Accessibility Guidelines (WCAG). These guidelines provide valuable criteria for making digital content accessible to individuals with disabilities.

Following these standards ensures that your designs are usable for everyone.

5. **Seek Feedback from Diverse Users**: Engaging with users from different backgrounds throughout the design process is crucial. Regularly seek feedback on your designs to identify areas for improvement. User testing with diverse groups can uncover insights that may not have been considered otherwise.

6. **Avoid Stereotypes**: Stereotyping can alienate users and hinder inclusivity. Avoid making assumptions about users based on their gender, ethnicity, or any other characteristic. Instead, focus on individual needs and preferences, and ensure your designs reflect this understanding.

7. **Create an Inclusive Culture**: Foster a culture of inclusivity within your design team. Encourage open discussions about diversity and provide training on inclusive design practices. A team that values inclusivity will naturally produce more empathetic and user-centred designs.

Case Studies in Inclusive Design

To illustrate the impact of inclusive design, let's look at a few case studies:

- **Airbnb**: Recognising the importance of diversity, Airbnb implemented features that cater to users with different needs. This includes the ability to filter listings by accessibility features, such as wheelchair access and step-free entrances. By prioritising inclusivity, Airbnb has not only attracted a wider audience but has also enhanced user satisfaction.

- **Microsoft**: Microsoft has taken significant steps toward inclusive design with products like the Xbox Adaptive Controller. This controller is specifically designed for gamers with limited mobility, allowing them to customise their gaming experience. By actively involving users with disabilities in the design process, Microsoft has created a product that truly meets their needs.

- **The BBC**: The BBC has a long-standing commitment to inclusive design. They regularly conduct user research to understand the needs of diverse audiences. Their website includes features such as text-to-speech and adjustable font sizes, ensuring that everyone can access their content. This commitment to inclusivity has helped the BBC remain a trusted resource for people of all backgrounds.

Conclusion

Designing for inclusivity and diversity is not just a moral obligation; it is a strategic advantage. By prioritising the needs of diverse users, designers can create products that are more accessible, engaging, and effective.

CHAPTER 72: DESIGNING FOR INCLUSIVITY AND DIVERSITY

In today's global landscape, inclusivity in design is essential for fostering a sense of belonging among users. As designers, we must embrace our responsibility to create solutions that empower everyone, regardless of their circumstances. By understanding the principles of inclusive design and learning from successful case studies, we can pave the way for a more inclusive future in the design industry.

73

Chapter 73: UX Beyond the Screen: Voice and Gesture Interfaces

Understanding Voice Interfaces

As technology advances, we find ourselves interacting with devices in new and exciting ways. One of the most significant changes in user experience (UX) design has come from the rise of voice interfaces. Voice interfaces allow users to interact with devices using spoken commands, creating a more natural and intuitive way to communicate. Think about how easy it is to ask your smartphone a question or to tell your smart speaker to play your favourite song. This chapter will explore how voice interfaces work, their advantages, and how designers can create effective voice user experiences.

Voice interfaces rely on speech recognition technology, which converts spoken language into text. This technology has improved significantly over the years, thanks to advancements in artificial intelligence (AI) and machine learning. Now, devices can understand various accents, dialects, and even different languages. This ability to comprehend spoken language makes voice interfaces more accessible and user-friendly.

One of the main advantages of voice interfaces is their convenience. Users can complete tasks without needing to use their hands or eyes, which is particularly beneficial when they are multitasking. For example, cooking in the kitchen while your hands are covered in flour makes it challenging to scroll through a recipe on your phone. With voice commands, you can easily ask for the next step without interrupting your workflow. This hands-free capability opens up new possibilities for users, making their daily lives easier and more efficient.

Additionally, voice interfaces can provide a more personalised experience. Many voice-activated devices learn from user interactions, allowing them to recognise individual voices and preferences. This means that users can receive tailored responses based on their specific needs. For instance, a smart speaker might offer different music recommendations depending on who is speaking. This level of personalisation helps build a deeper connection between the user and the device, enhancing the overall experience.

However, creating an effective voice user experience is not without its challenges. Designers must consider the nuances of spoken language, such as tone, pitch, and context. Unlike written language, spoken language can be more ambiguous. A command like "turn it up" could refer to the volume of music, the brightness of lights, or even the temperature of a thermostat. Designers need to ensure that voice interfaces can interpret commands accurately and provide appropriate responses.

To address these challenges, designers should focus on creating clear and concise voice interactions. When designing voice commands, it is crucial to use simple and straightforward language. Users should be able to understand how to interact with the device without needing extensive instructions. Designers can also implement visual aids, such as displaying the available voice commands on a screen, to guide users in their interactions.

Moreover, it is essential to consider the context in which users will engage with voice interfaces. For example, a user may want to adjust their smart thermostat while relaxing on the couch. In this case, they may prefer to use a casual tone when speaking to the device. On the other hand, if someone is using a voice interface in a professional setting, they might adopt a more formal tone. Designers must take these variations into account to create a more natural and effective user experience.

In summary, voice interfaces represent a significant shift in how we interact with technology. By understanding the advantages and challenges of voice user experiences, designers can create intuitive and effective voice interfaces that enhance usability. As we continue to move beyond traditional screens, voice interactions will undoubtedly play a vital role in shaping the future of user experience design.

Exploring Gesture Interfaces

In addition to voice interfaces, gesture interfaces are another exciting area of UX design that extends our interactions beyond the screen. Gesture interfaces allow users to control devices using physical movements, such as swiping, tapping, or waving. This form of interaction is becoming increasingly popular, especially with the rise of smart TVs, gaming consoles, and virtual reality (VR) systems. In this section, we will explore how gesture interfaces work, their benefits, and considerations for designing effective gesture-based experiences.

Gesture recognition technology relies on sensors and cameras to track users' movements. These sensors can detect hand gestures, body movements, and even facial expressions, allowing for a wide range of interactions. For example, users can navigate a virtual environment by simply moving their hands or bodies, creating a more immersive and engaging experience. This interaction style mimics real-world movements, making it feel more natural and intuitive for users.

One of the key advantages of gesture interfaces is the level of engagement they provide. By allowing users to interact with devices using their bodies, gesture interfaces can create a more immersive experience. For instance, in a VR game, players can physically swing their arms to swing a virtual sword or leap to jump over obstacles. This physical engagement can lead to a heightened sense of presence and enjoyment, enhancing the overall experience.

Another significant benefit of gesture interfaces is their accessibility. For users with disabilities or limited mobility, gesture-based interactions can offer an alternative way to engage with technology. By using simple hand movements or body gestures, these users can access content and control devices in ways that may be challenging with traditional input methods. Designers should consider inclusivity when developing gesture interfaces to ensure that they cater to diverse user needs.

However, designing effective gesture interfaces comes with its own set of challenges. One of the main concerns is the accuracy of gesture recognition. Users may perform gestures differently based on their unique styles and preferences. For example, one person may swipe left to navigate a menu, while another might use a circular motion. Designers need to ensure that the system can accurately recognise various gestures and interpret them correctly.

To achieve this, designers should focus on creating a limited set of gestures that are intuitive and easy to remember. Overly complicated gestures can lead to frustration and confusion for users. For example, using a simple swipe or pinch to zoom is more effective than implementing a series of intricate hand movements. It is also helpful to provide visual feedback to users, confirming that their gestures have been recognised. This feedback can be in the form of animations or sounds, assuring users that their actions have been acknowledged.

Another consideration when designing gesture interfaces

is the environment in which they will be used. Gesture recognition systems can struggle in poorly lit or cluttered spaces, making it essential to ensure that the technology can operate effectively in various conditions. Designers should test their systems in different environments to identify any potential issues and make necessary adjustments.

Additionally, cultural differences can influence how users interpret gestures. A gesture that is common in one culture may be unfamiliar or even offensive in another. Therefore, designers must conduct thorough research to ensure that their gesture interfaces are culturally sensitive and do not inadvertently exclude or alienate users.

In conclusion, gesture interfaces represent a dynamic and engaging way to interact with technology. By understanding the benefits and challenges of gesture-based interactions, designers can create intuitive and effective gesture interfaces that enhance user experience. As we continue to explore new ways of interacting with devices, gesture interfaces will undoubtedly play a crucial role in the future of UX design.

The Future of UX: Integrating Voice and Gesture Interfaces

As we look to the future of user experience design, it is clear that voice and gesture interfaces will play a vital role in shaping how we interact with technology. The integration of these two interaction styles presents exciting opportunities for designers to create seamless and intuitive experiences for users. In this section, we will explore the potential future of UX design by examining how voice and gesture interfaces can complement each other and enhance user interactions.

The combination of voice and gesture interfaces can create a more holistic user experience. For instance, imagine a smart home environment where users can control their lights, thermostat, and entertainment system using both voice commands and gestures. A user could simply say, "Turn on the living room lights," while simultaneously waving their hand to indicate the desired brightness. This multimodal interaction allows users to choose the method that best suits their preferences and the context of their tasks.

Furthermore, the integration of voice and gesture interfaces can enhance accessibility. By providing multiple ways for users to interact with technology, designers can cater to a broader range of needs. For example, a user with hearing impairments may prefer to use gestures to control a device, while another user with limited mobility might find voice commands more effective. By offering a combination of interaction methods, designers can create inclusive experiences that accommodate diverse user preferences.

As AI and machine learning continue to advance, we can expect voice and gesture interfaces to become even more sophisticated. Future systems may be able to anticipate user intentions based on their behaviour and context. For example, if a user consistently plays a specific playlist during their morning routine, a voice-activated system might proactively suggest that playlist as soon as they enter the room. This level of anticipation can create a more personalised and intuitive experience for users.

Moreover, advancements in haptic feedback technology could further enhance gesture interfaces. Haptic feedback provides tactile sensations that mimic physical interactions, adding another layer of realism to gesture-based experiences. For instance, when a user waves their hand to swipe through a virtual menu, haptic feedback can create the sensation of resistance, making the interaction feel more tangible and satisfying. This combination of visual and tactile feedback can significantly improve user satisfaction and engagement.

Despite the promising future of voice and gesture interfaces, designers must remain vigilant about privacy and security concerns. As voice and gesture recognition technologies become more prevalent, the potential for misuse and data breaches increases. Designers should implement robust security measures to protect user data and ensure that interactions remain secure. Transparency is also essential; users should be informed about how their data is being used and have the option to control their privacy settings.

In conclusion, the future of user experience design lies in the integration of voice and gesture interfaces. By combining these two interaction styles, designers can create intuitive, engaging, and accessible experiences that enhance how we interact with technology. As we continue to explore the possibilities of voice and gesture interfaces, it is essential to prioritise user needs, privacy, and security. The journey ahead promises to be exciting, as we redefine the boundaries of user experience design beyond the screen.

Summary

- **Voice interfaces** allow users to interact with devices using speech, offering hands-free, personalised experiences.

- **Gesture interfaces** enable users to control devices using physical movements, creating immersive and accessible interactions.

- The **integration of voice and gesture interfaces** holds great potential for the future of UX design, offering more holistic, engaging, and inclusive experiences.

- Designers must focus on creating clear, intuitive interactions while addressing privacy and security concerns in the evolving landscape of UX design.

VIII

Book References

Explore the key resources that shaped the insights and principles in this book.
*This section provides a curated list of books, articles, and other resources that have informed the content of **"The Rules of UX Design."** It serves as a guide for readers looking to deepen their understanding, explore further reading, or reference foundational texts and studies within the field of UX design.*

74

A Good Book Reading List

Here's a list of each book from the previous reference with a brief one-line description of what it focuses on:

1. **"Don't Make Me Think" by Steve Krug**
   Focuses on usability principles and the importance of intuitive web design.

2. **"The Design of Everyday Things" by Don Norman**
   Explores how design affects human behavior and usability in everyday objects.

3. **"About Face: The Essentials of Interaction Design" by Alan Cooper**
   Covers interaction design principles and how to create user-friendly interfaces.

4. **"Lean UX" by Jeff Gothelf**
   Introduces a collaborative approach to UX design that integrates Lean principles.

5. **"A Project Guide to UX Design" by Russ Unger and Carolyn Chandler**
   Provides a comprehensive guide for managing and executing UX projects effectively.

6. **"The User Experience Team of One" by Leah Buley**
   Offers strategies for solo UX designers to conduct research and design user experiences.

7. **"Designing for Interaction" by Dan Saffer**
   Discusses the importance of interaction design and practical techniques for creating interfaces.

8. **"Seductive Interaction Design" by Stephen Anderson**
   Explores how to create engaging experiences that draw users in and keep them interested.

9. **"The Elements of User Experience" by Jesse James Garrett**
   Outlines a framework for understanding user experience and its components.

10. **"Rocket Surgery Made Easy" by Steve Krug**
    Provides practical guidance on conducting usability testing with minimal resources.

11. **"Just Enough Research" by Erika Hall**
    Advocates for using lean research methods to inform design decisions without overdoing it.

12. **"User Story Mapping" by Jeff Patton**

Introduces story mapping techniques to prioritize user needs and enhance product design.

13. **"Designing with the Mind in Mind" by Jeff Johnson**
    Examines cognitive psychology principles that inform user-centered design practices.

14. **"The UX Book" by Rex Hartson and Pardha Pyla**
    A comprehensive guide covering the entire UX design process from research to prototyping.

15. **"The Art of UX" by Andrew Maier**
    Discusses the creative aspects of UX design and how to blend art with usability.

16. **"Designing Interfaces" by Jenifer Tidwell**
    Offers design patterns and best practices for creating user-friendly interfaces.

17. **"Mobile First" by Luke Wroblewski**
    Advocates for designing mobile experiences before scaling to desktop.

18. **"Letting Go of the Words" by Janice (Ginny) Redish**
    Focuses on effective content strategy and writing for user-centered design.

19. **"The Inmates Are Running the Asylum" by Alan Cooper**
    Critiques the software development process and advocates for user-centered design.

20. **"The UX Research Playbook" by Jennifer Hanzlik**
    Provides actionable insights on conducting effective UX research.

21. **"Designing for Emotion" by Aarron Walter**
    Discusses how to create emotionally engaging designs that resonate with users.

22. **"Smashing Book #4: New Perspectives on Web Design" by Smashing Magazine**
    A collection of articles offering insights into modern web design practices.

23. **"Design is a Job" by Mike Monteiro**
    Covers the business side of design, including client relationships and project management.

24. **"The Laws of Simplicity" by John Maeda**
    Discusses principles of simplicity in design and how they can enhance user experience.

25. **"Designing Web Usability" by Jakob Nielsen**
    Offers guidelines and principles for creating user-friendly websites.

26. **"Universal Principles of Design" by William Lidwell**
    A reference guide covering fundamental design principles applicable across disciplines.

27. **"Storytelling for UX" by Whitney Quesenbery and**

Kevin Brooks
Explains how storytelling techniques can enhance user experience design.

28. **"The Lean Startup" by Eric Ries**
Introduces a method for developing businesses and products through validated learning.

29. **"Product Design for the Web" by Andrew Maier**
Focuses on web-based product design processes and best practices.

30. **"The UX Design Process" by David Farkas**
Provides an overview of the stages involved in the UX design process.

31. **"Creative Confidence" by Tom Kelley and David Kelley**
Encourages individuals to unleash their creativity in design and innovation.

32. **"Eye Tracking in User Experience Design" by Andrew Duchowski**
Explains how eye-tracking technology can enhance user research and design.

33. **"Sketching User Experiences" by Bill Buxton**
Discusses the importance of sketching in the design process and its impact on UX.

34. **"Microinteractions" by Dan Saffer**
Explores small design details that enhance user

interactions and experiences.

35. **"Designing for Growth" by Jeanne Liedtka**
Introduces design thinking as a strategy for innovation and problem-solving.

36. **"Hooked: How to Build Habit-Forming Products" by Nir Eyal**
Examines the psychology behind habit-forming products and user engagement.

37. **"The Smashing Book 5" by Smashing Magazine**
Features expert articles on the latest trends and techniques in web design.

38. **"The Phoenix Project" by Gene Kim**
A novel that illustrates the principles of DevOps and their impact on productivity.

39. **"User Experience 101" by David M. Kelly**
An introductory guide to the principles and practices of user experience design.

40. **"Evil by Design" by Chris Nodder**
Discusses how design can manipulate users and explores ethical considerations.

41. **"Lean Analytics" by Alistair Croll and Benjamin Yoskovitz**
Explains how to use analytics to validate business decisions and improve products.

42. **"Visual Thinking" by Ruth Culham**
Focuses on how visual thinking can enhance communication and creativity in design.

43. **"The UX Guide to Web Design" by Michal Levin**
Provides practical advice on creating effective and user-centered web designs.

44. **"The Non-Designer's Design Book" by Robin Williams**
A beginner-friendly guide to graphic design principles and best practices.

45. **"Thinking, Fast and Slow" by Daniel Kahneman**
Explores the two systems of thought that drive decision-making and user behavior.

46. **"Inclusive Design Patterns" by Heydon Pickering**
Discusses how to create inclusive and accessible design patterns for users.

47. **"Designing with Web Standards" by Jeffrey Zeldman**
Advocates for best practices in web standards to enhance usability and accessibility.

48. **"Content Strategy for the Web" by Kristina Halvorson**
Covers strategies for managing web content effectively to enhance user experience.

49. **"The Graphic Design Idea Book" by Gavin Ambrose**

and Paul Harris
A collection of design principles and case studies to inspire graphic design.

50. **"Build Better Products" by Laura Klein**
    Provides a framework for building user-centered products through design and research.

51. **"The Design of Everyday Things: Revised and Expanded Edition" by Don Norman**
    A detailed exploration of user-centered design and its application in everyday objects.

52. **"User Experience Revolution" by Johnathan Nightingale**
    Discusses the evolution of user experience and its impact on product development.

53. **"The UX of EdTech" by Robert T. Brown**
    Focuses on user experience design principles specific to educational technology.

54. **"Design Sprint" by Jake Knapp**
    Introduces the design sprint method for rapidly solving design challenges.

55. **"The Art of Product Design" by Hardi Meybaum**
    Explores the creative processes involved in product design and innovation.

56. **"Drive: The Surprising Truth About What Motivates**

Us" by Daniel H. Pink
Examines the psychology of motivation and its implications for product design.

57. **"The User Experience Book" by Gavin Doughtie**
A practical guide to understanding and implementing user experience design principles.

58. **"The Product Book" by Josh Anon and Robert Blake**
Covers the essential elements of product management and user-centered design.

59. **"Build Your Own Website" by David K. Laidlaw**
Offers step-by-step instructions for creating a personal website without coding.

60. **"The Designer's Guide to Marketing and Pricing" by Ilise Benun**
Provides insights into effectively marketing and pricing design services.

61. **"Building a StoryBrand" by Donald Miller**
Discusses how to clarify messaging and engage customers through storytelling.

62. **"The Visual Display of Quantitative Information" by Edward Tufte**
A guide to effective data visualization and presentation techniques.

63. **"User Experience Design" by Anjali Ghosh**

Explores the principles and methodologies of user experience design.

64. **"Designing Interfaces: Patterns for Effective Interaction Design" by Jenifer Tidwell**
    Offers design patterns to improve the usability of user interfaces.

65. **"Product Management's Sacred Seven" by Parth Detroja**
    Outlines essential skills for product managers to lead successful product teams.

66. **"Learning Web Design" by Jennifer Niederst Robbins**
    A comprehensive guide for beginners on the fundamentals of web design.

67. **"Designing UX" by Ben Shneiderman**
    Focuses on creating user experiences that are both enjoyable and effective.

www.ingramcontent.com/pod-product-compliance
Lightning Source LLC
Chambersburg PA
CBHW031602210526
45464CB00004B/1399